Lesson Plans for Creating Media-Rich Classrooms

Lesson Plans for Creating Media-Rich Classrooms

Edited by

Mary T. Christel
Adlai E. Stevenson High School, Lincolnshire, Illinois

Scott Sullivan
National-Louis University

National Council of Teachers of English
1111 W. Kenyon Road, Urbana, Illinois 61801-1096

Staff Editor: Bonny Graham
Interior Design: Doug Burnett
Cover Design: Jody A. Boles
Cover Icons: iStockphoto.com/Bulent Ince

NCTE Stock Number: 30483

It is the policy of NCTE in its journals and other publications to provide a forum for the open discussion of ideas concerning the content and the teaching of English and the language arts. Publicity accorded to any particular point of view does not imply endorsement by the Executive Committee, the Board of Directors, or the membership at large, except in announcements of policy, where such endorsement is clearly specified.

Every effort has been made to provide current URLs and email addresses, but because of the rapidly changing nature of the Web, some sites and addresses may no longer be accessible.

Library of Congress Cataloging-in-Publication Data

Lesson plans for creating media-rich classrooms / edited by Mary T. Christel, Scott Sullivan.
     p. cm.
   Includes bibliographical references and index.
   ISBN 978-0-8141-3048-3 (pbk)
   1. Mass media in education—United States. 2. Media literacy—United States. 3. Critical thinking. 4. Media literacy—Study and teaching (Secondary) I. Christel, Mary T. II. Sullivan, Scott, 1966–
   LB1043.L465 2007
   373.13'3—dc22
                                                         2007024263

When people talk to me about the digital divide, I think of it not so much about who has access to what technology as about who knows how to create and express themselves in the new language of the screen. If students aren't taught the language of sound and images, shouldn't they be considered as illiterate as if they left college without being able to read and write?

George Lucas, filmmaker
Life on the Screen, *Edutopia*

Contents

Acknowledgments

In compiling and editing these lessons into a single text, we answered the charge of both the National Council of Teachers of English's Executive Committee and the Commission on Media to provide high-quality teaching materials that promote "field-tested" strategies for both novice and experienced teachers to effectively integrate media literacy into existing English language arts curricula in both high school and middle school settings. We appreciate and value the support we have received throughout the process from Kurt Austin in NCTE's Books Program as well as the leadership and members of the commission.

The single greatest challenge in compiling a series of lesson plans is to ensure a consistency in style and level of detail across all the lessons that represent a diverse set of experiences. We would like to express our sincere gratitude to Mark Dolce, who served as our "editor in training" by providing the critical eye that made sure all the elements of the text work in concert in a seamless fashion.

We do appreciate that the NCTE Books Program gave us the green light to assemble a companion disk of handouts and sample videos that make this work especially useful to the classroom teacher. As teachers, we appreciate PDF handouts, and nothing replaces a sample of a video project that has been assembled by a teacher or capable students who have worked through the steps of an assignment. The companion disk would not have been a reality without the patience of Charlene Chausis from Stevenson High School and valued assistance and advice from Jay Rajeck at New Trier High School.

Finally, we must acknowledge the fine folks at the Borders Café in Highland Park, Illinois. They graciously allowed us to meet every several weeks over the course of more than a year even though we made few purchases of coffee or sweets.

Introduction: Media Literacy: Finding a Foothold in the English Classroom

Scott Sullivan
National-Louis University

The day I founded the field of media literacy is one I'll likely never forget. I was planning a new course with colleagues, and we'd been discussing a variety of topics to teach in this course, to be called "Critical Thinking in the Modern Age." The main focus of the course was going to be based on David Shenk's book *Data Smog*, which speaks to the overwhelming flow of information that surrounds us in our daily lives. We'd also been reading Deborah Meier's *The Power of Their Ideas* and trying to incorporate the five habits of mind that drove the evaluative portfolio framework of the Central Park East Secondary School; those habits are evidence, viewpoint, connections, conjecture, and relevance. Using these works as a framework from which one could examine nearly any "text," we felt we had a decent intellectual under-pinning for the course, but we were still missing something that would allow us to connect these ideas to curricula. We were searching for a unifying element that remained elusive.

The planning process wasn't going particularly well at first, pri-marily because we were struggling to come up with a common language to discuss what we felt was important to cover in the course. One per-son was interested in the profusion of news, another, the effects of ad-vertising on teens' self-image, and the list went on and on, each of us contributing our pet peeve to the list of ways we felt the media intruded on us, or showed us a skewed reality, or in some way misrepresented life as we lived it.

We decided to let the planning rest overnight while we thought a bit more, and we agreed to reconvene the next day. To prepare, I felt I needed to get a grasp of the content we'd been discussing as a group. I started thinking about how we discussed reading the media as we would any other text, how images had codes, how we interpret nonprint text to make sense of some picture, symbol, or visual. What we'd been dancing around and talking about, really, was a literacy involving the media. It was a type of media literacy. I thought I was onto something new.

This epiphany occurred in the spring of 1998, decades after the field of media literacy started gaining a foothold in the United States. It had existed even longer in other countries: Great Britain, Canada, Australia, and other nations have all had courses and programs in media literacy since the cultural studies movement of the late 1960s. An organization called the National Telemedia Council was founded in the United States in 1953, proving that, over the course of the last fifty years, media and education have been inextricably linked in the minds of educators, though never, till that moment, in mine.

I sat down at the keyboard of my computer and waited to access my dial-up AOL account. The Internet, while no longer in its infancy, was not the omnipotent well of information it is today, and it was still a bit novel to go to it for teaching ideas and materials. I slowly typed my new phrase, "media literacy," into the search box and hit Return, and with all the excitement of an explorer entering uncharted territory, awaited the results. I didn't expect much, as I was sure I'd just invented the concept and named an entirely new academic field of study. I was dumbfounded to get 1,100 hits for my query. Today, that phrase, properly formatted for Google in parentheses, garners over three million hits. To put it mildly, the field has grown.

Others had beaten me to the punch. My initial disappointment at not having actually invented a new field of academic study was quickly overcome by my excitement at finding a treasure trove of materials that would finally help me get my mind around the course I would be teaching. Some great sites popped up: the Media Literacy Clearinghouse, the Media Awareness Network, and the Center for Media Literacy, just to name a few. Those sites still flourish today along with dozens of others.

It took me a while to get up to speed on media literacy issues. I was looking for obvious connections to the English curriculum, for a more settled and established way to teach media literacy. I was hunting for ideas, lessons, and materials that would allow me to use media effectively in my classroom. But, good resources and all, it seemed it would be impossible to teach this class without an in-depth knowledge of media and media production, something I didn't have at that time, nor did my colleagues.

As a team, we struggled to find a place for the course, to design an experience that would allow us all to find ourselves in the curricula, and to create an in-depth, interactive, and valuable experience for our students. We came up with some basics that I have since found in a variety of media education courses: units on advertising, Disney, consumerism, gender and race representations, and a project involving a production component. The course turned out to be an enriching experience for us as teaching professionals and also a terrific place for students to find their voices in the classroom, some for the first time. We found, over time, that using media as an additional text in English class is a surefire way to increase the level of involvement for even the most reluctant students. It begins to change the student–teacher, master–apprentice mindsets that take over many classrooms.

I no longer teach that course, nor am I at that school, but the course still exists. Media literacy as a movement in schools and as an academic field continues to grow. I went back to that school recently to discuss media education with one of the teachers who taught the course during the previous school year. It was an informative discussion, one I wish I had had when I was planning the course, but one remark the teacher made stood out. He said, "No one goes to school to become a media literacy teacher. You come to this course through your own critical use of the media." It was a crystallizing moment for me. We'd been discussing the big issues that come up in class, the challenges of teaching a nontracked English course, the accessibility of materials, and the unpredictable nature of student responses, but, it was clear, not many people are trained to do this kind of work in the English language arts (ELA) classroom.

Some teachers, and English teachers in particular, seem a bit divided on the issue of using media as a text in the ELA classroom, believing that media isn't a subject worthy of in-depth study. The "low" nature of media art makes it pale in comparison to the great works of Tolstoy, Shakespeare, and Hemingway. Everyone, it seems, is aware that media consumption is like mind candy—you use it when you want to shut off your mind and relax. How could we justify a situation in which students might not read some of the great authors of the age but, horrors, have spent time in class actually watching TV? How does that meet the definition of what English class is supposed to be and do? Could a case be made for giving students the chance to apply to popular culture texts the skills of analysis, explication, and creation that we spend all of high school indoctrinating them in?

Media literacy has come a long way in the United States since my course was founded in 1998. The International Reading Association (IRA) has adopted language supporting the reading of nonprint texts; the National Council of Teachers of English (NCTE) adopted a resolution calling for instruction in a variety of media formats ("Resolution on Composing with Nonprint Media"); and a study by Robert Kubey and Frank Baker found that nearly all state curricular frameworks call for some manner of media education in either their English or social studies courses. The College Board is adding a question on the English AP exam asking students to interpret a visual image, and the National Board for Professional Teaching Standards has included a standard for media literacy as well. It would seem that the movement to include media literacy in the ELA classroom is beginning to take hold.

The world of media and the rate of media consumption by our students are growing at an unprecedented rate. Things unimaginable when my school started its media course are commonplace today; who imagined that one day you could download the entire text of *The Great Gatsby*? Or burn your own CDs of music? Or trade files with strangers over the Internet? Students are becoming increasingly adept at using media and even creating it, but there's been little effort to teach them how to compose, create, and interact with media in a thoughtful and reflective way.

Communication, technology, and language are always moving faster than the life of the English classroom. Through a variety of means, such as instant messaging, peer-to-peer file sharing, podcasting, blogs, TiVo, the list goes on and on, students today are faced with a media-rich world that is vastly different from the world most English professionals today inhabit. Students are no longer passive consumers of media products, and the "inoculation" theory of media education—i.e., arm children with critical thinking skills that will protect them from the devious, and often subliminal, messages of the media—is no longer the driving force of media education. Students live in a media-driven world, and the issue is no longer about trying to protect students from media, or convince them that popular culture isn't as worthy of examination as high art. The questions really lie with us, the classroom teachers. If we are to take our jobs as English teachers and educators seriously, we have to examine the type of world our students are going to be living in. What skills do they need? What production capabilities must they have? How does the English curriculum help prepare students for that world? Or should it?

English class has traditionally been the site in school where issues of culture can be discussed; where literature, art, society, and experience intersect; where the arts of persuasion and rhetoric are taught and refined. Media literacy is an essential component of those discussions. An understanding of media and its principles is integral to the understanding and development of our students, who we are, ostensibly, preparing for the world beyond school. But if our students spend more time in a media-saturated world than in our classrooms, what do we owe them? How do we best fulfill our mission to prepare critical thinkers for a future world if we resist embracing that future world?

There is a growing understanding that we now live in the grandiosely named Information Age, that the workplace has changed from one of production of products from raw materials to one of information management, but schools haven't changed much to address this reality. There hasn't been a concerted effort to analyze the needs of this newly emerging media-rich world and address it through our curriculum, which is still rooted firmly in the traditional reading and writing paradigm. Our tactics haven't changed to meet the rapidly developing form of literacy that our students cultivate independent of us and our classrooms.

According to a Harris Interactive and Teenage Unlimited Research poll conducted in 2003 (Indiantelevision.com Team), teenagers spend 16.7 hours a week surfing the Web and 13.6 hours a week watching television. Compare that to the average high school day, which is broken down into 50-minute class periods. With six courses a day, students have 300 minutes of teacher–student interaction a day, 1,500 minutes a week. Divide that by 60 and you get 25 hours, or 5.3 hours *less* than the time they browse the Net and watch TV. As the teacher of a single class, the competition is even worse, because you are able to teach students for only 250 minutes a week, or just over 4 hours. How does school compete? This survey included other forms of media that students involve themselves in: reading, talking on the phone, and listening to the radio, which covers another 20.5 hours. When you add it all up, the big picture is that we traditionally ignore in the school curriculum the media that occupies 50.8 hours a week of our average student's life. That's a full-time job plus overtime, yet we don't make a rule of teaching media texts or the processes of media production to our students. We don't require them to read or write for 50 hours a week. It would seem we owe it to them to use media as a text in our classrooms.

When we set the curriculum, why don't we consider the world our students will be entering? Aren't schools supposed to be about preparing our students for the "real world"? Shouldn't we be trying to make learning relevant to our students and drawing connections between the reading, composing, and thinking we do every day in the ELA classroom and the world that consumes our students and that our students consume? Isn't media literacy a skill that we should develop not only in our students but in our own lives as well?

This book attempts to bridge the gap between a curriculum that studies only media and the one that never studies media. As the teachers whose lessons appear in this text show, there is an enormous variety of work being done in the ELA classroom that makes connections between the literary texts that are the stock in trade of the profession and the media texts that our students interact with on a daily basis. There are logical steps to follow, connections to be made, and relevancy to be developed that make the teaching of media literacy skills an integral part of the ELA classroom.

National organizations for ELA teachers have, over time, passed a number of resolutions concerning the need to use media as a text and media literacy as practice in the ELA classroom. In 1975, NCTE passed a resolution on media literacy skill development:

> Resolved, that the National Council of Teachers of English, through its publications and its affiliates, continue to support curriculum changes designed to promote sophisticated media awareness at the elementary, secondary, and college levels; . . . that NCTE continue to encourage teacher education programs which will enable teachers to promote media literacy in students; and that NCTE cooperate with organizations and individuals representing teachers of journalism, the social sciences, and speech communication to promote the understanding and develop the insights students need to evaluate critically the messages disseminated by the mass media. ("Resolution on Promoting Media Literacy")

Then, at the 2003 NCTE Annual Convention in San Francisco, this call for media literacy developed further and was passed as the "Resolution on Composing with Nonprint Media." It called for all members of NCTE to:

- encourage preservice, inservice, and staff development programs that will focus on new literacies, multimedia composition, and a broadened concept of literacy;

- encourage research and develop models of district, school, and classroom policies that would promote multimedia composition;

- encourage integrating multimedia composition in English language arts curriculum and teacher education, and in refining related standards at local, state, and national levels; and

- renew the commitment expressed in the 1983 Resolution on Computers in English and Language Arts to achieve equity of access to the full range of composing technologies.

Clearly, the tide in the field of English is beginning to change. There are places where the study of media is treated with the seriousness it deserves. The skills of composition, analysis, and interpretation that we associate with the traditional study of printed texts are beginning to be applied to a wide variety of media texts, and the crucial links of relevancy between the lives of students and the texts we teach are beginning to be made.

To assist in this transition within, or addition to, the ELA classroom, this text is geared primarily toward ELA teachers who are either just beginning their exploration of media literacy or interested in finding more ways to bring media into their classrooms. Because education is such a unique endeavor, context is often crucial to the success of any classroom practice. Therefore, each contributor describes the context in which he or she teaches as a frame of reference. Each lesson also contains many other features that will allow you to adapt and restructure each lesson to fit your individual needs. We've adopted a basic lesson plan format that provides information on each of the pertinent features of the lesson and allows the teacher contributors to offer suggestions for differentiation and extension of skills.

After describing the context in which the lesson has been taught, each teacher contributor gives the rationale of the lesson, which is where you will find the genesis of the ideas presented in the lesson as well as the relevance of the skills to the lives of students and their connection to the ELA curriculum. The objectives will state clearly what skills and concepts the teachers are trying to accomplish with their lessons. Next, the specific NCTE/IRA standards are listed so that teachers who need to show how they are teaching to the standards in their curriculum can do so (the numbers map to the standards reprinted on pages xxv–xxvi). Listing the standards also helps reinforce the understanding that media is a subject worthy of study in the ELA classroom. After the standards, you'll find laid out the necessary materials and processes for each of the lessons. Then a time frame for planning the lesson is suggested, and the instructional activities are described in depth. At the end of the instructional activities section, you will find suggestions for assessment and connections to other texts or activities and other ideas for adapting the lesson to specific needs. Finally, contributors include a brief works cited list for each lesson; some lessons also include a supplemental reading list. Note that at the end of each section summary, we've provided a list of recommended resources for the general topic.

These lessons are designed to be introductory activities that will give you a starting point for bringing media literacy instruction into the classroom. Feel free to change, adapt, or mutate them as you see fit.

Works Cited

Indiantelevision.com Team. "US Youngsters Hooked on to Net, TV Say Researchers." *Indiantelevision.com* 16 Aug. 2003. 30 Jan. 2007 <http://us.indiantelevision.com/headlines/y2k3/aug/aug124.htm>.

Kubey, Robert, and Frank Baker. "Has Media Literacy Found a Curricular Foothold?" *Education Week* 27 Oct. 1999: 56+.

Meier, Deborah. *The Power of Their Ideas: Lessons for America from a Small School in Harlem.* Boston: Beacon, 2002.

National Council of Teachers of English. "Resolution on Composing with Nonprint Media." NCTE Position Statement. Urbana, IL: National Council of Teachers of English, 2003. 7 June 2006 <http://www.ncte.org/about/over/positions/category/media/114919.htm>.

National Council of Teachers of English. "Resolution on Promoting Media Literacy." NCTE Position Statement. Urbana, IL: National Council of Teachers of English, 1975. 7 June 2006 <http://www.ncte.org/about/over/positions/category/media/107519.htm>.

Shenk, David. *Data Smog: Surviving the Information Glut.* San Francisco: HarperEdge, 1997.

Copyright, Fair Use, and Classroom Media Production

Scott Sullivan
National-Louis University

One of the very real issues teachers need to address when they begin to incorporate media production into class is copyright. Copyright laws govern the use of images, sound, and a wide range of intellectual properties. A variety of laws govern your ability to tape programs for classroom use, use copyrighted imagery in media productions, or use music for sound tracks in film production. These laws limit your ability to reproduce articles for class discussions, images that can be placed on classroom websites, and even the movies you show in your classroom.

While we compiled this text, our contributors ran into many issues concerning copyright and fair use. When we began selecting sample materials for the companion disk, we had to reject many good media texts because they would violate copyright law. The first Power-Point example from Jacqueline Cullen's lesson had all images of Nemo, the cartoon fish, stripped out of it, as well as the images from *The Wizard of Oz* from the student sample. The sound tracks were removed from David L. Bruce's video themes, as the songs used exceeded the limit suggested by educational fair use guidelines. We did include the musical tracks on the sample PSA (Chapter 27) and movie trailers (Chapter 13) because they were in line with the proposed "30-second rule" (Stim 7/17–18). Since we felt strongly about offering media texts to illustrate the end result of several production-oriented lessons, we went ahead and included these "modified" examples.

Deciding how to encourage or discourage the use of copyrighted materials in student work is a complex situation that may affect your instruction to a degree, but it doesn't have to be prohibitive. The decision to permit the use of copyrighted materials is not as much of an issue if its use is confined to face-to-face instruction in a classroom setting. The problem arises when the work goes "public" on a class or personal website, and many corporations regularly troll the Internet for copyright violations. A number of sites on the Internet post stock photos, musical loops, or templates that can be used by anyone to create a media text. Knowing the rules and laws will help you and your students avoid making mistakes.

Many educational institutions, especially in higher education, have developed their own criteria for fair use and copyright compliance, so there are many resources available on the Web. Depending on where you teach, your school may already have designed and implemented its own policies, so we strongly suggest that you begin there as well.

The following list is in no way meant to be exhaustive but serves as a place to start your thinking on fair use and copyright. Here are a few informative sites where you can begin your study:

> http://www.copyright.gov/
> The official site of the United States government on copyright has a wide variety of information on all aspects of copyright procedures and laws.
>
> http://cyber.law.harvard.edu/media/files/copyrightand education.html
> Harvard University has put together an informative handout on the effects of copyright on educational settings that gives some specific limits and suggestions for conforming to copyright law.
>
> http://www.techlearning.com/db_area/archives/TL/2002/ 10/copyright.php
> This site explores the original intent of copyright law and how it may impact your classroom practice.

One last site has a handy, printable reference sheet that looks at basic media usage in the classroom and offers brief insights and recommendations on making sure you are conforming to the laws of the land. The site was created and is maintained by the Association of Distance Learning Educators and is located at http://www.nccei.org/black board/copyright.html.

Copyright and fair use may be great issues for you and your students to explore together. There is a growing movement among some segments of the computer community to begin what's called "open source" programming, meaning that the essential code written to run a program will be made available to anyone who wants to tweak or improve the program or adapt to some other use. Creative Commons, at www.creativecommons.org, is a place that offers open source software and licensing, as is Copyleft, located at http://www.gnu.org/copyleft, where a "reciprocal license" allows people to build, expand, and improve on existing creations.

The moral and ethical ramifications of copyright laws and fair use provisions may provide fertile ground for exploration in the classroom, as well as a valuable learning experience for teachers and authors of both print and nonprint texts.

Work Cited

Stim, Richard. *Getting Permission: How to License and Clear Copyrighted Materials Online and Off.* Berkeley, CA: Nolo, 2001.

NCTE/IRA Standards

M ost teachers are expected to align their curriculum with a variety of national, state, and local standards. Since NCTE/IRA standards have been widely accepted by professionals in the English language arts field, all of the lessons included in this volume are linked to them. This component will be helpful in developing a rationale for implementing media literacy into existing or developing curricula.

1. Students read a wide range of print and nonprint texts to build an understanding of texts, of themselves, and of the cultures of the United States and the world; to acquire new information; to respond to the needs and demands of society and the workplace; and for personal fulfillment. Among these texts are fiction and nonfiction, classic and contemporary works.

2. Students read a wide range of literature from many periods in many genres to build an understanding of the many dimensions (e.g., philosophical, ethical, aesthetic) of human experience.

3. Students apply a wide range of strategies to comprehend, interpret, evaluate, and appreciate texts. They draw on their prior experience, their interactions with other readers and writers, their knowledge of word meaning and of other texts, their word identification strategies, and their understanding of textual features (e.g., sound-letter correspondence, sentence structure, context, graphics).

4. Students adjust their use of spoken, written, and visual language (e.g., conventions, style, vocabulary) to communicate effectively with a variety of audiences and for different purposes.

5. Students employ a wide range of strategies as they write and use different writing process elements appropriately to communicate with different audiences for a variety of purposes.

6. Students apply knowledge of language structure, language conventions (e.g., spelling and punctuation), media techniques, figurative language, and genre to create, critique, and discuss print and nonprint texts.

The standards are reprinted from NCTE and IRA's *Standards for the English Language Arts* (Urbana, IL, and Newark, DE: NCTE and IRA, 1996), 3.

7. Students conduct research on issues and interests by generating ideas and questions, and by posing problems. They gather, evaluate, and synthesize data from a variety of sources (e.g., print and nonprint texts, artifacts, people) to communicate their discoveries in ways that suit their purpose and audience.

8. Students use a variety of technological and informational resources (e.g., libraries, databases, computer networks, video) to gather and synthesize information and to create and communicate knowledge.

9. Students develop an understanding of and respect for diversity in language use, patterns, and dialects across cultures, ethnic groups, geographic regions, and social roles.

10. Students whose first language is not English make use of their first language to develop competency in the English language arts and to develop understanding of content across the curriculum.

11. Students participate as knowledgeable, reflective, creative, and critical members of a variety of literacy communities.

12. Students use spoken, written, and visual language to accomplish their own purposes (e.g., for learning, enjoyment, persuasion, and the exchange of information).

Companion Disk Directory

The following lessons are linked to a series of handouts and media samples on the companion disk that is packaged with this text. For best results, view these files by using one of the following Web browsers: Internet Explorer (PC), Safari (MAC), or Firefox (PC or MAC). Also, make sure you have access to the following "plug-ins": Adobe Reader and QuickTime Player. Both of these tools are available for fair use download. Video files are best viewed by using an LCD projector to enlarge the image. If you don't have Internet access, you can view files by opening up individual folders on the disk. Files are identified by figure number.

Part I: Getting Started	
1 Capturing the Pulitzer Prize Photo: An Exercise in Photo Manipulation	Figure 1.1. Cropping Tool Figure 1.2. Capturing the Prize: A Photo Analysis
2 Snapshot Stories	Figure 2.1. Extension Activity
4 Building Active Viewing Skills: *An Occurrence at Owl Creek Bridge*	Figure 4.1. Annotated Viewing Guide for Instructors
5 Video Themes: An Introduction to Composing with Images	Figure 5.1. Sample Rationale of Shots Figure 5.2. Video Theme Rubric Figure 5.3. Sample Heuristic for "Isolation" Figure 5.4. Student Essay Sample 1 (video) Figure 5.5. Sample Heuristic for "Nourishment" Figure 5.6. Student Essay Sample 2 (video)
6 Truly an iMovie: Composing Video Diaries	Figure 6.1. Diary Sample 1 (video) Figure 6.2. Diary Sample 2 (video) Figure 6.3. Diary Sample 3 (video) Figure 6.4. Video Diary Rubric

	Figure 21.3. Media Economics Word Search
22 I Ate the Ad: Media Literacy and the Marketing of Junk Food	Figure 22.1. Advertising Concepts and Terminology
23 Inadequacy Illustrated: Decoding Teen Magazine Covers	Figure 23.1. Cover Text Analysis Figure 23.2. Cover Image Analysis Figure 23.3. Sample Magazine Cover
24 From Sammy Sosa to City Hall: Detecting Bias in Print News	Figure 24.1. Key Newspaper Terminology Figure 24.2. Sample Student Response Figure 24.3. Extension Activity
25 Deconstructing Broadcast News	Figure 25.1. Television News Analysis Figure 25.2. Television News Essay
26 Video News Releases: When Is News Really News?	Figure 26.1. What Is a Video News Release? Figure 26.2. VNRs and Media Ethics
27 Creating a Public Service Announcement: Powerful Persuasion in 60 Seconds	Figure 27.1. PSA Building Blocks and Appeals Figure 27.2. Ad Analysis Worksheet Figure 27.3. Creating a Public Service Announcement Figure 27.4. PSA iMovie Peer Evaluation Figure 27.5. PSA Evaluation Rubric Figure 27.6. Sample PSA (video)

I Getting Started

"When Was I Supposed to Learn That?"

Scott Sullivan
National-Louis University

English teachers aren't trained to be media literacy teachers. Many of us find our way to using media in the classroom for a variety of reasons: we are outraged by an issue in the media; we recognize that media texts surround our students and feel a vague tug to make our curriculum more relevant by using media; or we were forced to because it became part of our curriculum. Whatever the reason, very few media literacy training programs exist, and hence, very few teachers trained in the ways of media literacy are in English language arts (ELA) classrooms today. As a colleague of mine, Warren Wolfe, once said, "I was trained how to teach literature, but media literacy I just do because I'm interested." That sentiment is likely true for many of us.

Media literacy has been defined in various ways over the years, but a common definition is the ability to access, analyze, evaluate, and produce communication in a variety of media formats. But what does that mean? Showing a movie in class? Does having students use a picture as a writing prompt constitute a media literacy activity? If I have students make a collage out of advertisements, am I doing media literacy? The lack of training in media literacy is a concern for classroom teachers who are now expected by professional organizations from the National Council of Teachers of English (NCTE) to the National Board for Professional Teaching Standards (NBPTS) to teach media literacy in their classrooms.

Addressing that training gap is the ultimate goal of this text. In this first section, "Getting Started," we show how teachers, few of whom were formally trained in media literacy, began using media literacy as a tool to increase student understanding and performance in their class-rooms. The lessons progress from smaller, shorter lessons, designed to be done in a single period, to longer, more involved projects. From developing skills in analyzing a single photograph, to using media as writing prompts, to developing a video diary project, we show how, through your existing curriculum, you'll be able to use media literacy as a tool to enrich and improve the experience of your students.

A good place to start working with media literacy concepts is in examining a single static image. Students and teachers alike aren't threatened when facing a photograph, and photos are something nearly everyone has had experience with, so using them as a tool in class should be fairly easy. Belinha S. De Abreu's lesson, "Capturing the Pulitzer Prize Photo: An Exercise in Photo Manipulation," is a logical starting point for learning media literacy skills. One of the major concepts she raises is that photos are compositions, staged and edited for effect. Students, and many adults, tend to believe that all photographers do is point a camera and click a button, and that the photograph itself is then a realistic representation of the moment the photographer was lucky enough to catch. The idea that photos can be staged, or that decisions made after taking the picture might influence how a viewer sees the photo, rarely occurs to us. This lesson takes you through some basic terminology and some photo editing concepts and then asks students to begin working with pictures in an attempt to understand how photos achieve particular effects. Students work with Pulitzer Prize–winning photos to discuss their meaning, how that meaning can change based on decisions made by the photographer and editors, and whether those considerations influence our understanding of the reality of the photographs.

Taking the study of photographs one step further, Louis Mazza's "Snapshot Stories" asks students to use photography as a tool for exploration through the written word. Students create stories about the photographs, hypothesize about the artistic intent of the photographers, and produce finished writing products that have a clear connection to the photograph.

These two lesson plans allow both teachers and students to become more comfortable with the idea that photography is a proactive, constructivist activity. Pictures aren't produced simply by someone clicking a camera at just the right time; to create an overall mood or effect, it's necessary to build the picture by knowing your audience, understanding your intent, and using the most effective techniques to create the effects you are after—just like the composition process.

Furthering students' and teachers' understanding of photography, William Kist's exercise on developing vocabulary media journals is the next logical step in the progression of how to use both print and nonprint media to convey meaning. Kist's lesson is an easily adaptable strategy for allowing students to begin composing in a nonprint medium. Essentially, students create vocabulary definitions using images. One of the traditional complaints about teaching vocabulary is that students can memorize a definition of a word, even write it correctly in a sentence, but not really have a feel for the true essence of the word. Kist's lesson allows students to make their own connections with new vocabulary, and it provides an excellent opportunity for teachers to assess the students' ability to make sense of new words and incorporate them into everyday usage. Composing with nonprint texts is an excellent way to check for understanding of key concepts while breaking the traditional cycle of "study the list, take the quiz, forget the words" vocabulary exercises that many students have experienced.

While exploring meaning in nonprint media may be unfamiliar to some ELA teachers, using film as a companion to a piece of literature is something most of us have done from time to time. We all know the teachers who view movie day as a day off, or a "reward" for the students because they worked hard in reading and discussing the novel or short story. But simply popping in a DVD or videocassette and letting the students watch the film is not being media literate, nor does it promote media literacy. Mark Dolce's lesson using the short film *An Occurrence at Owl Creek Bridge* is an insightful introduction to the concept of active viewing, and in line with the NCTE resolution on teaching with nonprint texts. By linking the film and the short story, Dolce shows teachers how to use the film as another text, an active exercise in creating meaning and understanding, just as we hope to do whenever we discuss a piece of literature in the classroom. Movie day should be seen as a chance to continue learning, to supplement understanding of the text, and to create active and engaged minds, not an opportunity to take a day off.

Generally, the final recognized principle of media literacy is production, and judging from discussions with teachers unfamiliar with the field of media literacy, production is the element that most worries them. Having been taught to explicate text, to teach composition, and to assess the progress of our students, we aren't sure how to actually produce media. Digital video cameras and easy-to-use editing software make shooting videos easier than ever before. The cliché in using technology in the classroom is that if you don't know how to do it, just ask your students. While that has an element of truth to it, it would behoove most of us to take the few hours necessary to learn how to use a digital camcorder and editing program so that you can use them as teaching tools in your own classroom.

Here is where you might want to integrate into your curriculum some attention to being/getting comfortable with technology. The last two lessons in this section both deal with using video technology as a composing tool. Creating video, and doing it well, is one way for students to synthesize information, respond to it, edit that response, and create a product that represents their best thinking on a subject. Many ELA teachers are apprehensive about bringing technology into the classroom; many have stories of the day the connection to the Internet didn't work, or the projector wouldn't show the PowerPoint presentations. But technology isn't something to fear in the classroom, it's something to embrace and make use of in order to teach students how to compose messages more effectively. The easiest and simplest program for creating video pieces is the Apple iMovie program. Although there are many tutorials available online for learning the basics of the program, one of the best is found at www.atomiclearning.com and is free to use. Tutorials for a variety of other production programs are available as well, but make sure to search for the one that helps you use the program your school owns. Take a few minutes to play around with the program and tutorial, and to shoot some film, until you get comfortable. Most ELA teachers aren't trained to be filmmakers, but with a little time and effort, you can become one.

David L. Bruce's "Video Themes" is an effective exercise for introducing the basics of video composition, as well as introducing and reinforcing the concept of theme. This versatile lesson can be used in a variety of ways to explore any number of thematic elements. As you become more comfortable with video production, the possibilities of this lesson grow exponentially.

The final lesson in this section, Stephen Murphy's "Truly an iMovie: Composing Video Diaries," is a project designed to help students fully integrate their growing media literacy and production savvy into their knowledge base by creating projects that help them begin to define who they feel themselves to be. Murphy's project can be seen as a creative culminating exercise, an effective form of assessment, and an integration of all the components of media literacy we've covered in this section. It is also adaptable for a variety of purposes and can be used to create a number of projects that will help students become proficient in their growing media literacy skills.

Ideally, the lessons in this section scaffold your level of comfort and expertise in media literacy and its integration into your curriculum. The study of static images, advertising, and moving images is crucial for students to begin developing the skills needed to navigate our media-rich society. Print and its primacy in our classrooms haven't been replaced, but they are enhanced when students have the necessary understanding and skills to also compose in other forms prevalent in today's world. Students deserve to be able to develop a full range of composition, comprehension, and production skills, and the lessons in this section are the beginning of supplying you with the skills needed to help them do just that.

Recommended Resources

Print

Alvarado, Manuel, and Oliver Boyd-Barrett, eds. *Media Education: An Introduction.* London: British Film Institute, 1992.

Buckingham, David. *Media Education: Literacy, Learning, and Contemporary Culture.* Cambridge, UK: Polity, 2003.

Kist, William. *New Literacies in Action: Teaching and Learning in Multiple Media.* New York: Teachers College P, 2005.

Potter, W. James. *Media Literacy.* 3rd. ed. Thousand Oaks, CA: Sage, 2005.

Worsnop, Chris M. *Screening Images: Ideas for Media Education.* 2nd ed. Mississauga, ON: Wright Communications, 1999.

Websites

Action Coalition for Media Education. <http://www.acmecoalition.org/>.

Center for Media Literacy. <http://www.medialit.org/>.

Media Awareness Network. <http://www.media-awareness.ca/>.

Media Literacy Clearinghouse. <http://www.frankwbaker.com/>.

1 Capturing the Pulitzer Prize Photo: An Exercise in Photo Manipulation

Belinha S. De Abreu
Walsh Intermediate School
Branford, Connecticut

Context

Walsh Intermediate School is a suburban, shoreline school of 1,200 students encompassing grades 5–8. The following activity has been developed for use in English or social studies classes that are discussing the topic of visual literacy or historical accuracy in photographs. The lesson has been used in both a seventh- and eighth-grade classroom and can be adapted for older students.

Through this activity, students are able to explore the nuances of the media as they impact their lives in a variety of different formats and within the different academic content areas. My role as a media literacy specialist has been to develop curricula that can be implemented as a collaborative effort in the classroom. Walsh Intermediate School is an open space school that relies on a team-teaching approach. In essence, my specialization allows me to work with all grade levels and provide unique opportunities for learning.

Rationale

My fascination with Pulitzer Prize photos developed four years ago when I visited the Freedom Forum in New York City. They were having a celebratory program for the Pulitzer Prize and showcased the photographs, along with the photographers' stories, blown up to life-size proportions. The experience was like walking through moments of history while feeling joy, pain, suffering, war, love, and peace. The photographs in that particular size are impressive and intense. My goal was to try to duplicate that intensity in the classroom while discussing the importance of photographs such as these in comparison to ones that have been changed to conform to an idea or preference of an editor.

Photography developed early in the nineteenth century as an important visual medium. It is a format that transmits a variety of feelings and emotions while communicating news and information. As we have stepped into the twenty-first century, however, photos have become a source of contention. Questions frequently arise regarding whether a photo is "real" or if it has been manipulated. What does photo manipulation actually mean? What do extremely cropped photos leave out? What has been changed about a time or place captured on film? The concerns in the news industry have grown accordingly because of the availability of new photo manipulation technologies. This lesson teaches students about photo manipulation through the simple method of cropping. Second, it asks students to look at Pulitzer Prize photos, read the photographers' stories while studying the photographs, and then chose two pictures for closer analysis.

This is an introductory lesson on the importance of photographs, not a lesson on photography. Photographs are all around us both in our personal lives and as a source of messages displayed through media networks. Therefore, as a baseline lesson, it is an easy way for any educator to provide a general lesson on media literacy instruction through understanding and analyzing this particular medium's construction, message, and point of view.

Objectives

Students will be able to:

- Understand photographic terms such as
  - ◆ *cropping*: omitting parts of an image when making a print or copy negative in order to improve or change the composition of the final image
  - ◆ *composition*: visual arrangement of all the elements in a photograph
  - ◆ *photo manipulation*: telling a lie through a camera; altering images so that they misrepresent the information presented
  - ◆ *air brushing*: method of retouching black-and-white or color photographs in which dye is sprayed, under pressure, on to selected areas of the negative or print
  - ◆ *camera angles*: various positions of the camera with respect

to the subject being photographed, each giving a different viewpoint and perspective

♦ *ethics*: a set of moral principles or values; the principles of conduct governing an individual or a group

■ Analyze a photograph and detect where information has been manipulated and changed

■ Appreciate aesthetically a good-quality photograph and understand its societal and historical importance

NCTE/IRA standards addressed: 1, 3, 6, 12

Materials/Preactivity Preparation

For the first class period, the teacher will need to provide:

■ Selection of front covers from newsmagazines such as *U.S. News & World Report*, *Time*, *Newsweek*, etc.

■ June 27, 1994, covers of *Newsweek* and *Time* depicting the two variations of the O. J. Simpson mug shot ("Trail of Blood"; "An American Tragedy")

■ Copy of the video *Is Seeing Believing?* distributed by the Newseum

■ Selection of photographs from magazines or newspapers, enough for the whole class

■ Cropping template (see Figure 1.1 on the companion disk)

For the second class period, the classroom is converted into a museum. Pulitzer Prize photos should be hung throughout the classroom. They should be placed both high and low so that students can spend time reading and studying the photographs while sitting or standing. The following materials will be needed for the second class:

■ *Capture the Moment: The Pulitzer Prize Photographs*, edited by Cyma Rubin and Eric Newton

■ Pulitzer Prize photos matted on 11" × 17" hard bond paper, which will then be hung throughout the classroom museum style

■ Student reflective worksheet for analysis (Figure 1.2 on the companion disk)

Time Frame

This entire lesson should take no more than three class periods. The first period is an introduction to examining the role of photographs in the media and addressing conceptual understanding of how photographs are taken and then changed. The video selected for this lesson is approximately 18 minutes long but can be stopped after 10 minutes, which covers all the key concepts needed for this lesson. The duration of the entire lesson is based on students' discussion and their ability to master the information in order to complete the analysis. Consider that the actual museum element of the project, which takes place on the second day of the lesson, is a quiet time for student reflection, as they work their way around the room examining each Pulitzer Prize photograph.

When this lesson was first implemented, it was based on a 50-minute period, and we used only two class periods. Consider your own schedule and adapt the lessons accordingly. Each of the three activities has the ability to take up more class time, but only you can decide how they best fit your instructional needs.

Description of Activity

Day 1

To begin this lesson, you'll need to cover certain photographic terms, such as *crop*, *air brushing*, *photo manipulation*, and so forth, to evaluate and include students' prior knowledge as well as to establish a common vocabulary and preparation for viewing the video. Then ask students why photographs are meaningful. This will generate a lot of discussion, including information about the kinds of cameras that are used today: e.g., digital, instamatic, 35mm film. Introduce the magazine covers featuring O. J. Simpson.

The O.J. Simpson photo was taken at police headquarters as he was being processed, by a camera owned by the department. When the photo was distributed to magazines, many news organizations used the original photo, but others chose to manipulate it. The major source of contention about the photo occurred when both *Newsweek* and *Time* appeared on the newsstand together. It was apparent that one photo had been darkened.

Introduce the *Time* and *Newsweek* cover photos of O. J. Simpson. Ask students:

- What is the difference between the presentations of the same image?
- Which do you think is the real photo?
- Why would someone choose to darken the picture of a person?
- What is the message to you, the reader?
- Introduce the concept of ethics: what does it mean and should photographers follow a specific ethical standard?

At this point, you can begin introducing the video *Is Seeing Believing?* I have used this video with both seventh- and eighth-grade students and have found it to be just as valuable for both grade levels. The video covers a wide variety of photo editors' and journalists' points of views, but more important, it presents actual examples of photos that have gone to press changed from their original version. The video is approximately 18 minutes long, but showing just the first 10 minutes would work well too. Balance this viewing with the planned activity within the time available.

Once the video is finished, discuss with students what they think of photo manipulation. Students will express both pro and con points of view, and asking them to explain why they support one view over the other reveals their philosophical beliefs on this issue. Bring the conversation around to the news and the importance of news photos. Ask the students:

- Should news photos be changed or cropped?
- Under what circumstances might cropping be appropriate or necessary?
- What are some concerns about cropping too much content from a photograph?

Students understand the idea of eliminating a bad shot or an angle from a shot, but when you start to discuss important issues such as war or the World Trade Center bombings, their feelings begin to change. This is where the cropping exercise is most appropriately integrated into curriculum content.

Place on each student's desk a picture with the cropping box or framing tool on top (see Figure 1.1 on the companion disk). Group the students in pairs or in fours, depending on the time you have for this activity. Model an example with the students so that they understand the significance of how too much cropping can remove information and thus tell a different story.

Have the student groups discuss amongst themselves how little or how much a photograph can reveal depending on how it is presented. Ask students to uncrop their photos and talk about what they are seeing as they uncover the image. Have students experiment with different ways to crop the same image for different effects.

Visit each table to sit in and assist students in answering these questions:

- What is the message when the photo is cropped? What is emphasized in the image?

- Is it positive or is it negative?
- What makes the image important?
- Why would a photographer or editor choose to crop or eliminate information from a particular photo?
- To what extent is that an ethical choice if the image is a news photograph?

As you work your way around the classroom, students will voice a variety of thoughts on the stories they see reflected in the images. Discuss with students how each person has a unique perspective and may not see things the way someone else might. Close the class period with the question: what did you learn from this assignment about the impact of cropping an image?

The Pulitzer Prize photography book you purchase for this lesson should contain the stories of the photographers. For instance, Robert Akeret's *Photolanguage* is a wonderful resource because it gives the context or circumstances surrounding the picture, which is just as important as the picture itself. The stories provide background information on how the photographer came to be at the location where the picture was taken, and also how he or she managed to capture the shot that won the prize.

Day 2

On the second day of this assignment, ask students to examine the Pulitzer Prize photos. The classroom should be set up like a museum so that students have uninterrupted access to the photos. They should feel free to walk around, sit or stand while looking at the photos, and consider the photographers' stories that accompany the images.

As the students settle into their seats, hand out the analysis sheet titled "Capturing the Prize: A Photo Analysis" (see Figure 1.2 on the companion disk). Point out the many photographs mounted around the room. The images show times of triumph and sadness and some of the darkest moments in our history. These are images captured on film by photographers who were willing to go the extra mile to show the world these events through their lenses. The students' job is to walk around the room, look carefully at the photos, and read the stories associated with the photographer who snapped the picture. Students are to select two photos and write about them. They are to answer the following questions:

- What made you stop to look at these specific photographs?

- What ultimately made you decide to pick these photographs to write about? What about them struck you?
- How did the photographs make you feel?

They are to write as much as possible, but encourage them to compose a minimum of two paragraphs.

Remind students that photographs are a personal experience. Students are not to pick a photo just because their fellow classmate or friend did. Making a truly personal choice is something that needs to be emphasized in grades 7 and 8 but not usually with older students. Instead, tell students to pick photos that made them think or that provoked a strong emotion.

This exercise will take almost the entire class period. You will need to walk around the room and in some cases give further direction, but for the most part you can watch students as they react to the images and the stories presented before them. Leave 10 minutes at the end of class for students to share their thoughts on the photos. You can ask for volunteers to share their choices, but in my experience this activity becomes very personal for students. Many feel that their reflection is almost like a journal entry that they would rather not share and instead just give to the teacher.

End the class with a reminder of the true testament of photographs and why Pulitzer Prize photos have had such an impact on our society.

Assessment

Assessment needs to focus on class discussion, observation of students' collaborative efforts in coming up with responses for the cropping activity, and their written analyses of the two selected photographs. Use continuous informal teacher assessment throughout the two class periods, through your conferencing with the working groups, listening to students' conversation and observing their responses, and watching them interact with the Pulitzer Prize photos.

Connections and Adaptations

Using photographs in different curricular areas has several practical purposes. In the English language arts classroom, studying images is an investigation of a visual text and its purpose in society. Teachers can use photography to discuss messages and content, even to consider the adage "A picture is worth a thousand words," and as a method for discussing language, voice, theme, and point of view. In a history classroom, pictures can be used to discuss propaganda, political motivations, and even stereotyping. Certainly pictures are a window into the past. They explain events in history, they reflect the passing of time, and they open doorways to change.

Photographs can also be regarded as an art form and can be helpful if you are interested in teaching production. Using this lesson on the meaning of photographs as an introduction, ask students to snap pictures and adapt them for use in class projects, as a creative outlet, or for the purpose of telling a personal story. These are just a few examples of what a lesson on photography can offer students and teachers.

Works Cited

Akeret, Robert U. *Photolanguage: How Photos Reveal the Fascinating Stories of Our Lives and Relationships*. New York: Norton, 2000.

"An American Tragedy." Cover. Mug shot of O. J. Simpson. *Time* 27 June 1994.

Is Seeing Believing? How Can You Tell What's Real? Video Recording [Curriculum Package]. Washington, DC: Newseum, 1997.

Rubin, Cyma, and Eric Newton, eds. *Capture the Moment: The Pulitzer Prize Photographs*. New York: Norton, 2001.

"Trail of Blood." Cover. Mug shot of O. J. Simpson. *Newsweek* 27 June 1994.

2 Snapshot Stories

Louis Mazza
University of the Arts
Philadelphia, Pennsylvania

Context

"Snapshot Stories" is a lesson created for a sixth-grade English class at Dimner Beeber Middle School in West Philadelphia, Pennsylvania. The lesson is designed to bring a visual component to teacher Samuel Reed's annual playwriting workshop. In this context, the lesson has helped students build skills in character creation. By projecting personalities and characteristics onto images of people, students can experience the creative process of creating characters for a play.

Beeber Middle School is a large, predominately African American middle school that struggles to balance discipline with meaningful instruction and classroom experiences. The school spans grades 6–8 and scores 31 percent and 16 percent on the Pennsylvania Standard Assessment tests in English and math, respectively.

Learning is often disrupted by behavioral problems that make it difficult for teachers to teach and students to learn; however, for the past three years, Samuel Reed's English classes have participated in a playwriting and poetry workshop that has students enthusiastically engaged in writing, reading, and performing.

My involvement with the school and Mr. Reed's class has been facilitated by the Graduate Art Education Department at the University of the Arts in Philadelphia, where graduate students are placed in service-learning positions as part of their preservice graduate course work.

Rationale

How has visual culture affected our society? Has the ubiquitous camera clarified or complicated our perception of reality? What does a snapshot say about its subjects? How many meanings can you derive from one picture? These are some of the questions we address in "Snapshot Stories," a lesson about storytelling through photographs.

Next to visual art, stories are our oldest and most enduring form of cultural communication. One need only look at the pervasiveness of films to see that this remains the most popular and universal art form in our modern times. This lesson refines students' visual aesthetic skills and ties together writing, storytelling, and visual art. Students can identify with the pictures because chances are they have similar snapshots in their own homes.

Art teachers are in a particularly advantageous position when it comes to media literacy and visual culture. The modularity of our subject area allows us to plan lessons that address formal and aesthetic issues in art and also to connect with other content areas such as English, science and civics. We should remain aware of the enormous influence our visual culture exerts on our students, and we must use teaching strategies that give them the capacity to decipher, decode, and deconstruct the vast amounts of visual information they face. Critical thinking and aesthetic fluency as well as the ability to filter information are the most important skills the twenty-first-century student needs.

Objectives

Students will be able to:

- Utilize visualization skills and practice independent thinking and constructive imagination skills
- Learn about the many ways we communicate through visual images
- Develop a sense of different cultural customs and family structures while noticing and discussing our common traits as human beings
- Apply visualization and imagination skills to writing assignments
- Exercise metacognitive skills such as critical thinking and aesthetic response
- Develop critical thinking skills (comparing, contrasting, and analyzing)
- Develop problem-solving skills and nurture curiosity and openness about the unfamiliar

NCTE/IRA standards addressed: 4, 5, 6, 7, 8, 9, 12

Materials/Preactivity Preparation

You should spend some time on the Snapshot Stories website (www. snapshotstories.net) a week or so before you plan to introduce the lesson. View all the pictures and explore some of the links on the homepage. Click on the links, numbered 1 through 20, to view the photos. The links on the left take you to websites with other snapshots of people from around the world.

Teachers should visit the computer lab before class to test the website, confirm Internet connection, and determine whether students need to pair up on computers and take turns writing their stories. Two or more students can also collaborate on one story if necessary.

To keep everyone on task, you should have a supply of photographs printed from the Snapshot Stories website available for students who don't have access to personal photos or who neglect to bring them in.

The last class in the lesson series will require the following: construction paper, photo mounting corners, and glue sticks.

Time Frame

This lesson fits into a larger unit about the photographic image and the principles of narrative, or storytelling, in photography and art. The cumulative goal is to develop in the students a keen sense of detail in what they notice and in how they convey what they notice through what they write. Paying attention to detail requires focus and concentration as well as developing rational problem-solving and visualization skills. These kinds of skills develop over time. This lesson would ideally span four class periods, and it is well worth the time spent in classroom discussions. The discussions will prove to be very interesting as long as you remain open-minded about student responses and stay focused. The lesson is not about setting up materials for a final project; it is more about the process of thinking that students will develop along the way.

Description of Activity

Day 1: Preparatory Class

Most preadolescent students think that art is painting and drawing. They may not be used to the idea that the photograph can be art. To introduce the idea of photography as art, show works by Robert Frank, Diane Arbus, Lee Friedlander, and so on. While viewing those works, ask the question, "What is going on in this photograph?" Repeat students' answers out loud so you are certain you heard them correctly and so that the rest of the class can hear the comment. There is no need for judgment, agreement, or evaluation by the teacher or other students.

Students are simply telling what they see. Ask students to volunteer. They will usually be excited to tell you what they see by naming items. Remind them that you are not looking for answers, but observations. The purpose of the exercise is for students to become more confident speakers and more astute viewers. Also, explain to students that in discussing art in a group setting, all ideas and opinions are equally valid and that ridicule is not tolerated.

At the end of class, ask students to bring in a couple of snapshots (personal photographs) from home, as long as they have parental or caregiver approval. The photos do not have to be of themselves. It is important for them to know this, as students may feel embarrassed to show photos of themselves. It is most important to create a classroom environment in which students feel safe to show and talk about art and images.

In preparation for the second class, print out and save eight or ten photos you find on the Web (some good places to start are linked from the Snapshot Stories website) in case students arrive without photos of their own.

Day 2: Second Preparatory Class

Students bring snapshots to class. Collect student photos and redistribute them throughout the class so that students have one anothers' pictures and no one has his or her own. Students use their writing journals for a two-step writing assignment:

> Step 1: Have students record exactly what they see in the photograph. Tell them to be as detailed as they can. Ten to 15 minutes should be plenty of time for this.

> Step 2: Tell students you will give them 20 minutes to write what they imagine is going on in the picture. Have students avoid writing in the familiar style of "It looks like that kid is tying his shoe." Instead, have students write in the main character's "voice," telling what is happening from his or her point of view. Remind them that, as a writer, they should know what is going on in each character's mind. They are masters of their own universe! Anything can happen, but it has to be believable. What are the relationships between the characters in the picture? How are they reacting to one another during this "event"?

Collect journals with the photos left in them at the end of this class.

Day 3: Creating Snapshot Stories

Class meets in the computer lab. Ask students to keep their computers off or in sleep mode while you introduce the lesson and discussion. Go to the Snapshot Stories website (www.snapshotstories.net) and have it projected at the front of the class. The following statement appears at the front of the website:

> Since the birth of photography, snapshots in the family album have become so common that we rarely think about them more closely. Looking at other people's snapshots gives us the opportunity to look through a window into their lives and imagine that we know something about them.
>
> These pictures remind us that there are many different kinds of people in the world, and yet we are all the same in many ways.
>
> Our friends and families are important to us. We are proud of the towns and cities we live in. And we all have the desire to record the highlights of our lives in photographs.

Ask students to recall snapshots they have taken or seen in their own homes of their own families and friends.

Read the following quote by art critic Charles Caffin, written in 1901: "There are two distinct roads in photography—the goal of one being a record of facts, and the other an expression of beauty." Ask students if they think this statement is true. Ask them if they think that snapshots can be beautiful. If so, which of the two categories does the snapshot fit into? Is photography only for capturing memories, or can photos reveal more than just a moment in time? Are there ways to find more meaning by noticing the style of someone's manner of dress, the environment (setting), or a situation (context)?

Explain to students that a writer can look at a picture of a stranger and the image will produce a flood of creative possibilities. Writers can pretend they are someone else. To make the connection between writing and images, you might talk about how screenwriters are people who write in pictures. Screenwriters do not *tell* what is going on; they *show* it. This lesson asks them to take one frame of the "movie" and describe what is happening by looking carefully at the image. Using the comparison of a movie often helps students shift from reporting what they see to telling a story.

Tell students that they must know their characters' personalities: their likes and dislikes, their favorite color, the names of their family members, the kind of clothes they wear, the kind of food they like best. Tell students what they will do in the Snapshot Stories exercise: "You will choose a snapshot and imagine; you are the writer who has created the characters in the picture."

Some questions for students to ask themselves as they contemplate their stories:

- What are your characters' names?
- Where are they?
- What just happened or is about to happen?
- What are they thinking?
- What is their relationship to the other characters in the picture?

Instructions for the Snapshot Stories Website

1. Click on the numbers to the left and browse through the pictures until you find one that interests you.
2. When you have chosen one, make up a name or names for your character(s) and enter them into the space provided.
3. Be sure to enter the number of the photograph you chose in the space provided.
4. Decide what your story event is and type a short description in the large space provided.
5. When you are finished, click on the "submit" button.
6. You will be automatically taken to the "story log" page where you can read your entry along with others who have participated.

Day 4: Sharing Snapshot Stories

Class meets again in the computer lab. You should have the Snapshot Stories website projected on the screen. Students will evaluate the work of others that has been posted on the website. Go to the "story log" section of the site and have students volunteer to read random entries. Since the postings are anonymous, there is little risk of embarrassing someone. A number is linked to each entry. Click on the number to reveal the photograph the entry refers to. After a student reads an entry, ask him or her the following questions:

- Can you identify the main character in the story?
- Does the story seem real or is it too outrageous to be true?
- If something sounds outrageous, does that mean it *isn't* true?
- What are the ways we might be able to tell a successful story from one that seems fake?
- If you do not believe the story you've read, can you explain why?
- What do *you* think is going on in this picture?

After the class has talked about several entries on the website, you can hand back students' journals from the second class. Then hand out colored construction paper and four self-adhesive photo corners for each snapshot. Explain that on a piece of colored paper, students will be mounting the stories they wrote in their journals next to the photograph. Demonstrate this using a photograph and four adhesive corners. The corners are used to preserve the photos. Next, cut out the journal entry and, using a glue stick, affix it to the paper next to the photo. As an alternative, students could rewrite their story using colored pencils directly on the colored paper.

As a culmination of this exploration of photography and narrative, students' work can be mounted and displayed in the school and, eventually, given back to the photograph's owner.

Assessment

Students will be evaluated with a clear rubric, which consists of the following criteria:

Preparedness

- Student has the requested snapshot(s) from home.
- Student has his or her art journal with pencil.
- Student is lacking one or more of the required materials.

Participation

- Student participates actively, offering thoughtful comments and showing good listening skills while others are talking.
- Student is attentive but is not adding his or her own thoughts to the discussion.
- Student is disengaged and does not participate.

Following Directions

- Student can successfully complete the lesson without disruption, confusion, or misconduct.
- Student has trouble listening to directions, hindering his or her ability to use the website successfully.

Journal Entries

- Student hands in journal with complete entry using descriptive words and details to describe the classmate's photo (snapshot).
- Student has only a few sentences and few descriptive words and/or ideas.
- Student displays little or no interest and has not written more than two or three sentences.

Connections and Adaptations

Through this assignment, students will learn speaking and listening skills, critical thinking skills, story structure and design, and character study. Characteristics and functions of the English language are implicitly reinforced. Students develop interpretation skills when they evaluate the artistic and aesthetic qualities of photographs. An "Extension Activity" worksheet, Figure 2.1, is included on the companion disk to encourage students to write about their own image and connect it to others at the site.

Social and cultural issues are addressed during discussion of the photographs and the many different kinds of people in them. Links to other snapshot websites in other parts of the world may enrich the discussion at the end of the project (links are on the front page of the Snapshot Stories website: www.snapshotstories.net).

This lesson could be used as a companion to a writing or drama workshop within a language arts curriculum. Additionally, it could be used within the context of an art and/or media class as part of a unit in which students are taught about the importance of inquiry and critical thinking in art and media.

Work Cited

Caffin, Charles H. *Photography as a Fine Art: The Achievements and Possibilities of Photographic Art in America.* New York: Doubleday, Page, 1901.

Suggested Resources

Eggleston, William. *Los Alamos.* Photographs by William Eggleston. Text by Walter Hopps and Thomas Weski. New York: Scalo, 2003.

Housen, Abigail, and Philip Yenawine. *V.U.E: Visual Understanding in Education* [online curriculum]. 2001. <http://www.vue.org/whatisvts.html>.

McKee, Robert. *Story: Substance, Structure, Style, and the Principles of Screenwriting.* New York: HarperCollins, 1997.

Millstein, Barbara Head, and Sarah M. Lowe. *Consuelo Kanaga: An American Photographer.* U of Washington P, 1992.

Sultan, Larry, and Mike Mandel, eds. *Evidence.* New York: DAP, 2003.

Winogrand, Garry. *The Man in the Crowd: The Uneasy Streets of Garry Winogrand.* Ed. Jeffrey Fraenkel and Frish Brandt. San Francisco: Fraenkel Gallery in association with DAP, 1999.

3 Vocabulary Media Journals: Finding Multimedia to Define Words

William Kist
Kent State University Stark Campus

Context

I work in teacher education for Kent State University. One of my assignments over the past few years has been to teach methods courses at our Stark Regional Campus, located in Canton, Ohio. At the Stark campus, we have developed a partnership with three school districts: Canton City Schools (urban), Northwest Local Schools (rural), and Jackson Local Schools (suburban). The lesson I describe here has been used in these different school districts at various grade levels (4–9) and in various subject areas (English language arts, social studies, math, and science). Teachers at all grade levels and in all subject areas need to teach vocabulary, and this lesson has grown out of the need to teach vocabulary in a way that involves new media. This lesson can be used at the beginning, middle, or end of any unit. Its length can be simply determined by the number of vocabulary words you desire to teach.

Rationale

Certainly, teaching students to understand the words they will encounter is a key skill in reading comprehension instruction. This skill shows up in most state standards across the nation in all subject areas. Teachers of all topics and at all levels are searching for the best strategies for teaching vocabulary. Blachowicz and Fisher describe four components of word study instruction that should be present when teaching vocabulary: (1) creating a word-rich environment in which students are immersed in words for both incidental and intentional learning; (2) helping to develop independent word learners; (3) modeling good word-learning behaviors; and (4) using assessment that matches the goal of instruction (7). Increasingly, researchers are also urging that some kind of visualization technique be used to help students comprehend what they read, such as having kids draw what they read as in a sketch-to-stretch activity (Short, Harste, and Burke), by making extensive use of picture sorts (Bear et al.), or by creating images in their vocabulary squares (Burke). This trend coincides with our growing metamorphosis from a page-based society to a screen-based society (Kress). Teachers are increasingly attempting to incorporate new media into their classrooms as our definitions of *reading* and *writing* broaden to include both print and nonprint elements (Kist). This lesson plan grew out of these foundational elements of both word study instruction and new literacies instruction.

Over the years, I have urged my preservice students to develop lessons that use new literacies. While much has been written on the theoretical need to do so, there hasn't always been a large amount of information on how to use new literacies on a daily basis. Several years ago, two of my students, Melissa Eddy Billington and Brian Lundgren, developed this lesson. Since then, many of my students have used the lesson in various settings.

Objectives

Students will be able to:

- Determine the meanings and pronunciations of unknown words by using dictionaries, thesauruses, glossaries, and/or technology
- "Define" words using images (and perhaps sound or other multimedia)
- Identify appropriate electronic resources and search techniques for gathering images
- Identify the connotations and denotations of new words in relation to the related images they have secured
- Discuss the merits of various forms of representation (e.g., print, images) for various communication purposes
- Discuss the differences between literal representation and abstract representation

NCTE/IRA standards addressed: 3, 8, 12

Material/Preactivity Preparation

- Computer(s) with Internet access and browser

- Computer(s) with Word or some word-processing program
- LCD projector and screen
- List of vocabulary words

Time Frame

This lesson has been taught in a variety of schools and lengths of instructional periods. The teacher really just needs a few minutes to model how to do a Google image search and to go over some of the parameters of the assignment. Teachers can spend as much or as little time as needed to demonstrate this skill. Many students have probably already done a Google image search. For students who are not familiar with Google, the teacher can quickly demonstrate how the image search works: Simply click on "Images" on the main Google screen, and a new screen will pop up. Students type a word or phrase into the box, hit enter, and the resulting images pop up. Once students get the hang of the skill, they will run with it. The teacher must also allot time for explaining how the resulting document should be formatted. Once the activity is initially explained, students can complete their search either in class or on their own time.

Description of Activity

This assignment allows students to define words using nonprint media. Doing a Google image search allows them to match vocabulary words with images. Students choose the image that best matches the definition and paste the image into their Word documents. This gives the participant a visual reminder of what the word means. This activity also allows for some discussion of the advantages and disadvantages of using print or images to communicate.

Teachers usually begin by talking about the words that need to be learned. Most students are well aware of how we look up words in dictionaries and thesauruses. But it's worth discussing whether a dictionary definition can ultimately capture the true essence of a word. Ask students to brainstorm about a word as simple as *pizza* and whether the true nature of "pizza" can really be completely summed up with words.

To complete this model, the teacher could demonstrate how to do a Google image search for *pizza*. There isn't much to this task and, depending on the age of the student, most students will already know how to do an image search. Students should also be taught how to copy an image and paste it into a Word document. It might be a good idea for the teacher to harvest a set of images in advance to go with certain words on the vocabulary list. This will aid in modeling the activity. Also, having a set of images stored in advance might work better in districts that have strict policies related to Internet use.

In districts with more Internet freedom, teachers will still be concerned about the images that might crop up when doing such a search. Fortunately, Google is currently offering a SafeSearch option. According to the Google website, users can currently choose from among three SafeSearch settings by clicking on "Preferences":

- *Moderate filtering* excludes most explicit images from Google Image Search results but doesn't filter ordinary Web search results. This is the default SafeSearch setting; users receive moderate filtering unless they change it.
- *Strict filtering* applies SafeSearch filtering to all the search results (i.e., both image search and ordinary Web search).
- *No filtering* turns off SafeSearch filtering completely.

Once the task of doing a Google image search has been thoroughly demonstrated, students can be turned loose to find images to match any number of vocabulary words.

After students begin to surf and find images that match words, they will probably have several questions. One question may concern how literal the images need to be. If a student types in "igneous," he or she will simply get pictures of igneous rocks. While this might not be a waste of time, it still might not satisfy the goal of amplifying what exactly is an igneous rock. Students may soon prefer to be more creative at linking an image that is only indirectly or even abstractly related to the word being defined. It's up to the teacher to decide how literal the image definitions need to be. And, in fact, this can open up a discussion focusing on the various advantages and disadvantages of abstract representation and literal representation.

Many additional activities can be offered as spin-offs of this lesson:

- Students could take one image that is linked to a word and make a poster out of it. The classroom walls could, in fact, be turned into a gallery for the week's vocabulary words.
- A contest could be held for the most abstract or indirect picture–word definition tie-in, and other students could be asked to figure out what the image–word link is before being told.
- In language arts class, students could use images to link to adjectives such as *delicious* or *fantastic*. Discussion could follow about what an adjective really means.

- Students could branch out to other media, such as sound files (music and/or sound effects) or video clips to define words.
- "Sentences" could be formed as a group of students links their images together in ways that form a complete thought. Other students in the class would have to guess what the "sentence" is saying.

Once the activity is completed, the following questions could be asked to generate discussion:

- What do images provide that other words cannot when we are searching to define words?
- What do images fail to provide? What is lacking when we define a word by using one or more images?
- Is there a difference between an abstract linking of an image and word and a literal linking of an image and a word? Which types of images better help you understand the meanings of words?
- Are some words impossible to truly define, using words or images?
- How will this activity help you remember the definition of a word? Or will it?

Assessment

A simple rubric can be developed around the following criteria:

- Is there a demonstrable link between the image(s) and the word being defined?
- Does each word defined have an image linked?
- Have the words been defined in a creative, perhaps even indirect, fashion (if so desired by the teacher)?
- Have all the words been defined?
- Have the definitions been recorded in the expected format?
- Is the image appropriate for a family audience?

Beyond a teacher-generated rubric, students and teachers together could generate a rubric. In addition, to provide a kind of meta-analysis for the students to reflect on how the use of the images has shaped their learning of vocabulary, students could be asked to think about this activity in an exit slip or a blog entry. Students could be asked to write about their reactions to thinking about images and how they intersect with words. How has this activity improved (or not improved) students' deep understandings of the words being studied, not only on a rote memory level but also on a deeper structural level? Also, as mentioned above, students might be further assessed on one or more of the enrichment activities described. One advantage of this lesson is that students of all ability levels are interested in it and can be assessed. The activity is both fun and challenging for all ability levels.

Connections and Adaptations

Our preservice teachers who have used this activity and who are now working in schools rave about this activity. Jim Ryan writes:

> Vocabulary journals are a great way to teach/uncover new vocabulary in a way that makes sense for students. They are student directed (although the teacher may assign the words, the students pair these words with images of their choosing). Vocabulary image journals are another great avenue when trying to distance oneself from the old vocabulary books and incorporate technology in the classroom. This may be a good way for teachers that lack some of the more advanced computer skills such as iMovie or web page design to get their feet wet with technology.

Tracey Lehr adds:

> On the surface this activity may seem like it would be relatively easy, but coming up with a picture to define a given word is not always that simple. . . . One must give careful thought to the meaning of the word, and then put it into context before an image comes to mind. By the time a student has a picture in mind, they have a good grasp on the meaning of the actual word. This activity is actually much more meaningful (no pun intended) than it might seem at first glance, and more importantly, the students generally *enjoy* this hands-on method of learning spelling/vocabulary. It requires higher level thinking rather than rote memorization, so my students learn more than just how to spell a word. Awesome!

This activity can be used with any student old enough to navigate the Internet and with any class in which students need to learn vocabulary words. Try it yourself sometime—you may find that Google image searching is addicting! Whoever thought teaching vocabulary could be fun? Or that it could be done using new literacies?

Works Cited

Bear, Donald R., Marcia Invernizzi, Shane Templeton, and Francine Johnston.
    Words Their Way: Word Study for Phonics, Vocabulary, and Spelling

Instruction. 3rd ed. Upper Saddle River, NJ: Prentice Hall, 2004.

Blachowicz, Camille, and Peter J. Fisher. *Teaching Vocabulary in All Classrooms.* 2nd ed. Upper Saddle River, NJ: Merrill/Prentice Hall, 2002.

Burke, Jim. *Reading Reminders: Tools, Tips, and Techniques.* Portsmouth, NH: Heinemann, 2000.

Kist, William. *New Literacies in Action: Teaching and Learning in Multiple Media.* New York: Teachers College P, 2005.

Kress, Gunther. *Literacy in the New Media Age.* London: Routledge, 2003.

Short, Kathy G., Jerome C. Harste, and Carolyn Burke. *Creating Classrooms for Authors and Inquirers.* 2nd ed. Portsmouth, NH: Heinemann, 1995.

Supplemental Reading

Allen, Janet. *Words, Words, Words: Teaching Vocabulary in Grades 4–12.* York, ME: Stenhouse, 1999.

Alvermann, Donna E., Jennifer S. Moon, and Margaret C. Hagood. *Popular Culture in the Classroom: Teaching and Researching Critical Media Literacy.* Newark, DE: International Reading Association, 1999.

Cope, Bill, and Mary Kalantzis, eds. *Multiliteracies: Literacy Learning and the Design of Social Futures.* London: Routledge, 2000.

Cunningham, Patricia M., and Dorothy P. Hall. *Month-by-Month Phonics for Upper Grades: A Second Chance for Struggling Readers and Students Learning English.* Greensboro, NC: Carson-Dellosa, 1998.

Lankshear, Colin, and Michele Knobel. *New Literacies: Changing Knowledge and Classroom Learning.* Buckingham, Eng.: Open University, 2003.

4 Building Active Viewing Skills: *An Occurrence at Owl Creek Bridge*

Mark Dolce
National-Louis University

Context

The following lesson was implemented in eighth-grade language arts classes at Sunset Ridge School in Northfield, Illinois. Class sizes ranged from seventeen to twenty-three students. The class periods for eighth-grade language arts consisted of two nonconsecutive 42-minute periods daily.

In the course of a ten-week student teaching stint, I used the film *An Occurrence at Owl Creek Bridge* near the end of a unit on the Civil War novel. All eighth graders were studying the Civil War in their social studies classes at more or less the same time I held my Civil War novel unit.

Rationale

The challenge for teachers who want to integrate film and other visual media into the English language arts curriculum is how to transform the passive adolescent spectator into an active, engaged viewer. Such a metamorphosis does happen, but gradually, after many opportunities to practice, not unlike a beginning student of piano working through a rendition of "Für Elise." We ask students to reread poems and sections of books to squeeze out some kind of meaning, so we should be prepared to have them do the same type of "rereading" of films and media to build active viewing skills.

What constitutes "active viewing"? Simply, active viewing is the attentive engagement with a visual text so that meaning is constructed and remembered. When we first begin building these active viewing skills, we should be prepared to guide students with questions that invite them to make meaning from the film or video. Most adolescent (and adult) viewers are passive precisely because they do not process these questions automatically while watching a film or video. The average person can follow the average fiction or nonfiction visual text with little or no difficulty. However, unless we take the time to examine how meaning is constructed through visual means, most students will retain only a superficial understanding of visual texts. The wonderful thing about the film *An Occurrence at Owl Creek Bridge* is that the surprise ending forces the viewer to go back and rethink or reinterpret the images just viewed. That process of viewing and reassessment or reflection—a process triggered first by how the teacher frames the viewing and second by the surprise ending—lies at the heart of building active viewing skills.

Part of the process of building active viewing skills also includes judiciously choosing the films we show in class. *An Occurrence at Owl Creek Bridge* is an ideal choice for classroom use primarily because the film's scant dialogue, coupled with the economic but rich use of visuals, allows adolescents to focus on the visual details and the sound effects to construct meaning. There's no extended exposition given through dialogue. In addition, the brevity of the film forces the filmmaker to present the conflict up front, so there are no long explanations, no unexplained narrative twists in the rising action, and no extended or superfluous sequences that might confuse the adolescent viewer.

Another, no less important part of this process of building active viewing skills involves how, when, and where the films are presented and what we ask students to look for in the films. Outside the world of jockeys, one rarely hears the phrase "shorter is better." However, when asking middle or high school students to decode the visual language of any electronic media, especially narrative films, shorter is most assuredly better, at least in the beginning. With a running time of around 25 minutes, the short film *An Occurrence at Owl Creek Bridge* makes a great choice for the classroom in which instructional time is at a premium.

The endorsement of this film also comes with a warning: asking the class to read the Ambrose Bierce short story beforehand will dampen somewhat the impact of this lesson, which is contingent on the surprise ending. At the end of the film, as soon as the viewer realizes that all the narrative action, which was believed to be a certain reality, is in fact the doomed man's fantasy, the viewer immediately reexamines the film in search of (mostly visual) clues that the experience is all just a dream. This search for clues—the practice of active viewing skills—is the guts of the lesson, which will be lost or severely diminished if the story is read ahead of time. That does not mean the short story by Bierce cannot or should not be read either before or after the film. Refer to the "Connections and Adaptations" section below for suggestions on how to integrate the printed source material into the lesson.

Objectives

Students will be able to:

- Actively view the 25-minute film with mostly undivided attention
- Discuss and record details of visual effects that create meaning
- Write about those details to solidify and transfer the visual information learned

NCTE/IRA standards addressed: 1, 6, 11

Material/Preactivity Preparation

- Read and study the Annotated Viewing Guide for Instructors (Figure 4.1 on the companion disk) to this film after a first viewing of the film. Use the guide to watch the film again.
- Check with other teachers to see if this film has been used in any previous classes. This is vitally important because the success of the exercise is dependent on the surprise ending, which triggers a reexamination of the previous narrative action. It is also a good idea to ask students if they have seen the film. If they have, you might have to alter, truncate, or append some of the activities detailed below.
- Secure a DVD or VHS copy of the short film *An Occurrence at Owl Creek Bridge* (1964), directed by Robert Enrico.
- Secure a television or LCD projector with appropriate VCR or DVD player.
- Read the short story by Ambrose Bierce on which the film is based but, as previously suggested, to fulfill the objectives of this lesson in active viewing, don't have students read it.

Time Frame

The lesson was implemented in three 42-minute class periods.

Description of Activity

Day 1: Introducing the Film

Cue up the film and have it ready to go. To set the expectations of active rather than passive viewing of the film, write the title on the board and establish that this will be a graded viewing through written or spoken instructions. Refrain from giving out too many details about the film before you start it. Trivial background details, such as that the actors and crew are all French, are not cogent to the objective for this first class:

watching the film attentively. However, before you start the film, I would suggest pointing out a few things to guide or focus students' viewing. I asked my students to pay attention to how the filmmaker establishes the setting. (These are the shots that tell us where the story is taking place, e.g., longer distance shots, and details that would indicate when the story is taking place, e.g., full or medium shots showing costumes or props.) Since my students had not read the story, I told them to notice where the soldiers were stationed, how many there were, and how they handled their prisoner. It is imperative to tell students that the big payoff occurs in the last five seconds of the film so it is critical that they pay attention through the very last seconds. Again, our job when showing the film is to build anticipation and pique their curiosity. Thus, pointing out that there is a climactic ending contributes to increased attention. I did not, however, narrate the film in any way during the first viewing. With about 20 seconds left in the film, I shouted out to the class to pay attention, that the big payoff was coming. Literally, the ending— the whole point of the film—could be missed by simply looking down for a second or two. Therefore, it's essential to cue the students to pay extra close attention as the surprise ending approaches.

Immediately following the end of the film, there will be audible gasps, chatter, and objections and protestations of disbelief. That's all good! I did nothing to squelch student reactions as I turned on the lights, stopped the tape, turned off the television, and shuffled a few papers around. I let the students decompress and debrief among themselves for a minute or two before initiating a full-class discussion for the balance of the period.

The first time I used this lesson, each of my classes started—without prompting—to identify many clues that indicate that the protagonist's escape is merely fantasy. One student stated, "When he untied himself underwater, it looked like he was under an ocean." Another chimed in, "And that river was too slow-moving to carry him so far down the river." I asked why he knew it was slow moving. He referenced shot 22 (see Figure 4.1 on the companion disk), in which a large branch barely moves in the slow-moving current in the river. This observation about the branch in the stream represents the heart of the lesson: noticing visual details and how those details provide vital narrative information to the viewer. If students need prompting or if the discussion stalls, which happened a few times, use the following questions to get the discussion moving:

- What do we learn about the main character and the setting before the noose is put around his head?

Here you are concentrating on the first seven minutes of the film. This is when the filmmaker establishes setting and the main conflict. It is also when the filmmaker provides numerous clues that the man is doomed to die, that escape is impossible. See the "Annotated Viewing Guide" included on the companion disk for more detailed information.

- What images and sound effects tell you that his escape is a fantasy or dream and not real?

My students started naming things like the depth of the water and the noose being tightened and tied over the planks. At this point, it is just a discussion, so encourage students to name as many things as possible. This is good practice at recalling images.

- What do you think it meant symbolically when they took his pocket watch?

For my eighth graders, this was not so obvious. They had a hard time figuring out what this gesture meant symbolically. For older audiences, you could leave out the "symbolically" and just ask what it meant.

In the last minute or so of class, I previewed the next class period, telling students that we would review key parts of the film and take notes on what we notice. For longer language arts periods (80 minutes or more), I would recommend planning a different activity for the remainder of the period.

Day 2: Re-viewing the Film

For the second viewing of the film, I handed out a viewing packet with questions and spaces to write in answers. Here is a sampling of the questions I used for the packet:

- What is the setting of the film and what shots specifically tell us about the setting?
- In the beginning, what images tell us that escape is unlikely or near impossible?
- What sound effects are used up until the actual hanging? List them.
- What do we know about Peyton (the condemned man) from what we see of him?
- What is the symbolism of the soldier's removing Peyton's timepiece (pocket watch)?
- What sound effects are used during Peyton's escape in the river? State whether those sound effects are realistic or unrealistic.
- What details (or images) indicate that his escape is not real? List them.

- What is the symbolism of a spider wrapping up his prey in a web? Why would this be ironic in this context?
- What is the effect of repeating—four times—the shot of Peyton's wife walking to him with her arms outstretched?

Most students, especially middle schoolers, will be unused to taking notes while watching a film, so it might be wise to pause now and then to allow them to write. You might pause the film after the setting is established, just before the soldiers lead Peyton to the middle of the bridge. Stop again just before the hanging; this will give students a chance to note how well the noose is secured around Peyton's neck. Before starting, tell them to pay attention to sound effects and the reactions of the soldiers to the escape. Pause again when Peyton washes up on shore. Play until the end. Ask the students if they need to repeat any scenes for review. This process of pausing while playing the film pushes the time to about 40 minutes.

Day 3: Summative Discussion

After you have graded and handed back the packets, I would suggest a 20-minute discussion of the answers, keeping the film cued up in case review of key scenes is necessary. I encouraged the students to add to their notes in order to be prepared for the test, in which some of the questions might arise (see assessment suggestions below).

Assessment

You have a multitude of options for assessment. I suggest grading the packets mostly for completion and less for accuracy, keeping in mind how new students are to the whole process. Because of time constraints, I did not give an assessment separate from the packets and points for the viewing. I did, however, use a few short-answer questions, lifted verbatim from the packet, and a few multiple-choice questions about the film on the Civil War novel unit exam. I recommend using a variety of multiple-choice questions, ranging from easy plot-level questions, like "Peyton Farquhar is condemned to death by [hanging]," to more analytical questions, like "What is the purpose of showing us a branch barely moving in the slow river current?" Testing viewing in this context is no different from asking literal and analytical questions on quizzes and tests covering literature. We want students to become fluent in recalling visual images and the meanings those images create. Therefore, it is valid as well as fair to students to use the same type of assessment tools for films and visual media as we do for literature.

Connections and Adaptations

I did not use the printed text except as an extra credit option in which students were asked to craft a brief essay about specific differences between the short story and the film. For older students, I would add to that prompt by considering whether those differences show a limitation of the printed word or the film or both. This type of analysis requires a bit more sophistication since it would involve making judgments on both form and content. I would also let older students make a judgment with regard to this short story and film adaptation, whether one form is superior to the other in terms of dramatic storytelling and impact. For a purely literary analysis, older students could examine the use of visual imagery and shift in tenses (there is one) in the short story. Subsequently, the students could make the same type of analysis of visual imagery and tenses. This would illuminate the question of dramatic impact, since most film action, even told in flashback, has the immediacy of the present tense.

If I were to use the printed text with a middle school audience, I would include a read-aloud, pausing after the first paragraph to ask for volunteers to stand in for the characters—the condemned man, the sergeant, the sentinels—and arrange themselves in the room as Bierce describes the scene. Having students demonstrate the opening tableaux would create a visual reference point that would help draw contrasts in the students' minds as they watch the film. Another exercise I would consider is to have groups of students storyboard the story from beginning to end (see Chapter 7, "Visualizing the Literary Text Using Storyboards and Basic Cinematic Techniques"). This exercise might illuminate the process of filmmaking more vividly for students who are new to interpreting and deconstructing visual texts.

Work Cited

An Occurrence at Owl Creek Bridge. Dir. Robert Enrico. 1964. DVD. Monterey Video, 2004.

Supplemental Reading

Sousa, David A. *How the Brain Learns*. 2nd ed. Thousand Oaks, CA: Corwin, 2000.

5 Video Themes: An Introduction to Composing with Images

David L. Bruce
Kent State University

Context

I used this lesson at the suburban high school of approximately 1,800 students where I taught for over a decade. The courses in which I used this lesson were Communications I and II. Each was a yearlong media literacy elective offered through the English department. I currently use video themes in my undergraduate/graduate teacher education program. This lesson serves as an introduction to using video equipment, as well as to digital composition exploring a concept or theme.

Rationale

This lesson serves as a starting point in the reading of and writing with video, focusing particularly on composing with images. In this activity, students create a thematic essay using the medium of video. They select a topic, a concept, or an idea that has broad connotations (freedom, isolation, nourishment, happiness, success, etc.). Through the use of visuals, graphics and text functions, audio (music and ambient sound), and visual transitions, students are able to compose a multilayered approach to exploring elements of their chosen topic.

I began using video themes almost as an afterthought, as a means of quickly introducing my students to various production elements—namely videography and editing. My reasoning was that the sooner they became familiar with the equipment, the sooner they would become conversant with technology in telling their stories. The video theme project went from an exercise to an integral course scaffold: meaningful group work, ownership of topic and projects, and ongoing discussions of composition processes (with both print and video). Because of the relative brevity of the assignment, I now use this and/or video poems (see Chapter 12, "Creating Video Poetry") as essential projects for other nonproduction courses I teach.

I have found the video theme assignment to be indispensable in setting up the class dialogue for the larger concept of "composition." When we discuss compositional issues such as audience, point of view, transitions, specific details, etc., the video theme provides a useful framework for discussion. This is especially crucial if the course work involves print compositions. For those students who struggle to get their ideas on paper, I have found it helpful to refer back to their videos as a reference point; for example, "You have two ideas in this paper but so far have not connected them. How did you connect the different ideas or visuals in the video theme? Likewise, how could you create a transition with words?"

Objectives

Students will be able to:

- Brainstorm potential images that fit a concept or theme
- Create a working storyboard
- Videotape appropriate images using a digital video camera
- Edit the appropriate scenes using a nonlinear video editing system
- Select music that thematically fits the concept or theme
- Analyze their compositional choices of the finished video theme

NCTE/IRA standards addressed: 4, 6, 12

Material/Preactivity Preparation

To implement this lesson, students must have access to a nonlinear video program such as iMovie, Movie Maker, Final Cut Pro, etc. Note: This activity can be adapted using digital stills and PowerPoint. However, PowerPoint has limitations that make it much more cumbersome to use than the video editing programs.

Materials/Equipment Needed

- Computers for groups of approximately three students
- Storyboard sheets (see handouts 7.1 and 7.2 for Chapter 7 on the companion disk)
- Digital video cameras

- LCD projector (to model the program features and to show final projects)
- Librarian, media aide, and/or student experts for help with technical assistance

Depending on the availability of digital video cameras, this lesson can be modified by using digital still cameras. Video editing programs (iMovie, Movie Maker, etc.) work with digital photos as well as with video.

There is no better way for teachers to become familiar with the technology than to create one of these assignments themselves before introducing them in class. Editing programs are user-friendly, and by composing a video theme, teachers will have an example to show the students.

For teachers who need assistance with the technology, I suggest enlisting expert students or a colleague to help during this process. Many students may already be familiar with video editing programs. I have found that students who feel disenfranchised in a school environment often feel empowered when they are able to share their technological expertise. This is especially helpful if there are a number of questions about how to use technology effectively. When students help teach one another the equipment, the teacher is free to focus more on the compositional aspects of the project.

Time Frame

When I taught this unit in my high school classroom, this lesson typically lasted one week, with a schedule as follows:

Day 1	Introducing assignment, examples
Day 2	Videotaping images
Days 3–4	Editing/video theme written reflection
Day 5	Viewing final projects

Description of Activity

The project begins with a brief discussion of words and ideas that cannot be defined easily. Your guiding questions might include:

- What words are difficult to briefly define?
- Why are these words difficult to define in a few words?
- How can visuals help describe or define words and ideas?
- What is a "theme"? What does it mean in music? literature? film? essays?

At this point, I describe the overview of the assignment. Students are to choose one word that has no quick definition and create a video that uses images and sounds that help convey some of the nuances of the term. I usually provide a word or topic for each group but will allow them to come up with an idea of their own.

Selecting a Topic

I have found it extremely beneficial to have the students brainstorm a list of images they might potentially videotape prior to leaving the classroom to film. When I first began using this assignment, I did not have students preplan potential shots. Students tended to wander around looking for ideas and consequently had less usable footage than they might have. After I began having them list images, students tended to be more focused. A brief planning time yields much better footage for use in the editing stages.

In selecting topics, I suggest choosing a theme or concept conducive to the school surroundings, such as "conformity." This particular theme is ideal given the number of uniform images in the school environment (bricks/tiles, desk arrangements, rows of lockers, cafeteria tables, trophy cases, parking lot rows, etc.). Other stock themes suitable for a school setting include success, happiness, and time passing. In the dozens of times I have provided these examples to students, although the images they have videotaped have often overlapped, the students' interpretations of these themes have varied tremendously. Sometimes students will explore or define their theme by providing images of what the theme is not. Sometimes I have students select their own themes, which have included isolation, nourishment, freedom, love, peace, rebellion, change, art, creativity, movement.

Videotaping Images

In introducing composing with the video camera, I begin with a simple and brief exercise. Have students use their thumbs and forefingers to create a "frame" (students could also cut out a square or rectangle from a sheet of notebook paper to use as their frame). As students frame objects within the classroom, we discuss what is pictured within and outside of their finger frames. It is important to emphasize that what the camera sees in the viewfinder is what the viewer will ultimately watch during the final film. Time permitting, I have students sketch storyboards to practice their framing ideas.

You will need to provide a brief tutorial of the camera's most basic functions such as loading the tape or disk, turning the camera on and off, zooming, and using the record or play mode. In the ideal demonstration, we use several cameras; I demonstrate with one while groups of students follow along with the other cameras.

I always set a limit around the amount of time students can videotape during the school day. This tends to make them more focused and economical with their time and footage. If possible, allow students to videotape outside of the normal school day. For students who have access to camera equipment at home (or for those at schools that allow students to sign out equipment for class projects), having additional time to videotape allows them to be more creative with the cameras and their footage.

Camera Suggestions

- Make sure batteries are charged before class begins.
- Allow students to bring cameras from home (with parental permission). This will provide more resources for groups.
- Insist that each student in the group get camera experience by videotaping images.
- Encourage students to get close-ups. Specific images are effective.
- Encourage students to try different angles or perspectives of each shot. This provides more choice during editing, and it is easier to discard footage than to shoot additional video.
- If students will be taping on more than one occasion, make sure they cue the tape to the end of the footage so they do not tape over their existing videotape (I cannot count the number of times this has happened over the years).
- Cameras have limitations—if students use the camera to videotape an object sideways, it is almost impossible to reorient the footage so that it appears horizontal (unlike a still image, which can be reoriented easily).
- Caution students against using the built-in camera special effects. It takes too long to go through the various functions, and all of those effects can be created more effectively during the editing process.

Editing

In introducing the editing aspect of the video composition process, I begin with a brief tutorial (about 10 minutes for an overview) of the editing program, such as downloading footage, trimming clips, adding transitions, and adding sound. The sooner students begin to experiment and play with the program, the sooner they are able to shape their video. As students return to the classroom from their videotaping (and they always take different amounts of time), I work with each group to have them begin loading their footage into the editing program.

I have found that during the editing process, I take on the role of a coach. I offer pointers about rudimentary editing while also encouraging students by pointing out interesting camera work and editing sequences. It is important to remember that although the students are using computers to complete this project, the point is not the technology—the point is to use the technology to create a *composition*.

Editing Suggestions

- Identify those students who are familiar with the editing program. Place these students in different groups to allow for student leadership. Make sure that *all* students get to edit.

- Encourage students to be selective in the footage they use for their final version. Use only the footage that emphasizes the topic. Remind students that their final video may include only a small portion of their original footage.

- Encourage experimentation—have students try different perspectives of the same shot to see which is most effective, or have them try using a slow-motion effect to emphasize a scene.

- Tell students not to use special effects simply because they are available. If the effect does not enhance the theme, they shouldn't use it. This is especially true with transitions; the basic ones (dissolve, wipe, fade in/out) are effective and do not tend to draw attention to themselves.

- While they are editing, have students ask themselves if their footage, transitions, and special effects all contribute to (rather than detract from) their video composition.

- It is helpful to have a variety of music CDs (instrumentals are especially effective) available that students can use with their compositions. To allow for more student choice, I often tell them ahead of time to bring in music that might fit the mood of their project.

Final Viewing

It is important to capitalize on the visual nature of these projects by allowing the final versions to be made as public as possible. At the very least, have the students gather around the individual computers to view each finished project. For best results, use an LCD projector. I have seen students enjoy showing off their projects to others and receiving the immediate feedback.

Before the film viewing, I encourage all students to watch and listen carefully. After we have watched the film, I prompt students for examples of effective videography, audio, and so on. I then ask students what they felt the authors of the video theme were trying to convey about their topic.

Some Teaching Considerations

Once this project has been completed, the teacher can use an example of past projects to model the assignment for subsequent classes. I try to select samples that are creative in both production elements and interpretation of the theme.

Time permitting, an interesting comparison can be made between projects, particularly if there is more than one film on the same theme (from that same year or from a compilation of several years). Students often have lively discussions about how the authors' compositions differed from one another in interpretation, use of camera work, arrangement of sequences, etc.

Assessment

Students should complete a written reflection explaining each shot (see Figure 5.1 on the companion disk for a student sample). Have students describe and evaluate their videography by answering the following questions for each shot (or shot sequence):

1. Describe the shot (or draw it).
2. Why did you choose to film the scene in this manner? What were you trying to show?
3. Evaluate the shot. How pleased were you with the final result? Explain.

Evaluation of the public viewing discussion should include students' comments on effective videography and editing as well as on how the video defined and explored the concept or theme.

The teacher can use the "Video Theme Rubric" that is included on the companion disk (see Figure 5.2) to evaluate the overall effectiveness of the finished product. Based on teacher preference, students could receive this handout prior to final submission.

For sample heuristics and student video essays, see Figures 5.3–5.6 on the companion disk.

Connections and Adaptations

While this lesson can be used as a stand-alone activity, I have found its most important connection to be as a setup for broader discussions of composition. I have used this lesson with all grade levels from 9 to graduate school. Although I have not taught this lesson directly to middle school students, it could be adapted for their skill level and curriculum.

A possible adaptation could be to have students select a theme from a piece of literature they are reading and use the video project as a means for exploring that theme. So, for instance, if teaching *To Kill a Mockingbird*, a theme for exploration could be "discrimination." The students could follow the general guidelines as explained here, but this time explicitly tie their response to how it fits thematically with the novel.

Supplemental Reading

Bruce, David. "Visualizing Success: Using Video Composition in the Classroom." *Ohio Journal of English Language Arts* 44.1 (Fall 2003/Winter 2004): 51–56.

Goodman, Steven. *Teaching Youth Media: A Critical Guide to Literacy, Video Production, and Social Change.* New York: Teachers College P, 2003.

Kist, William. *New Literacies in Action: Teaching and Learning in Multiple Media.* New York: Teachers College P, 2005.

6 Truly an iMovie: Composing Video Diaries

Stephen Murphy
New Trier High School
Winnetka, Illinois

Context

New Trier High School is located in the suburbs sixteen miles north of Chicago on Lake Michigan. Over 4,000 students attend the school on two campuses, one in Winnetka and a first-year campus in Northfield. Video Art has been in the curriculum of the art department for three years. Sophomores, juniors, and seniors can take the class as an elective, and students of all abilities are welcome.

Rationale

The video diary project is an engaging, non-printcentric project in which students use video, technology, and text to create and articulate as knowledgeable, reflective, creative, and critical members of literacy communities. As students engage in media techniques employing the use of spoken, written, and visual language, they learn to communicate their discoveries effectively in ways that suit their purpose and audience. Students become comfortable thinking and composing in a nonlinear, nonprint medium.

The most successful of the video diaries produced by students in my Video Art classes achieve this effect. They leave me variously speechless and awestruck. They shed light on the radiant identities and lives of the young filmmakers (see three samples of video diaries on the companion disk). The diaries travel an arc of storytelling that is not necessarily narrative or linear but that is always supported by students' visual imagination. The diaries represent authentic learning about the medium, the integration of text and image, and the students themselves. Students write and rewrite, they shoot video and reshoot, they edit and they reedit. The creative self-exploration the students engage in to produce their diaries is astonishing to witness.

The video diary project that follows was conceived as the culminating phase of a project funded by the Urban /Suburban Consortium of Northwestern University. Students from New Trier and Evanston Township High Schools—century-old rivals—participated in the project. The goal in the last phase of the project was to debunk the misconceptions each school held about the other and at the same time have the students turn the camera on themselves to address a more personal topic: *"You are wrong about me; I am not the sum total of your perceived stereotypes—THIS is who I am."* Excited by the possibilities of a handful of completed diaries and some promising starts, I set out to develop Video Diaries as a stand-alone unit for my Video Art class. I must acknowledge the contributions of Alice George, visiting artist/writer/poet, with whom I worked closely on the planning and text component of the diary samples included; her residency was supported in part by a grant from the Illinois Arts Council.

Objectives

Students will be able to:

- Identify and analyze characteristics of effective print and nonprint diaries
- Develop subject matter for a video diary
- Shoot, import, and edit video footage
- Compose effective nonprint texts
- Incorporate multiple literacies in their work (e.g., text, sound, motion and still visuals)

NCTE/IRA standards addressed: 4, 6, 11, 12

Materials/Preactivity Preparation

- Video cameras, microphones, videotape
- Access to a computer lab (preferably MAC)
- iMovie or Final Cut Pro software
- Video and print examples of diaries
- DVD-Rs to burn final projects for archiving and screening
- Samples of memoirs from text-based sources
- Samples of video diaries drawn from professional videographers

Time Frame

This schedule is based on 40-minute periods, five times per week.

Week 1: Introduction of print diaries and writing to prompts.

Week 2: Introduction of video and radio diaries, including a selection from Stan Brakhage's *By Brakhage: An Anthology* or *Bill Viola: The Eye of the Heart* directed by Mark Kidel.

Week 3: Composing first draft of the text component, storyboarding same, and beginning to shoot video footage outside of class. Check drafts and storyboards with teacher.

Week 4: Instruction in editing software, importing of student footage, and initial assemblage of video diary.

Week 5: Continuation of editing process; investigation of sound options: composition of sound in an ancillary software package or experimentation with musical options.

Week 6: Text and video check with teacher individually. Continuation of editing process to combine text and visuals.

Week 7: More editing, as well as small-group peer screening or export of projects to class tape for screening.

Week 8: Screening of near-completed work and feedback from peers.

Week 9: Final edit and export of projects to class tape or DVD. Option of festival the following week.

If the project were to be implemented as a production component in a semester-long English class, there would be more time for the teacher to devote to student diary or journal writing as well as to exploring more examples of compelling diary writing. Students could be asked to begin keeping a journal after the introduction of the diary and then mine this journal for project ideas. I could easily envision this project adjusted in length to allow the English language arts teacher to have students do several drafts of the textual component.

Description of Activity

The best way to have students begin their video diaries is to expose them to a cross section of text-based diaries. I suggest compiling and presenting the students with some excerpts that span a range of styles. I have used excerpts from *The Adrian Mole Diaries* by Sue Townsend, *The Diary of a Young Girl* by Anne Frank, *The Unabridged Journals* by Sylvia Plath, and a poem, "Spring Comes to Chicago," by Campbell McGrath. Once the excerpts are selected, students can read them, react to them, and identify key characteristics of good diary writing: keen observation of the outside world balanced by honest revelation of the diarist's inner world. Students can also listen to some teenage voices in *Radio Diaries*, a now-dated feature from National Public Radio but available online at www.radiodiaries.org. These radio diaries may be even more challenging for students because audio relies on spoken word and sound alone, placing students in a situation not unlike that of pre-television families gathered around the wireless.

It is important to schedule a few days of writing in the classroom to give students their first stabs at the direction and style their diary entry will follow. These preliminary activities may ultimately develop into students' final diary form. I've used prompts such as explaining your latest theory (teenagers are rife with theories); describing something weird you noticed, something you regret, a daydream, a night dream, someone you got angry with. These are the examples my class came up with; you may just as easily generate a similar list with other teachers or with students in class discussion.

To balance the textual component of stand-alone written diaries, it is important to screen some selections of the video diary genre. In my class, students would have already been introduced to some of the major players of video art and art film, including Nam June Paik, Stan Brakhage, and Bill Viola; they already would have had their approach to film and video production shaken to its foundation. This parallels the aesthetic development and maturation that occurs in a photography course when students realize that photography is not about taking happy snapshots of friends but rather about delving into the underpinnings of the art form. After examining some classics, students are then ready to examine the work of some more contemporary and edgy diarists such as Sadie Benning, George Kuchar (*Weather Diary 1* and *Weather Diary 2*), Mike O'Reilly (*Glass Jaw*), and Jem Cohen. These examples can be secured through Video Data Bank in Chicago (see the references). While screening these examples, discuss ways to avoid the "see dog, say dog" syndrome—the rookie pitfall of seeing on screen what the narrator/text or dialogue is depicting—and how to previsualize images for their inherent power, which may not be directly linked to what the viewer is hearing.

At this point, it is important to complete a round of text checks—checking in with individual students about their diaries to determine whether the seed has germinated. Once students have their scripts written, the next step in the process is to storyboard their images to help previsualize their videos and make an effective, successful transition from print to nonprint modes (see Chapter 7, "Visualizing the Literary

Text Using Storyboards and Basic Cinematic Techniques" for a definition of storyboarding, as well as for storyboarding forms).

By this stage, approaches and ideas should be taking root; footage should be shot, rethought, reshot, and imported. Topics that my students have developed in their diaries have included what it is like to live in America and not be American, revealing a not-so-obvious Chinese ancestry; identity as an adopted child; exploring physical difference; the challenges of a varsity wrestler; and a meditation on facelessness, to name a few. These are some very private pastures that need tending but have to lay fallow a while to bear the fruit that is beginning to form.

As footage is being shot and assembled, ask students questions and make suggestions about the transition from text to image. A common suggestion is "Don't just rant. Reveal something meaningful about your life." Counsel students on the use of narrative strategies, including the element of surprise, repetition, and focus on key details, and address the difficulty of coming up with an ending. Some of these discussions may be met with brilliant silence, while others may lead to exciting revisions. Students clearly need some time to determine how personal they want to be and how comfortable they are sharing some private experiences with a wider audience. While they ponder this, they have plenty to do creating text, recording voice, composing sound, and exploring the intricacies of editing in Final Cut Pro, Adobe's state-of-the-art editing software.

Regarding the modes of literacy involved in the creation of these projects, I assume an age-appropriate mastery of writing skills. Teachers who cannot make this assumption will need to build in additional time for students to work on writing. Since the project takes shape in an art class with students of different abilities, their media production and writing skills are variable. Also, trying to get students to do something all too familiar from their major academic pursuits—that is, to write—means that teachers may run into another level of resistance. All students in my class have taken a yearlong prerequisite, either Photography I or Visual Art Studio, and consequently have a fairly broad baseline in visual literacy; they are used to creating, interpreting, and analyzing images. The media literacy component is new for some, both the deconstruction and decoding of messages and the developing facility with nonprint composition needed to build a text–image composition on the computer.

One frustration with the project for both students and teacher is the revision process. Students often feel that when they have completed a given project they are finished. Time and time again it is necessary to make the analogy to the English classroom and the need to revise and rework their papers to make them their best efforts—*writing is rewriting*. In Video Art, students experience the need to reshoot and reedit—*editing is reediting*. I often remind them of Soviet filmmaker Sergei Eisenstein's definition of editing: "the ruthless elimination of the unessential."

High school students cannot possibly anticipate the coverage—the variety of shots—they might need later as a piece takes shape. And, as so often happens in the individualized instruction and critiques during conversations that follow our viewing of the diary in progress, students slowly understand that they are not yet finished. An understanding comes into focus: how different shots could improve the piece or change the meaning; how reworking the existing visual elements—adding text, voice-overs, or sounds—can enhance their work.

When students share their nearly completed diaries, it is important to encourage peer feedback through constructive criticism. Questions for peers to consider: Do the visuals support the text? Does the sound—composed, musical, or natural—enhance or detract from the piece? Does the film need further editing or additional text or visuals to support the piece? The teacher's private suggestion to rework a piece is often echoed in the same feedback in a group critique. Resistance to rework generally diminishes when it comes from a student's peers. I sometimes give them a choice—this is B work but it could easily be A with some small improvements. The video diaries on the accompanying companion disk (Figures 6.1–6.3) represent a cross section of students, each of whom wrestled with the challenge of self-exploration and nonprint composition in a unique way.

Assessment

I assess diaries using a holistic rubric (see Figure 6.4 on the companion disk). Categories of achievement include "accomplished," "effective," "satisfactory," and "needs more work." Short evaluative statements in each category address the accomplishments of that category in terms of production value, use of text, editing, sound, etc.

All work is ultimately screened on an overhead projector. This is the first time students see their films on a big screen. Students make constructive comments about each film, and the filmmaker is invited to speak; popcorn is served.

Connections and Adaptations

Video diaries can be used as an alternative to the memoir writing common in many high school English courses. Working with a computer lab supervisor or other technical support personnel, students can be instructed in the basics of video production and editing. The lesson is adaptable to middle school students as well as for the university level. I would suggest using iMovie—an extremely user-friendly editing software program. Students could be given the option of using a pet, stuffed animal, or toy to "invent" a diary for if the teacher determines that it might be too challenging for some students to write about themselves. Or students could do a diary about key experiences—a memorable visit or a family vacation—with a grandparent, uncle, or aunt.

Another option is to do a project with animated stills. Students import digital still images (especially where video cameras may not be readily available) and "animate" them in an editing software program (wireframe editing in Final Cut Pro, the "Ken Burns Effect" in iMovie). Students can still use multiple literacies to create an effective piece with photographs, voice-over, text, and sound.

I recently traveled to China where I screened video diaries, translated into Chinese by New Trier's advanced Chinese language class, for Chinese and American educators. A Chinese teacher enthusiastically offered to have some of the students in a Beijing high school both respond to and create video diaries to begin a transpacific youth dialogue. The possibilities for video diaries are endless.

Works Cited

Print

Frank, Anne. *Anne Frank: The Diary of a Young Girl.* New York: Bantam, 1993.

McGrath, Campbell. *Spring Comes to Chicago.* Hopewell, NJ: Ecco, 1996.

Plath, Sylvia. *The Unabridged Journals of Sylvia Plath.* Ed. Karen V. Kukil. New York: Anchor, 2000.

Townsend, Sue. *The Adrian Mole Diaries.* New York: Grove, 1988.

Video

Bill Viola: The Eye of the Heart. Dir. Mark Kidel. Callipe Media, 2002.

By Brakhage: An Anthology. Dir. Stan Brakhage. Prod. Peter Becker and Kate Elmore. Criterion Collection, 2003.

Glass Jaw. Dir. Michael O'Reilly. Video Data Bank, 1991.

Jem Cohen: Early Works. Dir. Jem Cohen. Video Data Bank, 1992.

Nam June Paik. Dir. Nam June Paik. Creative Arts Television, 1975.

Sadie Benning Videoworks: Volume 1. Dir. Sadie Benning, Video Data Bank, 1990.

Weather Diary 1. Dir. George Kuchar. Video Data Bank, 1986.

Weather Diary 2. Dir. George Kuchar. Video Data Bank, 1987.

Primary source for videos:
Video Data Bank
112 S. Michigan Avenue
Chicago, IL 60603
312-345-3550
info@vdb.org

II Media and Literature

Read It, Watch It, Analyze It, Shoot It

Mary T. Christel
Adlai E. Stevenson High School
Lincolnshire, Illinois

For most conscientious English language arts teachers, the written word and the moving image have become contentious rivals for their students' attention. We certainly want students to appreciate the subtlety and complexity of a literary text, but in the recent wake of an abundance of film adaptations of classic and contemporary literature, watching the movie version can be the electronic equivalent of CliffsNotes, giving students easy access to broad outlines of plot, characterization, and theme. Isn't it more appealing to passively watch Gwyneth Paltrow and Ethan Hawke cavort in a modern reimagining of Dickens's "really long" and complicated novel *Great Expectations* than to read it? In *William Shakespeare's Romeo + Juliet*, Baz Luhrmann's postmodern substitution of guns and knives for swords and sabers brings a visual vitality to the opening scene, and the casting of Leonardo DiCaprio imbues the story with a pop culture currency that tops Zeffirelli's adaptation to raise interest in that staple of ELA curricula. But these natural rivals can easily be turned into peacefully coexisting companions that can encourage closer reading and better understanding of the written text, as well as allowing students to create their own media images inspired by the novels, plays, short stories, and poems that they read or that they write themselves.

Even though ELA teachers fully understand that media texts lure their students away from more conventional written texts, film is probably the medium that teachers are most comfortable integrating into a literature unit. Most of us have used film to analyze a novel's or play's narrative properties of character, plot, and theme, but we may not have explored the cinematic artistry of those filmic texts in much depth, usually due to a lack of experience in analyzing shot composition, sound elements, mise en scène, and editing. We also need to realize that video games and graphic novels use the same conventions of narrative that more traditional texts employ, as well as introducing conventions unique to these new forms. Integrating these less familiar media texts can provide rich possibilities for tapping into what students know and what they enjoy outside the classroom.

So, as we examine the range of media texts that can complement and enrich the study of literature, we need to examine how to set clear purposes for viewing that are just as meaningful and rigorous as the purposes we set for reading conventional literary texts. How do we set the stage for viewing in a way that achieves results that are similar to the results we see with activities we routinely employ before studying fiction or drama? How do we create ways for students to become active viewers of a cinematic text just as we encourage them to become active readers? What kinds of speaking, writing, and media production activities can we develop to assess their understanding of the connection between two different types of texts? This next collection of lesson plans has been selected to foster critical reading and thinking skills, and they can be used in a variety of settings with students of all abilities.

This section begins with "Visualizing the Literary Text Using Storyboards and Basic Cinematic Techniques," a multi-use lesson that focuses on storyboarding, a technique that creates a series of single-frame images that constitute a film sequence. Neil Rigler and colleagues Carol Porter-O'Donnell and Thomas O'Donnell explain how students can better understand the distinctions between print and nonprint text by translating words into images from small sections of texts like *To Kill a Mockingbird* and *Romeo and Juliet*. This strategy is also integrated into later lessons that require students to produce their own videos in response to a poetic or dramatic text.

In "Video Games as a Tool for In-Depth Plot Analysis," Nili Friedman uses a novel approach (no pun intended) to help students understand plot structure by having them create video games that are based on novels like *Carry on, Mr. Bowditch*. Middle school students are certainly well acquainted with the conventions of classic video games like *Super Mario Brothers* that include characters, setting, narrative lines, conflicts, and resolutions. They can use their expertise gleaned from the realm of popular culture to better understand its application in a more traditional text-based form. Jacqueline Cullen's lesson on examining the epic patterns of Homer's *The Odyssey* in contemporary films follows the same notion—that sophisticated literary texts that are the staples of high school curricula can intersect usefully with popular culture, such as contemporary films that draw on the tropes of epic journeys.

Elizabeth Kenney's lesson, "All about *Emma*: Using Multiple Film Adaptations to Teach Literary Elements," which examines two film adaptations of Jane Austen's novel, highlights the popularity of adapting classic novels to film in ways that illuminate a literary text in interesting and sometimes competing ways. Kenney shows how to view a selected sequence from two cinematic versions to explore elements of setting, tone, and characterization, as well as fidelity to the source material. Since many novels and plays have been adapted for theatrical release and televised presentation by the A&E network or PBS's *Masterpiece Theatre*, teachers are certainly not limited to using *Emma* to implement Kenney's template for viewing questions, discussion strategies, and writing assignments.

A book of this sort would be remiss if it did not address the role of the graphic novel in the ELA classroom. In "Reading Graphic Novels: An Approach to Spiegelman's *Maus*," Kathleen Turner offers a series of lessons to help students read the now classic graphic novel *Maus*, to carefully understand the interplay between image and text. Once both teacher and students grasp the unique conventions of the graphic novel, the reading experience the text provides is certainly as rich as its more traditional text-based counterpart, in this instance Elie Wiesel's *Night*.

Finally, students can apply their understanding of the grammar and syntax of the cinematic treatment of literature by producing video texts themselves. In "Creating Video Poetry," David Bengtson presents a fascinating way for students to immerse themselves in the poetic texts they study in their traditional print form by creating "cinepoems" based on works by renowned poets or works of their own devising. Scott Williams's lesson, "Turning Text into Movie Trailers: The *Romeo and Juliet* iMovie Experience," tests his students' understanding of the essence of a complex work like *Romeo and Juliet* by having them create movie trailers that highlight key concepts extrapolated from the play, translating them into words, images, and sounds.

This series of lessons will provide any teacher of literature a rich resource for helping students understand the influences of and interplay between print and nonprint narrative, poetic, and dramatic texts. As culture and technology evolve, so must the ways that writers express themselves across traditional and nontraditional forms. It is up to savvy readers and viewers of those texts to recognize the unique strengths of each form.

Recommended Resources

Print

Cartmell, Deborah, and Imelda Whelehan, eds. *Adaptations: From Text to Screen, Screen to Text*. New York: Routledge, 1999.

Christel, Mary T. "Film in the Literature Class: Not Just Dessert Anymore." *Seeing and Believing: How to Teach Media Literacy in the English Classroom*. Ed. Ellen Krueger and Mary T. Christel. Portsmouth, NH: Boynton/Cook, 2001. 68–88.

Corrigan, Timothy. *Film and Literature: An Introduction and Reader*. Upper Saddle River, NJ: Prentice Hall, 1999.

Harrison, Stephanie, ed. *Adaptations: From Short Story to Big Screen: 35 Great Stories That Have Inspired Great Films*. New York: Three Rivers, 2004.

Naremore, James, ed. *Film Adaptation*. News Brunswick, NJ: Rutgers UP, 2000.

Roberts, Graham, and Heather Wallis. *Introducing Film*. London: Arnold, 2001.

Tibbets, John C., and James M. Welsh. *Novels into Film: The Encyclopedia of Movies Adapted from Books*. New York: Checkmark, 1999.

Websites

British Film Institute. <http://www.bfi.org.uk/>.

The Film Foundation. <http://www.film-foundation.org/>.

7 Visualizing the Literary Text Using Storyboards and Basic Cinematic Techniques

Neil Rigler and Carol Porter-O'Donnell
Deerfield High School
Deerfield, Illinois

Thomas O'Donnell
Highland Park High School
Highland Park, Illinois

Context

School District 113 is located in the northern suburbs of Chicago and comprises two high schools. Deerfield is a school of about 1,700 students, and Highland Park is a school of 1,850 students.

The lesson that follows was originally developed for an integrated grade 11 American Studies class, a grade 9 English class, and a grade 9 reading class. As a result of our collaboration, however, we have adapted our original attempts to incorporate the general ideas to all grade and ability levels.

Rationale

The technique of storyboarding is primarily used in the creation of movies, as a way of preplanning ideas about the visual representation of a story, including camera work, costumes, scenery, and movement. Asking students to create a set of storyboards to depict a story they've read not only appeals to their artistic and visual talents and interests, but also asks them to engage in the text by making decisions about sequencing, perspective, and literary interpretation. Storyboards require that students portray their mental images of the text using basic cinematic techniques. When students discuss the ways in which they storyboarded a scene, they are enhancing the ways in which they usually approach the study of literature and creating a basis for discussion.

When students create and discuss storyboards, they are better able to see the tools that writers use and the decisions they make to influence the "text" that a reader creates. Students can discuss what is included in the image, what isn't included, whose perspective was chosen, and how the director's decisions influence the messages that are portrayed. This understanding of the methods available to directors and writers to express and influence ideas helps learners to critically analyze text in whatever form it is presented. As a strategy for discussion, storyboarding can elicit rich conversations related to scenes that were chosen and why, what choices the reader-illustrator made in terms of types of shots and camera angles, and how those choices alter the messages conveyed. We should note that although obviously there are other elements to consider (e.g., sound design or sound track music), the emphasis here, for clarity of discussion, is on the visual aspects.

Helping readers to visualize the text, to see the differences between surface, or literal, meaning and deep, or more abstract, meaning, and to distinguish between important information and less important information promotes some of the comprehension skills that storyboarding (and potentially the use of film as a parallel text) can provide to struggling readers. Since many students who struggle with reading tend to resist writing, students can use storyboards as an alternative method of developing this type of thinking. Students can reveal the important aspects of the plot, in addition to the author's craft, by creating storyboards for these scenes.

Objectives

Students will be able to:

- Create storyboards based on a given text
- Determine the most effective way to present their understanding of a text to an audience
- Explain choices concerning the director's craft: perspective, angle, focus, information included or excluded from the frame, and other visual elements
- Use storyboards to help articulate their interpretation and understanding of a text
- Demonstrate active reading strategies (e.g., predicting, making connections, generating opinions, reflecting, analyzing author's craft) to comprehend "text" in various formats

NCTE/IRA standards addressed: 3, 4, 6, 11, 12

Material/Preactivity Preparation

The following materials will be used in the range of activities presented in this lesson:

- Blank storyboards (paper or blank overheads, depending on whether you have a classroom projector; see handouts 7.1 and 7.2 on the companion disk)
- Copies of nursery rhymes
- Texts (e.g., short story, novel) to be discussed
- Markers/colored pencils
- Projector or ELMO
- VCR and/or DVD player and monitor
- Movies (any appropriate for your curriculum, or, as discussed below, *To Kill a Mockingbird* and *Romeo and Juliet*)

Time Frame

The introduction of the storyboarding technique, as well as the first use and discussion of it, can be completed in one (58-minute) or two (42-minute) class periods.

In the American Studies class, storyboarding is used throughout the year as a regular part of discussions. In the grade 9 English and reading classrooms, we introduce storyboarding at the beginning of the school year to encourage multiple ways of expressing interpretations and to help readers visualize as a way of comprehending a text. Storyboarding and the use of film as a parallel text are part of a *To Kill a Mockingbird* unit (grade 9 English) and a *Romeo and Juliet* unit (grade 9 reading) that are taught midway through the grade 9 year.

The technique of creating storyboards and discussing the results is flexible enough to use in a variety of time frames and contexts, and we have found that students can comfortably return to the strategy months after it is first introduced.

Description of Activity

Introducing the Storyboarding Strategy

We introduce the concept and techniques of storyboarding through an overview of some of the factors to take into consideration when creating a visual representation of a text. Each student receives the text of a nursery rhyme (e.g., "Little Miss Muffet") and creates a series of eight frames or shots to portray it, writing the corresponding text below the image. Students share their storyboards with the rest of the class (by hanging them on the wall, projecting them, etc.) and explain the decisions that went into them, answering questions such as the following:

- Why did you choose to break up the text in this way?
- Why did you choose to include these details?
- Whose perspective did you use to show the story and why?
- What images did you add beyond those specifically named in the nursery rhyme?
- What did you omit and why?

From this discussion, students are able to see a range of possible ways to visually portray a text, based on their understanding of it, as well as to determine which parts of it they wanted to portray. For example, students might create storyboards to show the perspective of the spider in "Little Miss Muffet," and they could talk about what this perspective says about the story. Students enjoy the opportunity to see one anothers' work, especially when it presents a perspective or concept they have not previously considered. The teacher often works to ensure that this insight occurs by providing sample work in a way that will not limit students' creativity.

Students can continue to develop the skill of storyboarding as a way to interpret text by pairing up or getting into larger groups to work with different nursery rhymes and then repeating the activity. As these are shared, the class can work together to name the different choices the "director" can make, including perspective, angle, focus, and information included or excluded from the frame. This basic film terminology forms the basis of discussion about the storyboards, which demonstrates to the students the various ways in which creating a visual portrayal of a written text represents an understanding of it, and how the choices made by the director shape an audience's perception.

Using Storyboarding to Promote Discussion of a Novel

After reading Harper Lee's novel *To Kill a Mockingbird* and watching the 1962 movie, students will likely notice that several characters were deleted and several key scenes cut from this excellent film. To address this issue and create a framework for discussion, divide students into pairs and let them choose some of the most important scenes that were cut from the movie but that played an important role in the novel. Once these scenes are identified, students can begin to storyboard the deleted scenes; while doing so, they should discuss with their partner a rationale for why their character(s) and scene(s) were important to the novel for illustrating a certain theme or motif.

For example, many students in the grade 9 English class chose to storyboard the Missionary Tea Society scene in Chapter 24 of the book, which was completely cut from the movie. The students reasoned that this chapter illustrated the small town prejudice of Mrs. Merriweather and other hypocrites who were worried about the poor Mrunas in Africa but put down the blacks in their own town; by not including the scene in the film, an important idea was lost.

For this lesson, students can be required to draw or sketch three to six shots that constitute a sequence of related shots. Also, for each shot, they need to be able to discuss in a larger group answers to the following questions:

- Why did you choose the scene depicted in the storyboards as one that should have been included in the movie?
- What kind of camera angle did you use and why?
- What mood or attitude did you want to demonstrate?
- What lines from the text helped you to see this?
- What sound effects would you include?
- What background music, if any, would you use?

After sufficient class time (two 42-minute periods, for example), students should be ready to discuss their storyboards for the deleted novel scenes using the preceding questions to guide their interactions. For students to value the strategies of storyboarding and discussion as tools for deepening and enhancing their understandings of the text, students might write a reflection using the following questions to guide their writing:

- How did creating storyboards help you to better understand the story?
- What were some of the different interpretations your group came up with?
- What cinematic techniques (lighting, camera angles, and special effects) were used to show these different interpretations?
- How did your discussion change your understanding of the literature?

This storyboarding activity helps students understand the difficult job of a director who makes the decision about how scenes are shot for a film. In addition, students use their creativity to make their shots from the novel interesting. Finally, we discuss the director's possible reasons for cutting characters and scenes, and the lesson on storyboarding motivates students to ask important questions as they analyze the novel.

Assessment

A storyboard rubric formatted as a grid can be found on the companion disk (Figure 7.3). This tool allows teachers to assess each storyboard based on the following criteria, which are met, partially met, or not met:

- Key parts of the plot are captured in the storyboard.
- A variety of shots, angles, and distances are used to show character relationships and the relative importance of different details and perspectives.
- Scenes are labeled with chapter numbers and a brief title that provides additional meaning.
- Drawings have details that show a careful reading and/or symbolic interpretation of the text.
- An explanation of "director's craft" is included that accounts for choices made in storyboards.

The written element can be in the form of a set of descriptions accompanying the storyboards (often called a "director's notebook") or as a self-reflection, using the questions in the previous section as a guide.

Connections and Adaptations

In the past, we have tried to teach the thought processes that effective readers use while working to comprehend text by modeling this thinking while reading aloud to students in a reading class or to students who are struggling with a difficult text in our English classes. For example, while reading a short story aloud, the teacher stops at the end of the first page and announces that she or he is confused and is unable to sort through all of the information that authors usually put on the first page. The teacher can then have students help sort through this information by assigning small groups to determine the surface meaning in the text up to that point—who, when, where, and what problems—or have students create a cluster on the inside front cover of their books with a circle for each of these aspects of the plot. As the teacher continues to read, she or he stops periodically to make a prediction or to ask students to make a prediction. We can also make connections, state opinions, summarize, ask questions, and analyze the author's craft when we stop to share our thinking, to both assist in comprehending the text and to consider more abstract meaning. One way for readers to practice these active reading strategies is to make predictions by drawing scenes they would expect to see in future chapters of a book. Furthermore, storyboards can also capture connections between the text and scenes from their own lives or scenes from another text. Students can analyze the author's craft by creating storyboards of the metaphors, similes, and other vivid language the author has used.

Struggling readers and students who watch a lot of TV often watch movies with the same passivity they exhibit while reading. While the class watches a film, teachers can model the dialogue strategy of stopping to ask questions to clarify understanding and interpretation, and they can push their students to do the same type of thinking if they pause the movie and ask students to share. We have found that students who struggle the most with thinking in these ways quickly and loudly voice their displeasure with interrupting the movie. "Can't we just watch it?" is a common request from students when the teacher first starts pausing the movie. After repeated interruptions for discussion, however, students seem to develop a need to process this "text" in the same way that effective readers "dialogue" with the text while they read. To assess students' ability to use the "in head" strategies that effective readers use, teachers need to capture the talk in the classroom while students are watching the film.

Another problem for struggling readers is that they are often given "easier" texts to read in their lower-level classes or as a way to differentiate instruction in a "regular" English class. However, rather than reading adapted or abridged versions of texts, which lose most of the literary qualities for which they were chosen, students can read these original texts with the supporting strategies of storyboarding and viewing a film version of the text.

Reading the text in its written form, creating and discussing storyboards, and then "reading" the film can continue in this manner until students have completed both versions. If students know they are going to storyboard, they might want to annotate or mark the text for scenes they will draw and the type of shot they are considering.

Work Cited

Lee, Harper. *To Kill a Mockingbird*. New York: Warner, 1960.

Supplemental Reading and Viewing

Costanzo, William V. *Great Films and How to Teach Them*. Urbana, IL: National
     Council of Teachers of English, 2004.

Golden, John. *Reading in the Dark: Using Film as a Tool in the English Classroom*.
     Urbana, IL: National Council of Teachers of English, 2001.

Krueger, Ellen, and Mary T. Christel. *Seeing and Believing: How to Teach Media
     Literacy in the English Classroom*. Portsmouth, NH: Boynton/Cook,
     2001.

Visions of Light: The Art of Cinematography. Dir. Arnold Glassman, Todd
     McCarthy, and Stuart Samuels. Twentieth Century Fox, 2000.

8 Video Games as a Tool for In-Depth Plot Analysis

Nili Friedman
Vanderbilt University
and
Akiva School
Nashville, Tennessee

Context

The Akiva School is a Jewish community day school in Nashville, Tennessee. The school is made up of eighty-six students in grades K–6 with varying degrees of religious observance. It is located in a suburb about 20 minutes from downtown Nashville.

This lesson was created for a fifth-grade language arts class. The class is divided into two periods. The first period focuses on writing. Students work on their writing using the writing process and the six traits of writing as a guide. They study the art of writing in a variety of genres, including essays, folktales, and biographies. The second half of the class is devoted to studying literature and building stronger reading skills. For each novel studied, students are expected to keep a structured reading journal, contribute to a class reading chart, and take part in a creative final project. The following lesson plan is an example of one such project.

Rationale

Most students seem to love action-packed adventure novels. The quick pace of adventure novels appeals to a generation of students who are used to constantly changing images on TV, movie, and computer screens. Despite the attraction of adventure novels, however, their complex plots often pose significant challenges to readers. In addition to requiring students to remember plot details over an extended period of time, adventure novels, and other novels as well, call on readers to make inferences about the impact of characters and settings on plot, and vice versa. It is easy to see how keeping track of all this information can be burdensome to a reader who is simply trying to get caught up in an adventure. I have found that using video games as a tool for in-depth plot analysis helps alleviate some of the burden of understanding complicated plots by allowing students to synthesize information about plot in a more familiar form. In addition, analyzing a complex story line allows students to gain a deeper understanding of how plots are constructed and how they relate to other structural elements of a novel.

Objectives

Students will be able to:

- Convert the plot of a novel into a video game format
- Prepare a detailed proposal of a video game based on a novel
- Display textual and graphic information on a project board
- Make an oral presentation to a mock board of directors
- Evaluate classmates' video games based on a specified rubric

NCTE/IRA standards addressed: 1, 2, 3, 4, 6, 11, 12

Material/Preactivity Preparation

Because adventure novels work best, some good choices might include:

- *Carry on, Mr. Bowditch* by Jean Lee Latham
- *The Lion, the Witch, and the Wardrobe* by C. S. Lewis
- *From the Mixed-Up Files of Mrs. Basil E. Frankweiler* by E. L. Konigsburg
- *The Wolves of Willoughby Chase* by Joan Aiken
- *The True Confessions of Charlotte Doyle* by Avi

Other materials include:

- Final project sheets (see Figure 8.1 on the companion disk)
- Note-taking packets (see Figure 8.2 on the companion disk)
- Project boards
- Drawing materials (markers or colored pencils)
- TV monitor or projector
- Video game system
- Video game with a clearly defined plot and a variety of levels (i.e., *Super Mario Brothers 3*)
- Student reading logs
- Class reading chart

I recommend that students keep individual reading journals as well as a class reading chart while they are reading the novel. This will provide students with two secondary resources to refer to when they are analyzing the plot of the novel and transforming it into a video game format.

Time Frame

The lesson takes approximately five one-hour class periods that ideally take place over the course of a week. The first class period should be spent going over the project, studying the format of a video game, and discussing how components of the sample video game could be applied to students' own games. Over the next three days, students should be given time to work on their video games in class. Teachers might also consider assigning the video games for homework. By the end of the fourth day, students should be ready to present their video games and evaluate one another's work the following day.

You might want to spread the project out over a longer period, depending on your allotted class time and curricular goals. Obviously, if students are given more time to work on the project, they will be able to analyze the plot in greater depth, create more detailed video games, and conduct practice runs of their presentations for one another. However, I do not recommend stretching the project out more than two weeks, because students might forget parts of the novel or lose interest in the project.

Description of Activity

When students have finished reading the novel, hand out a project sheet with a narrative similar to the following:

> PlayStation has decided to create a series of video games based on famous children's books (or young adult novels). Your team has been hired to transform *Carry on, Mr. Bowditch* into an action-packed video game. First, create a proposal for a video game that includes the guidelines listed below. Next, arrange all your information on a project board. Finally, prepare a presentation of your video game to be presented to the rest of the class.
>
> PlayStation Board of Directors

To help students understand what makes a successful video game, lead them in a discussion of what makes a successful novel. This will allow students to begin their evaluation process with a format more familiar to an English class, in addition to highlighting the parallels between novels and video games.

Begin the discussion by reviewing the six elements of fiction: character, setting, situation, problem, conflict, and resolution. Then ask students to consider what an author has to do to make each of these elements successful in a novel. The next step would be to ask students how each of these elements translates into a video game. Some examples might include the settings in a novel paralleling the levels in a video game, the situation in a novel paralleling the mission in a video game, and the resolution in a novel paralleling the resolution in a video game.

Next, divide the class into teams. If you already have your students divided into literature circles, keep the same groups. Depending on your style of classroom management, you might want to give each team member a specific role to perform or select one leader for each group.

Tell the class that to better understand the components of a successful video game, they will be taking notes while you play a video game. See the "Notes for Sample Video Game" handout (Figure 8.2 on the companion disk).

Have the students watch you or another adult play various levels of a video game. Be sure students get to see a variety of levels so that they are exposed to the creativity of this genre. The *Super Mario Brothers 3* game works well. Some other good choices might include *Sonic the Hedgehog* by Sega, *The Legend of Zelda* by Nintendo, or any of the other Super Mario Brothers games by Nintendo.

While students are watching the video game, have them fill out the information on the note-taking packet. Pause the video game periodically to have students share their ideas about how components of the sample video game could be applied to their own video games. For example, my students suggested that instead of Mario collecting gold coins, Nathaniel Bowditch could collect expectations from different ships.

After the students have watched the game and completed their note-taking packets, lead the class in a discussion of what qualities make a successful video game. List students' responses on chart paper. Post the chart paper on the wall so that students can refer to it when they are creating their own video games.

Give students the next three class periods to work on their video games. Make sure students are dividing up the work evenly, with different students responsible for different aspects of the video game. For example, one student might be responsible for dividing the game into a series of levels, while another student is responsible for creating different types of equipment.

Start each class period by reminding students of the list they created about the qualities of a good video game. Then monitor students to ensure that they are working toward their standards.

Once students have completed the video games, have them reconvene as the PlayStation Board of Directors. Remind students of their list of standards and explain that they will be filling out an evaluation sheet for each team's video game based on their standards.

Use a rubric to have students evaluate one anothers' video games, such as the one provided in Figure 8.3 on the companion disk. If you have the time, you could take a class period to help students create their own class rubric. Make sure to leave room for students to write in comments. Also, remind students of the difference between constructive and destructive criticism.

Have students present their projects and then display them out in the hall. Photocopy the rubrics both you and the students completed, giving each student a copy of his or her team's and keeping the originals for your records.

Conclude the activity with a brief discussion of what students learned. Some possible discussion questions include:

- How does a novel change when it is presented as a video game?
- How can the creators of video games preserve the elements of a novel when they are adapting it to a different medium?
- How effective are video games at communicating a plot?
- What are the challenges of telling a story through a video game?
- How do the different elements of a video game (levels, character, equipment, etc.) impact the plot of a novel?

As a follow-up activity, the class might want to send copies or photographs of the proposals to Sony PlayStation to see if the class gets a response.

Assessment

Assessment should focus on students' participation, project boards, and oral presentations. I recommend basing grades on presentation, creativity, and the extent to which the games adhere to the essential elements of the novel. As mentioned earlier, the whole class will take part in the assessment of the video games when they reconvene as the PlayStation Board of Directors. I recommend that after each group's presentation, you allow the class a couple of minutes to give verbal feedback on the group's proposed game, with some carefully chosen questions to guide a productive discussion. Then give students additional time to fill in an evaluation form such as Figure 8.3 on the companion disk.

During this time, you should also fill in an evaluation form for each group. Here are some questions to guide your response to students' work to supplement the evaluation form, especially if you are not familiar with the construction of video games:

Name of Video Game

- How does the name connect to the novel?
- To what extent does the name catch viewers' attention?
- To what extent does the name sound appropriate for a video game?

Summary of Book

- Did the group include the book's title and author?
- Is the summary written in students' own words?
- How does the summary capture the main ideas of the novel?
- Is the summary well organized and easy to understand?

Sketch of Main Character

- Does it look like the group put its best effort into the drawing?
- How does the drawing fit with character descriptions in the text?

Names and Pictures of Equipment

- How does the choice of equipment tie into the novel?
- How does the equipment assist players in achieving the object of the game?

Explanations of How Equipment Is Acquired

- How do the explanations tie into the plot of the novel?
- Are the explanations clear?
- Do the explanations make sense in the context of the video game?

Mission

- Is the mission clearly explained?
- How does the mission connect to the plot of the novel?

Descriptions of Levels

- How vivid are the descriptions of at least five different levels?
- To what extent are the levels based on scenes from the novel?

Description of Obstacles at Each Level

- How do the obstacles make sense in the context of the novel?
- Are the obstacles clearly explained?

Overall Map of Game

- Does it look like the group put its best effort into drawing the map?
- How is the map based on the setting of the novel?

Drawings of Levels

- Does it look like the group put its best effort into the drawings?
- How do the drawings tie into the plot and setting of the novel?
- How do the drawings correspond to the descriptions of the levels?

Your evaluation would also take into account the visual and oral presentation of this information.

Connections and Adaptations

The project is meant to provide authentic assessment following the study of a novel. The project incorporates multiple intelligences and is meant to stimulate student interest by bringing an increasingly popular form of media—the video game—into the classroom. The unusual pairing of the novel and the videogame is meant to excite even the most reluctant readers in your class. The project is also meant to be academically rigorous as students conduct in-depth plot analysis and demonstrate their understanding through an original and creative medium. Depending on your teaching style and curriculum standards, the project may be used instead of or in addition to the formal assessment of students' understanding of the novel.

Works Cited

Latham, Jean Lee. *Carry On, Mr. Bowditch*. Boston: Houghton Mifflin, 1983.

Nintendo. *Super Mario Brothers 3*. (Nintendo Entertainment System). Redmond, WA: Nintendo of America, 1990.

9 Analyzing Epic Patterns of *The Odyssey* in Contemporary Films

Jacqueline Cullen
Adlai E. Stevenson High School
Lincolnshire, Illinois

Context

Adlai E. Stevenson High School is a northwest Chicago suburban school of 4,500 students. This assignment has been used in Freshman Accelerated English, an honors English course, during a unit in which the students read *The Odyssey*.

Rationale

Connecting literature in the classroom to the lives of students allows for a deeper, more authentic understanding of the text. For some students who have only limited knowledge of Greek mythology, reading and analyzing *The Odyssey* can be a challenge. They may ask, "Why do we have to read about a one-eyed monster who kills and eats men?" But even though the story may seem foreign to them, the characteristics that Polyphemus, for example, possesses parallel the traits of most antagonists in contemporary films. In addition, literature becomes more accessible and manageable when students can recognize the common story lines in films. In turn, the best readers and viewers are those who have a wider range of experience in relation to the texts and who have studied them in depth.

Objectives

Students will be able to:

- Analyze a modern-day film in terms of how it parallels specific aspects (scenes, characters, theme) of *The Odyssey*
- Identify specific cinematic techniques that parallel literary elements (epithets, repetition, narration) of *The Odyssey*

- Produce a PowerPoint presentation that highlights the main areas of comparison and present it as a group to the class

NCTE/IRA standards addressed: 3, 6, 8

Materials/Preactivity Preparation

- Individual copies of *The Odyssey*, preferably written in verse form
- Access to PowerPoint and the technology to show PowerPoint presentations
- Various films (DVD/VHS) that have been approved by the teacher but chosen by students

Time Frame

The entire unit, which includes reading the text, lasts approximately 23 class days; each class at Stevenson is 50 minutes long. Within the unit, time is set aside once a week for groups to meet to plan the presentation. Groups are made up of four to five students and are formed by the teacher.

Description of Activity

For class time to be productive, the teacher must provide clear expectations and tasks that students can complete while meeting in groups. Therefore, during in-class meeting time, groups need to be very efficient in each of the following tasks.

Week 1: Get Started

Groups are formed, potential movies are considered, and specific parallels are identified between *The Odyssey* and films. This marks the first time the groups meet in class. Based on early discussion of *The Odyssey*, students should consider which parallels relate to which potential movies. They should turn in a calendar of the group's proposed activities and a list of potential movies by the end of class.

Week 2: Select a Movie

Based on the information generated during the previous meeting, groups are assigned a movie to analyze for the presentation. Each group gets a different film and must formulate a "to do" list that is turned in at the end of class. The list should also specify parallels between the selected movie and *The Odyssey*. Potential films for student selection include:

Live Action Films	**Animated Films**
O Brother, Where Art Thou?	*The Lion King*
The Blues Brothers	*Toy Story*
Raiders of the Lost Ark	*Toy Story 2*
The Lord of the Rings trilogy	*Finding Nemo*
The Princess Bride	*Shrek*
The Wizard of Oz	*Monsters, Inc.*
Star Wars	*Madagascar*

For more older or sophisticated students:

Thelma & Louise

The Outlaw Josey Wales

Amistad

The Dirty Dozen

Rabbit-Proof Fence

Walkabout

Week 3: Report on Progress

Groups should have viewed their film multiple times outside of class, and group members should compare notes to incorporate ideas into the presentation. Time in class may also be needed for students to develop the PowerPoint presentation. The teacher might want to assign specific sections of the PowerPoint presentation to be completed each week. I also ask students to respond to the following questions:

As far as you know,

- Who has watched the movie?
- Who has taken notes on the movie–book parallels to be explored in the project?
- What plans do you have for deciding who is presenting which part of the project, keeping in mind that everyone needs to play an equal role?
- What problems or concerns do you need to let me know about at this time in the project?

Week 4: Finalize Plans

This week groups determine when they will present, which film clip to show, and how to organize the presentation. An outline of the presentation should be turned in at the end of class.

Setting the Stage for Analysis

Since *The Odyssey* stems from oral tradition in literature, elements within the structure of the epic should be considered; for example, the use of epithets and repetition of text highlight the importance of sound in the tale. In the same way, films today use sound elements such as music to convey similar effects. Central to *The Odyssey* is the quest or journey, which the hero must go through to reunite with family or to attain a goal. In the course of the journey, the hero encounters multiple obstacles, which he miraculously overcomes. The superhuman traits that the hero embodies also define the main character in films that echo *The Odyssey*.

Having background knowledge of the elements of an epic will help students understand not only the structure of the tale but also the characteristics to pay attention to in viewing the film. So when the teacher introduces *The Odyssey*, students need to know the essential elements of an epic: the underlying theme concerns basic and eternal human problems; the narrative is a complex synthesis of experiences that may change narrators and include flashbacks; the hero embodies national, cultural, and religious ideals; the storyteller starts the story at a low point in the middle of the action (in medias res).

It is also helpful early in the unit to discuss characteristics of a typical adventure story. Students can generate a list of qualities from adventure stories or adventure movies they are familiar with (e.g., fight scenes, exotic settings, damsel in distress, etc.). By generating this list, students can then begin thinking of films that have some characteristics in common with *The Odyssey*.

Students also need a working vocabulary of cinematic terms, including *shot composition* (*framing, subject arrangement, camera placement, lighting,* and *color*), as well as *camera movement, point of view, editing,* and *sound.* A list of these terms with key questions is included in Figure 9.1 on the companion disk for students to use when analyzing at least one specific scene from the movie.

Monitoring Student Progress

During the weekly group meetings, one way I monitor progress is by sitting in on each group's meeting, at least for a short time. This gives the group an opportunity to ask me any questions regarding the presentation, and if I have concerns about a particular group or specific students, I can address my questions directly to them. It is important to reinforce for students how to use their time productively in and out of class.

Creating Presentations

Presentations usually last a minimum of 20 minutes but should not exceed 30 minutes; film clips should be included but not exceed 5 to 7 minutes. Using more than one clip is acceptable as long as the clips highlight different aspects of the epic. In selecting the clip, students should consider the importance of the scene as well as cinematic components such as use of color, sound, symbols, etc. In addition, the presentation must include a discussion of characters, scenes, and motifs within the film that are parallel to and significant in *The Odyssey*.

PowerPoint presentations must be well organized to be effective. (See Figure 9.2 on the companion disk.) It is essential to instruct the students on what goes into a PowerPoint presentation: what to include on the slides, how to order the slides, and how to build up to incorporating the film clip. The format of the slides should include bullet points rather than full text slides since students have a tendency to read from the slides when the slides contain a series of sentences; instead, students should expand on the ideas displayed in bullet points. Students also need to be aware of what their audience knows about the film they have selected. Knowing the degree of background information the audience has will help the group determine how much summary of the film is necessary in the beginning of the presentation.

Starting the presentation with information that provides the basic plot line is recommended. Essential information about characters should follow. The presentation can then examine specific elements such as scene parallels and cinematic techniques in more depth. By providing the basic information first, students also eliminate overlapping of material later in the presentation.

Whenever possible, the slides should combine information from the film and examples from *The Odyssey* to highlight the parallels. This can be accomplished by discussing parallel scenes and then showing the scene from the film to examine cinematic techniques. Before showing the film clip, however, students should let the audience know what to look for. This direction makes the film clips and presentation more effective by requiring the audience to process all that has been presented up to this point.

Showing a sample PowerPoint presentation does clarify for students what to include in their own work. As with any presentation, practice and preparation are essential, particularly because this involves a number of people. Everyone needs to know his or her part in the presentation, and that comes from planning the presentation together.

As a model, I created a PowerPoint presentation comparing *The Odyssey* to *Finding Nemo*. In it I compare plot similarities, character parallels, scene parallels, and stylistic devices from *The Odyssey* that are incorporated in the movie and translated into cinematic techniques. For example, the stylistic device of repetition builds throughout both works. The sentence "When young Dawn with her rose-red fingers shone once more . . ." (Homer 3.550) appears multiple times as a sign of passage of time. In *Finding Nemo*, Dory, the blue fish who suffers from short-term memory loss, repeats many things, which reinforces events and adds a comedic element to the journey to find Nemo. This sample presentation is Figure 9.3 on the companion disk, along with a student sample, Figure 9.4. Unfortunately, the presentations do not include the images due to copyright limitations. (It is lawful to use copyrighted images for such presentations *only* in face-to-face instructional contexts.)

PowerPoint technology fits in well with this assignment; however, if this technology is unavailable, students can still present an effective analysis of the film using visuals (e.g., poster board or handouts) that highlight scene and character parallels.

Assessment

Student Assessment

Although the primary focus of assessment for this project is the panel presentation, it is possible to have the group or individuals turn in a written analysis of the film as it relates to all of the aforementioned aspects of *The Odyssey*. It is also helpful to have students complete a reflective response that highlights how the process is working; think of this response as the eyes and ears during the project. This response could also allow more insight into how the project was actually accomplished.

Teacher Assessment

The group presentation should be evaluated based on the content of the PowerPoint presentation (60 percent of the overall grade) and on oral presentation (the remaining 40 percent), focusing on the discussion of character parallels, scene parallels, motifs, cinematic techniques, and the film clip. Figure 9.5 on the companion disk provides a sample evaluation form, which can be shared with students before final project submission.

Connections and Adaptations

Although this assignment is designed to revolve around *The Odyssey*, it could also be used with any literary text that involves an episodic journey or is an epic tale, such as *Beowulf, The Epic of Gilgamesh*, or *King Arthur and the Knights of the Round Table*.

Works Cited

Finding Nemo. Dir. Andrew Stanton and Lee Unrich. Disney/Pixar, 2003.

Homer. *The Odyssey*. Trans. Robert Fagles. New York: Penguin, 1996.

Kuhns, William, and Robert Stanley. *Exploring the Film*. Fairfield, NJ: Cebco, 1968.

10 All about *Emma*: Using Multiple Film Adaptations to Teach Literary Elements

Elizabeth Kenney
Stevenson High School
Lincolnshire, Illinois

Context

There are a lot of good reasons not to teach Jane Austen to high school students: archaic syntax, difficult vocabulary, and complex tone will challenge even the strongest reader. But after two years of teaching AP English language, I'd seen our juniors struggle to understand seventeenth-, eighteenth-, and even nineteenth-century prose passages, and I thought that more experience reading early nineteenth-century prose might help—the kind of experience you can only get by reading a long novel.

Rationale

Paradoxically, Austen's challenging language is both the reason I chose to teach *Emma* and the main obstacle to students' comprehension. The unfamiliar world of manners is a further obstacle—how would my students know whether a 15-minute visit was a compliment or an insult? Even for the most capable high school students, canonical texts can present significant challenges, including complex vocabulary, syntax, satire, and tone, as well as unfamiliar social customs. Careful use of film adaptations can help students overcome initial difficulties in reading and appreciate more subtle aspects of the work. Understanding tone is crucial for appreciating this novel. As Wayne Booth has observed, how Jane Austen manages to make the reader care about and even sympathize with Miss Emma Woodhouse—a hopelessly self-absorbed and insufferable snob—is a marvel of controlled narrative distance and tone.

When multiple film adaptations of a text are available, teachers can juxtapose different filmmakers' choices to highlight the complexities of the original. *Emma* was the subject of three different film adaptations between 1995 and 1997. The Miramax (1996) version is dominated by scenes filmed outdoors in bright sunlight; its sunny tone is further conveyed through broader comedy and an omission of the darker elements of Austen's novel. In contrast, the A&E (1997) production often looks like a Vermeer painting, with interiors subtly lit from a single light source. It includes some of the darker elements of the novel and tackles the thorny issue of Emma's (and Austen's) unrepentant class consciousness. But the film that began the wave of Austen adaptations was Amy Heckerling's 1995 *Clueless*, an updating of *Emma* to Beverly Hills of the 1990s, which uses much broader comedy and a lighter tone yet re-creates Austen's biting satire. This three-lesson sequence uses the two more literal film adaptations, but if time allows, *Clueless* could be used as well.

Objectives

Students will be able to:

- Identify several readily observable film techniques used in short scenes and explain what aspect of the characters' relationships are emphasized through the filmmakers' visual strategies
- View two different film versions of a scene, identify tone, and analyze how the filmmakers' choices convey one tone or another
- Discuss which of two film versions is closer to the tone of the original text
- Define what constitutes a "happy" or satisfying ending in literature, and analyze the extent to which a novel's ending fits this definition

NCTE/IRA standards addressed: 1, 2, 3, 6

Material/Preactivity Preparation

To compare filmmakers' choices, one must have at least two different film adaptations of the text, preferably films that are significantly different in their treatment of character, tone, or resolution of a challenge in adaptation. Students will also need to be provided with a basic working vocabulary for the film strategies the teacher wants them to notice and discuss. For this lesson, I provide a handout defining the terms *camera placement*, *framing*, *subject arrangement*, *lighting*, and *color* (refer to

Chapter 9 for definitions of these terms). I also provide a handout to help students structure their note taking while viewing the selected scenes (see Figure 10.1 on the companion disk).

Time Frame

The lessons that follow are intended for bright students who can be expected to read Austen's prose competently but with somewhat limited insight, and who can be expected to learn quickly to identify chosen visual elements of film; each of the three lessons takes one 50-minute class period. If these lessons were adapted for a less sophisticated group, they might need to be significantly altered to allow for more direct instruction of techniques.

Description of Activity

Day 1: Warm Up Visual Literacy

The sequence begins with a one-day examination of two early scenes from one film version (Miramax) to introduce a basic vocabulary for analyzing film. Used early in students' reading of the novel, the activity can help struggling students to visualize characters and setting.

Without any preparation, show the scene in which Emma and Harriet discuss Robert Martin while at their needlework. That the camera placement in this scene is very unusual is readily apparent to students. The camera begins at quite a distance before moving in toward the two women. Then, as Emma begins to weave her web of influence, the camera slowly circles around them. Show the scene twice: first, ask students to watch closely without taking notes; then, during the second viewing, ask them to jot down what they notice. They are then ready to discuss.

Discussion Questions

- Where is the camera during the scene? How does its placement change?
- What is the relationship between the characters? What's the conflict?
- How does their relationship change during this scene?
- How do the visual elements emphasize certain aspects of the developing relationship between Harriet and Emma?
- How does the setting affect the tone of the scene? (Imagine, for example, how it would be different if the conversation took place indoors while rain was visible through the window.)

Before viewing the second scene, have students reread Emma and Mr. Knightley's conversation at the Crown ball, after Harriet has been snubbed and rescued. If time allows, students can storyboard the scene (using handouts provided in the storyboarding lesson in Chapter 7). Otherwise, they simply write for five or ten minutes (and make a simple sketch) of how they would film it before watching the scene.

Discussion Questions

- What did you find interesting (visually) about the scene?
- What has changed in the relationship between Emma and Mr. Knightley?
- How do the visual elements in this scene emphasize certain aspects of their developing relationship?
- What does the film (and especially the framing) suggest about Emma's role in the change in the relationship?

Day 2: Comparing Tone in Two Versions

Anyone wanting to film *Emma* has a technical problem: in a novel in which much of the drama takes place inside the head of the protagonist, how do you convey the essential interiority of Emma's conflicts and growth? By asking students to reread the passage in which Emma realizes her love for Mr. Knightley, and then examining how the scene is rendered in the Miramax and A&E versions of *Emma*, they see two approaches to solving this problem and how the different choices dramatically affect tone.

Both scenes render the scene of Harriet's confession similarly but then diverge dramatically. The Miramax film has Emma immediately discuss her realization with Mrs. Weston, a conversation that does not take place in the book and that makes Emma seem much less isolated and forlorn than Austen does. The scene takes place in a brightly lit garden and almost immediately turns comic, which lightens the tone even further.

In contrast, the A&E film dramatizes Emma's realization in a series of flashbacks. The effect is darker and more psychological. The sequence ends with Emma alone in a dark parlor, with her father asleep in his chair; she looks out the window at the rain and speaks her realization aloud through tears. (This is actually the second time in the A&E version that we see Emma trapped behind glass, in tears. The first time is after Knightley's rebuke of her at Box Hill. It's an effective motif.) The A&E version of the realization scene is literally more faithful to the novel. Students can then debate which version is closer in tone. (If time allows, the teacher could show the parallel scene in *Clueless*, which makes effective use of voice-over to overcome the technical difficulty and combines the darkness of the original with broad comedy.)

Discussion Questions

Previewing

- Reread the passage in which Emma realizes her love for Mr. Knightley. What elements would be easy to translate to film?
- What would be the challenges of conveying Emma's developing realization?

Miramax Version

- What elements are different from the novel?
- How does the filmmaker overcome the challenges of filming Emma's realization?
- What are the effects of these differences, especially on tone?

A&E Version

- How does the filmmaker overcome the challenges of filming Emma's realization?
- What aspects of Emma and her situation does this version emphasize?
- How is the tone different?
- Which version is more (literally) faithful to the novel? Which version better conveys the novel's tone?

Clueless

- What is the effect of the voice-over?
- How does the scene use clichés for comic effect?
- Based on a typical scene, what seems to be the purpose of the film—parody or homage?

Day 3: Happily Ever After?

The ending of Austen's novel is problematic for many readers. Some dislike Emma and don't believe that she deserves the happiness promised by the ending. Others find it difficult to take the novel's last line at face value; they find the age difference and Emma's submission to Mr. Knightley troubling and believe that Mr. Woodhouse will create more difficulty than the narrator will admit. And yet I've always felt that anyone who understands what Jane Austen is about must acknowledge the marriages that conclude the novels to be a good thing for the characters involved, capable of creating if not the perfect happiness of a fairy tale then the best chance at happiness that these particular characters could hope for.

The Miramax and A&E versions of the story include very different endings which—taken together—create an interesting commentary on Austen's ending and the degree to which it satisfies its readers. The Miramax version ends with a short sequence very faithful to the novel: Harriet announces her engagement and Emma expresses her joy; Emma and Mr. Knightley walk out of the church as everyone cheers and throws confetti; they kiss as the narrator reads the last line of the novel in voice-over: ". . . the wishes, the hopes, the confidence, the predictions of the small band of true friends who witnessed the ceremony, were fully answered in the perfect happiness of the union."

The A&E version, however, does not end with the wedding, but rather invents a new scene: a harvest supper, which has no correlation at all in the novel. Harriet's announcement of her engagement is followed immediately by shots of happy peasants in the fields gathering the harvest. At the harvest supper, Mrs. Elton is shocked that she will be expected to sit down with the farmers; Mr. Knightley reassures the farmers with promises of stability; and Emma shocks and pleases Harriet and her fiancé by inviting them to visit her. This ending seems designed for a contemporary audience uncomfortable with Austen's class consciousness. Mr. Knightley is a patriarchal aristocrat, but he's a benevolent patriarch. The peasants are happy, and Emma and Mr. Knightley socialize with them in a way that does not happen in the novel. Emma's snobbishness is transferred to Mrs. Elton, the novel's comic villain.

Discussion Questions

Previewing

- What constitutes a happy ending? Think about the conventional endings of fairy tales, the conventions of Shakespearean comedies, and how these differ from what would be considered a happy ending in real life. Write a brief definition of a happy ending in literature.

- What is the difference between a "happy" ending and a satisfying ending?

- Which elements of *Emma* constitute a happy ending? According to whose conventions?

- What elements complicate the ending of *Emma*, working against a happy ending?

Miramax Version

- To what extent is the ending literally faithful to Austen's novel? To what extent is it faithful to the tone of the novel?

A&E Version

- List elements of the A&E ending that are different from Austen's original. How does each element contribute to the "happiness" of the ending?

- Why do you think the filmmaker added the harvest supper sequence?

- How does this version stand as a commentary on (or implicit criticism of) Austen's ending? How does the filmmaker try to "improve" the novel or its characters?

If time allows, show the ending of *Clueless*, both to enrich the discussion of the elements that constitute a happy ending for Emma and to extend the discussion of parody and homage.

Assessment

After viewing both versions of the ending, students write a one-page informal response to the following prompt: Which film version did you find more satisfying? Be sure to distinguish between "happy" and "satisfying," and use examples from both films to demonstrate how the filmmakers' choices lead to an ending that is more or less satisfying.

The entire sequence prepares students for a formal essay analyzing the ending of Austen's novel. Figure 10.2 on the companion disk combines the essay assignment and an assessment rubric.

Connections and Adaptations

This sequence could be endlessly adaptable to works of literature that are the subject of multiple film adaptations. What sets this sequence apart from other lessons that use adaptations is its narrow focus on one or two aspects of the literary work that are problematic for readers and critics, using contrasting film adaptations to highlight the complexities of the original. These lessons avoid simplistic responses (Which did you like better?) by keeping students' attention focused on specific literary elements, particularly tone. In another work, one might focus on a character's motivation (think of Othello's monologue before killing Desdemona), the portrayal of an unsympathetic character (*Frankenstein*), or the effect of an unreliable narrator (*The Great Gatsby*).

Follow these guidelines when adapting this sequence:

- Begin by warming up visual literacy, especially if this is the first time the class has examined a visual medium. Doing this early in the study of a novel or play also helps struggling readers to visualize distant places and unfamiliar customs. Choose scenes from the adaptation(s) that are visually rich.

- Juxtapose contrasting scenes from two (or more) adaptations that highlight the literary elements you want students to focus on.

- Always allow the students to watch a given scene at least twice. The first time through, have them watch without trying to take notes. Encourage them to jot down what they notice during the second viewing. Watch a third time if you have time, or after discussion to reinforce the observations that have been made.

Works Cited

Austen, Jane. *Emma*. 1816. *Emma: An Authoritative Text, Backgrounds, Reviews and Criticism*. 3rd ed. Ed. Stephen M. Parrish. New York: Norton, 1999.

Booth, Wayne C. *The Rhetoric of Fiction*. 2nd ed. Chicago: U of Chicago P, 1983.

Clueless. Dir. and writ. Amy Heckerling. Paramount, 1995.

Emma. Dir. Douglas McGrath. Miramax, 1996.

Emma. Dir. Diarmuid Lawrence. A&E, 1997.

Supplemental Reading

Pool, Daniel. *What Jane Austen Ate and Charles Dickens Knew: From Fox Hunting to Whist—The Facts of Daily Life in Nineteenth-Century England*. New York: Touchstone, 1993.

Troost, Linda, and Sayre Greenfield, eds. *Jane Austen in Hollywood*. 2nd ed. Lexington: U of Kentucky P, 2001.

11 Reading Graphic Novels: An Approach to Spiegelman's *Maus*

Kathleen Turner
Northern Illinois University

Context

Jefferson City High School is a local public school of approximately 2,400 students in Jefferson City, Missouri. The following activity has been developed for use in a sophomore English course during a unit on Holocaust literature that included the study of Elie Wiesel's *Night*. This particular sophomore class had a reading level of eighth grade or below, but this activity could easily be adapted to other ability levels by increasing the rigor of the questions or giving students a narrower focus.

Rationale

Our students live in a culture where they are bombarded by visuals from advertising, television, movies, video games, comic books, toys, and the Internet. Students watch more television and see more images on a daily basis than ever before; as a result, our students respond to visual images. However, although we live in a visual culture, we often don't take time to read critically the images around us. Reminding ourselves and our students of how to read visual images in a more sophisticated manner is important for the analysis of a graphic novel, in which the structure affects the content. Most students appreciate having a visual context when learning about anything, but they especially appreciate it for an abstract concept such as the Holocaust because visuals help make the Holocaust real. Many teachers accommodate this through the combination of a variety of written accounts and visual images. As an artistic rendering, Art Spiegelman's *Maus* adds an important layer to the visual depictions and to the verbal narratives of the Holocaust. While documentary or photographic footage provides a more real-life depiction of Holocaust events, the graphic novel gives Spiegelman's interpretation of these events that continue to have an impact on life today.

Art Spiegelman's graphic novel *Maus* tells the story of Art finding out about his father's experiences during the Holocaust in an interesting recombination of visual and written narrative. Reading portions or all of this graphic novel will help students consider visual images of the Holocaust in conjunction with written narratives. This lesson will not only help students consider the nature of graphic novels and how words form a cohesive unit with images to present a story, but it will also help them become better readers of our visual culture in general.

Objectives

Students will be able to:

- Analyze the visual and verbal context of *Maus* and consider the relation of the two elements within the text
- Examine historical intertextuality through the use of borrowed Holocaust images in *Maus*
- Identify the use of different technical devices in graphic novels

NCTE/IRA standards addressed: 1, 2, 3, 4, 6, 11, 12

Materials/Preactivity Preparation

- Drawing materials (i.e., paper and markers or colored pencils)
- Comic books, graphic novels, and newspaper funny pages
- *Maus*, volumes I and II
- Nazi propaganda images

If the teacher would like additional guidance regarding the form of comics and graphic novels before teaching *Maus*, I would suggest visiting the Chicago Humanities Festival lesson plan (www.chfestival. org/resources/content/ComicBookLessonPlan.pdf) or reading Scott McCloud's *Understanding Comics*.

Time Frame

This lesson takes approximately five to six one-hour class periods and ideally takes place over the course of a week or so. This schedule could be expanded or condensed, depending on how much of *Maus* the teacher wants to have students analyze. The first class period should be spent discussing visual culture and reading visuals. The second class period should access prior knowledge of the Holocaust. The third class period should establish some vocabulary and reading strategies regarding graphic novels. The teacher could then assign students to read *Maus* and begin a discussion of its visual elements as the students familiarize themselves with both the narrative and the presentation of the narrative. Students should be encouraged daily to reread key portions or all of the text so that they can relate new structural elements to previous ones and look for changes.

If time does not permit the teacher to implement the entire series of lessons, he or she could have students analyze only one volume of *Maus*, key passages or chapters, or selected images. Additionally, this lesson could be drawn out and students could be encouraged to find more examples of visual elements in the volumes.

Description of Activity

Day 1

Before students read *Maus,* have them access their prior knowledge. Focus on the concept of visual knowledge. Have students consider their experiences with visuals on a daily basis. Before this class, have students record in a personal log all the visuals they see in one hour, one day, etc. This activity will help them become aware of how important visuals are in our society. Using the following questions, encourage students to consider how we read some of these visuals:

- How many visuals did you record in your log?
- What types of visuals did you see?
- Which visuals had an effect on you and why?
- Which visuals are easy to decode? Which are difficult? What makes a visual message easy or difficult to decode?
- What was the meaning of the message? How did you know?

Class discussion should then focus on reading the funny pages, comics, and graphic novels. Have students share their experiences reading these visual and verbal texts. Ask them to think about how this kind of reading is different from reading a novel or a short story. Have students make two lists of strategies they use to read a novel versus a graphic text. (Some elements in the lists will overlap, so using a Venn diagram may be preferable to lists. Ask students to also consider why there is overlap.) Here is what a sample list might look like:

Visual text (i.e., funny pages, comics, graphic novels)	Verbal texts (i.e., poems, short stories, novels)
■ look at pictures ■ consider the position of characters in the frame ■ font of text ■ position of words in frame ■ visual depiction of characters/ setting	■ position of words on the page (for poetry) ■ foreshadowing/making predictions ■ visualize characters based on descriptions ■ visualize setting based on descriptions ■ consider word choice

The teacher may wish to provide some funny pages for students to look at as they consider different strategies. *Garfield* comics are always a good choice for demonstrating that something usually happens between the frames of the comics. For example, the *Garfield* comic from December 10, 2006, shows Garfield pushing buttons on a phone for five frames before John asks Garfield what he is doing. Garfield then explains that he is text messaging his Christmas list. The next frame shows a very frazzled Santa. What happens in between the last two frames of this comic? The middle action is not shown, yet everyone understands what happens between these frames. *Peanuts* cartoons are also great examples of something happening between the frames. Both strips are available in collected volumes for easy selection of examples and are available in archives on the official websites.

Here are a few questions you could provide students as they examine these typical daily strips:

■ Since space is limited in these strips, how much story do you get from one strip? (Students may look at an entire funny page and realize that some comics are self-contained stories, while others are serialized stories that are broken into smaller chunks.)

■ What happens in this comic? Is there a clear beginning, middle, and end? Does the action fit into a plot line? (Students may even draw a small plot line for a comic.)

■ How are the characters represented in the frame? What do the characters look like? Where are they positioned within the frame and within the setting?

As homework, have students begin reading the first volume of *Maus*. Ask them to read pages 1–70 (reading 70 pages of *Maus* is not overwhelming for less able students). Have students pay attention to the structural elements of the novel. Encourage students to use strategies from both of the lists they made in class so that they will slow down and read not only the words but the images as well. Have students pick some of the more important frames in these pages and write about them in their reading journals. Have students consider page 23 and talk about how real—how human—the story is as it is presented in the words and the images.

Day 2

Have students consider what they already know about the Holocaust. Ask your students the following questions and have them share their experiences:

- Has anyone studied the Holocaust in another class?
- Has anyone seen any movies that deal with the Holocaust (e.g., *The Diary of Anne Frank, Schindler's List, Life Is Beautiful,* etc.)?
- Has anyone read any books about the Holocaust (e.g., *The Diary of Anne Frank,* Elie Wiesel's *Night,* etc.)?
- What do you know about the Holocaust based on reading, viewing, or talking to people about it?
- What don't you feel you know enough about this historical event?

Ask students to draw or write about what they already know about the Holocaust. If student knowledge of the Holocaust is limited, it might be good to show portions of the following films: *Survivors of the Holocaust, The Diary of Anne Frank, Life Is Beautiful,* or *Schindler's List.* Or you could read portions of the following books: *The Diary of Anne Frank; Images from the Holocaust: A Literature Anthology; Voices from the Holocaust; The Lost Childhood: A Memoir.* Depending on how long class discussion lasts, this could be an in-class assignment or it could be a homework assignment.

Have students read the rest of volume I of *Maus* for homework (page 71 to the end). Have students consider how the Holocaust is portrayed in these chapters and make notes in their reading journals about it. Also, have them focus on the difference between "The Prisoner on the Hell Planet" and the rest of the story—how does this different comic affect reading a narrative of the Holocaust events and the ways the

Holocaust affects lives even into the present? Ask students to include in their journals any new facts they have learned about the Holocaust in reading this section.

Day 3

Using Figure 11.1 (see the companion disk) for basic vocabulary for graphic novels, introduce these structural elements of graphic novels:

> *Gutters*: Begin with reading silences, gaps, and gutters and making inferences. In literature, we often ask students to think not only about what is said but also about what isn't said, to think about the silences and gaps in novels. When we read graphic novels, we should pay attention to what is not presented in the frames. Often in graphic novels, action will occur in what is called the gutters, the spaces between the frames. Readers of graphic novels need to make inferences about what happens between the frames, so have students consider what happens in the gutters of *Maus*. Consider the scenario in *Maus* where a guard throws a prisoner's hat in one frame, and then in the next frame the prisoner lies dead (Vol. II, page 35). What action occurs in the gutter between these two frames? Why might this have been left out of the frames? As students continue to read in *Maus*, ask them to keep track in their reading journals of places where important action occurs between frames.

> *Bleeds*: In the terminology of publishing, an image "bleeds" if it extends to—and implicitly beyond—the edge of the page. Have students make notes in their reading journals of places where Spiegelman uses a bleed. Discuss how this affects the narrative. Consider the point when Vladek relates his war experience as Art lies by his feet (Vol. I, page 45). In this image, the past has a frame but the present bleeds into the past as Art's feet interrupt the space of the past. Encourage students as they read volume I to think about the subtitle, *My Father Bleeds History*, and how this subtitle is presented throughout the narrative of both volumes. Have students continue to make notes about this subtitle in their reading journals.

> *Frames*: Most panels are contained in frames. What effect does a frame create, and what effect does a bleed create? Look at the overlapping frames in volume I, page 83. How does superimposing the present frame on the frame of the past (of people hanging)

affect the reading of this scene? Additionally, consider the way in which Vladek and Art walk though the frame of the past (Vol. I, page 105). How does this affect the reading of Vladek's narrative within Art's book? Have students make notes of different uses of framing in both volumes of *Maus* in their reading journals.

After introducing these concepts, provide some class time for students to work in groups to find additional examples for each of the concepts. Let students present some of these examples to the rest of the class as a wrap-up activity and talk about the significance of these methods in the graphic novel.

The handout of supplementary vocabulary (Figure 11.2 on the companion disk) provides additional terms relating to graphic novels that the teacher may wish to cover in class, depending on time and student skill level. As homework, have students read pages 1–74 in volume II of *Maus*. In their reading journals, students should focus on finding and recording examples of structural elements covered in class. Make sure you tell students to write in their journal the page number, a brief description of what frame(s) they are talking about, and a record of why they thought these frames were important.

Day 4

Lead a discussion focusing on stereotypes and ask students about how Nazi propaganda stereotyped their "enemies" as animals in order to dehumanize them. Look at a few images of Nazi propaganda. Calvin College's *German Propaganda Archive* (www.calvin.edu/academic/cas/gpa/ww2era.htm) provides many images in an online database that could be used to facilitate this discussion. Nazi propaganda typically depicted Jewish people as rats and Polish people as pigs. Discuss how Spiegelman uses stereotypes and Nazi propaganda in his graphic novel.

Look at the epigraph in the second volume of *Maus*. What does reading this quotation about Mickey Mouse at the beginning of the second volume add to an understanding of Spiegelman's depictions of Jews as mice? For a detailed analysis of the use of Nazi propaganda in *Maus* and some images, the teacher can refer to Thomas Doherty's article "Art Spiegelman's *Maus*: Graphic Art and the Holocaust." The decision to depict people as different animals is discussed in *Maus* when Art is trying to decide how to draw his wife, who is French but has converted to Judaism (Vol. II, page 11). Also, focus on the moments in the text when mice wear disguises to try to escape the Nazis. Anja cannot hide the fact that she is Jewish and her tail sticks out of her coat (Vol. I, page 136).

Students should identify other instances of this technique and write in their journals about how these moments affect the story.

Additionally, you might consider the impact of Holocaust photos on the images in *Maus*. For more background information on the mirroring of Holocaust photos and sample images in *Maus*, the teacher can refer to Marianne Hirsch's article "Surviving Images: Holocaust Photographs and the Work of Postmemory." This article provides some images that the teacher can bring in to show students.

For homework, have students finish reading the second volume of *Maus*. Have them consider in their reading journals the following questions: How has Nazi propaganda influenced the creation of *Maus*? What instances of the effects of propaganda are seen in the last pages of the novels?

Day 5

Use the following guiding questions to lead your wrap-up activity and assessment of students. Have students pick one of the questions from the following list and work in pairs to draw an answer and write an explication of their drawing. After conferring, one student might do the drawing while the other writes the explanation. Or you can use these questions to form a more traditional test or writing activity:

Guiding Questions

- How is the Holocaust a part of the characters' lives after the Holocaust?

- In what ways does Art's life echo his father's experience during the Holocaust?

- How does learning his father's story affect Art throughout the graphic novel?

- Does Art change in the volumes of *Maus*? How? Why?

- How is reading *Maus* different from reading a verbal narrative of the Holocaust, such as *The Diary of Anne Frank* or a novel about the Holocaust? How does reading *Maus* change your experience of these other stories?

Assessment

Assessment of students' understanding of the connection between visual and verbal narratives and the choices made by graphic artists can be determined through class discussion, written responses to the guiding questions, or a more formal essay response that examines the ways in which visual elements are presented in the graphic novel. Students could also point out other techniques used in the graphic novel and how these effects add to the presentation of the narrative.

Additionally, students could be encouraged to create their own mini–graphic novel depicting their search to find out more about someone's life (this someone could be a family member or someone the student is close to).

Connections and Adaptations

This approach to analyzing graphic novels can be applied to a number of graphic novels and visual texts. Pairing a canonical work with a graphic novel can lend credibility to the use of this form in the English classroom. Portions of this lesson and *Maus* could be used in any class that deals with Holocaust narratives or images. When I taught *Maus,* we read Elie Wiesel's *Night* concurrently and discussed the similarities between the two, as well as the changes in impact and depiction of the narrative in a novel versus a graphic novel. You might try using *Capote in Kansas* and pair it with *In Cold Blood* or the section from *The Sandman* that retells *A Midsummer Night's Dream.*

Additionally, *Persepolis: The Story of a Childhood* (volume 1) by Marjane Satrapi would be an excellent graphic novel to teach in a high school or middle school classroom. This novel is an autobiographical story of growing up in Iran during the Islamic Revolution. Satrapi's *Persepolis* is often compared to Spiegelman's *Maus* for both its style and its content. This lesson could easily be reformatted to fit this graphic novel.

Works Cited

Chicago Humanities Festival. "Comic Books Programs." Study Guide. Chicago: Chicago Humanities Festival, 2001. 6 Feb. 2007 <http://www.chfestival.org/resources/content/ComicBookLessonPlan.pdf>.

Doherty, Thomas. "Art Spiegelman's *Maus*: Graphic Art and the Holocaust." *American Literature: A Journal of Literary History, Criticism, and Bibliography* 68.1 (1996): 69–84.

Garfield.com. Updated daily. 14 Dec. 2006 <http://www.garfield.com/>.

German Propaganda Archive. Calvin College. 22 Mar. 2006 <http://www.calvin.edu/academic/cas/gpa/ww2era.htm>.

Hirsch, Marianne. "Surviving Images: Holocaust Photographs and the Work of Postmemory." *The Yale Journal of Criticism* 14.1 (2001): 5–37.

McCloud, Scott. *Understanding Comics: The Invisible Art*. New York: HarperPerennial, 1999.

Snoopy.com. Updated daily. 14 Dec. 2006 <http://www.unitedmedia.com/comics/peanuts>.

Spiegelman, Art. *Maus: A Survivor's Tale: My Father Bleeds History*. New York: Pantheon, 1986.

Spiegelman, Art. *Maus II: A Survivor's Tale: And Here My Troubles Began*. New York: Pantheon, 1992.

Supplemental Reading and Viewing

Holocaust

Brown, Jean E., Elaine C. Stephens, and Janet E. Rubin, eds. *Images from the Holocaust: A Literature Anthology*. Lincolnwood, IL: NTC/Contemporary, 1996.

The Diary of Anne Frank. Dir. George Stevens. Twentieth Century Fox, 1959.

Frank, Anne. *Anne Frank: The Diary of a Young Girl*. New York: Bantam, 1993.

Gaiman, Neil. "A Midsummer Night's Dream." *The Sandman: Dream Country*. Illus. Charles Vess and Malcolm Jones III. New York: DC Comics, 1995.

Life is Beautiful. Dir. Roberto Benigni. Miramax, 1999.

Nir, Yehuda. *The Lost Childhood: A Memoir*. New York: Berkley, 1996.

Rothchild, Sylvia, ed. *Voices from the Holocaust*. New York: New American Library, 1981.

Schindler's List. Dir. Steven Spielberg. Universal, 1993.

Survivors of the Holocaust. Dir. Allan Holzman. Turner Home Entertainment, 1996.

Wiesel, Elie. *Night*. 1960. New York: Bantam, 1982.

Comics and Graphic Novels

Carter, James Bucky, ed. *Building Literacy Connections with Graphic Novels: Page by Page, Panel by Panel*. Urbana, IL: National Council of Teachers of English, 2007.

Eisner, Will. *Comics and Sequential Art*. Tamarac, FL: Poorhouse, 1985.

McCloud, Scott. *Reinventing Comics*. New York: HarperPerennial, 2000.

Parks, Ande, and Chris Samnee. *Capote in Kansas: A Drawn Novel*. Portland, OR: Oni, 2005.

Satrapi, Marjane. *Persepolis: The Story of a Childhood*. New York: Pantheon, 2003.

12 Creating Video Poetry

David Bengtson
Long Prairie-Grey Eagle High School (retired)
Long Prairie, Minnesota
and
Minnesota Institute for Talented Youth
St. Paul, Minnesota

Context

This project has been implemented in two different contexts, a traditional classroom setting and a gifted program.

Long Prairie-Grey Eagle High School, a rural school with 500 students in grades 9–12, is located in central Minnesota. The school day consists of seven 50-minute periods. The following activity has been used with juniors and seniors of all ability levels in language arts semester electives titled "Film/Video and Poetry" and "Video Production" and with seniors in a full-year "College Prep English" elective.

The Minnesota Institute for Talented Youth is a summer academic enrichment program. In a two-week class titled "Seeing Things with Video," students in grades 7–12 have an opportunity to work on a variety of video projects, including video poems.

Rationale

A video poem (also called a cinepoem) combines video and poetry in a powerful and magical art form. According to Herman Berlandt, the grandfather of the poetry-film movement, and George Aguilar, the San Francisco-based multimedia artist who coined the term *Cin(E)-Poetry* (for cinematic electronic poetry):

> Cin(E)-Poetry seeks a symbiotic relationship of image, word and sound + music. It uses cinematic rhythms in editing, as well as the tempo of music and the content of spoken word, to maintain mood and continuity. Any visual medium or genre can be used such as stills, animation, documentary clips, abstract computer-generated graphics, and narrative structure, all, potentially, harnessed to words and music to achieve a unique marriage of mood and style. (National Poetry Association)

The purpose of this activity is to introduce students to this new art form and the media literacy skills associated with it. The lesson plan focuses on creating a collaborative video poem as a class, and also on a project that can be done individually and in small groups.

Don't be afraid of the technology. There will always be someone—a student, a teacher, a custodian, the kid next door—who knows more than you do and to whom you can turn. This is a good thing. One of my most liberating moments occurred when I finally realized that I couldn't—nor did I need to—know everything.

I am indebted to Herman Berlandt, George Aguilar, and the National Poetry Association, and to Mike Hazard and Bob Holman for their pioneering work with video and poetry and for their generosity and encouragement to my students and me as we have explored the possibilities of this art form.

Objectives

Students will be able to:

- Analyze a poem with the goal of translating and illuminating the written text into a new text of moving and still images and sound
- Understand how the use of different kinds of shots and sounds controls meaning and apply that understanding to the production of the video poem
- Determine which images and sounds, literally and figuratively, are needed
- Understand how the rhythms of a poem can be emphasized by movement on the screen and the pace of the editing
- Select and arrange a series of shots and sounds into a finished video
- Recognize some of the similarities between art forms

NCTE/IRA standards addressed: 1, 2, 3, 4, 6, 12

Materials/Preactivity Preparation

- Digital video camera
- Tripod (if possible)
- External microphone (if possible, for recording the readings of the poem)
- Computer with editing software (iMovie is included with all Apple computers)

- FireWire cable to connect camera and computer
- Examples of video poems to introduce students to the wide range of possibilities

To find examples, conduct an Internet search for video poems and cinepoems. You might check local and university libraries for a video titled "The United States of Poetry." This five-part PBS/Washington Square Films television series, first broadcast in 1996, features more than 60 video poems. Also available are an anthology by the same title (with stills from the films) and a CD of many of the poems read by the poets. "The United States of Poetry" continues to be broadcast on public television stations. Check www.itvs.org/shows/ataglance.htm?showID =307 for stations and times. A piece called "At the Crossroads" is included on the companion disk in both print and video forms to offer an example of how words are translated into images and sounds. See Figures 12.1 and 12.2.

Time Frame

The creation of a collaborative video poem as a class activity can be completed in five sessions. In the first session, students select and begin discussing the poem and the possibilities for translating it into a series of images and sounds. The next three sessions are used for continuing the discussion, recording readings of the poem, recording the shots and additional sounds needed, and editing the video poem. During the fifth session, the class watches, discusses, and critiques the production.

This project can be accomplished entirely in the classroom by connecting a computer to a monitor or wide screen projector so the students can see the production in progress and come to a consensus about the selection and arrangement of shots and the use of sound. Of course, recording video and sound and some editing can also be done outside of class by teams of students.

Five sessions in a one-week period can be intense. If possible, you might take a break between any of the five sessions or increase the number of sessions to allow more time for filming, recording sound, editing, and discussion.

For individuals and small groups, the time frame depends on whether students have time in class to work on their projects. In a semester Video Production class in which students worked exclusively on video poems, we spent the first part of the semester learning about film and video, watching and discussing examples of video poems, and preparing to work on individual and small-group productions. During the rest of the semester, I expected the students to complete at least two projects.

Description of Activity

Class Project

First, select four or five *short* poems to hand out and read together. You might consider poems by local or regional poets. You might also use this project to help students bring to life poems that they consider difficult to understand. The poems should lend themselves to various visual interpretations. The students will become artistic and technical consultants, decision makers, cast (if needed), and crew.

Session 1

Once a poem has been chosen, read and reread the poem with two questions in mind: What do you see? What do you hear? You might hand out a worksheet with these questions so that as the poem is being read (or as an assignment), students can jot down their ideas to be shared later with the group.

Read the poem together and then have students read it individually, accumulating many voices through many readings. You might also record the poem at this time. Let the movie of the poem begin to run in each student's head.

In his poem "Second Childhood," Minnesota poet John Calvin Rezmerski writes, "Puberty binds our minds to our eyeballs." At the beginning of this project, we must try to free the mind, let the imagination loose, think figuratively. Enter the poem. Open the doors and windows of the poem. Look in the dark hallways and corners of the poem. We will not all find the same things, and this is good. Our responsibility is to interpret the poem and, at the same time, be true to the poem and what we perceive the poet's intentions to be.

The poem becomes the basic script for the production. Start to compile a list of images and sounds that are tied literally and figuratively to the text and that might find their way into the video poem. Often, the wilder the ideas, the more interesting the results. Think about locations and props. Encourage original artwork and music.

Session 2

Continue to brainstorm ideas. Once a list has been generated, talk about which ideas might be possible given the existing time and space restraints. The list will eventually be narrowed down to those shots and sounds/sound effects that are needed for the movie. Then put together a shot list. Assign students to bring in props, original artwork, etc.

Record a number of readings of the poem—readings by the group and by individual students—play them back, and decide which one to use. The class can listen to the audio by connecting the camera to a television monitor in the classroom. This recording should be done using a digital video camera so that once you make a decision you can import the audio to iMovie (or whichever editing software you are using). The length of time the reading takes will control, to some extent, the length of the production.

Begin, also, to record video. Do as much filming as possible in the classroom. In fact, the entire production could be filmed there. For each shot or series of shots, you might assign responsibilities, such as cameraperson, director, etc. Filming in the classroom provides opportunities to talk about some of the basics of photography and video: a steady camera, effective lighting, a variety of shots, what to include and what not to include in a shot.

If necessary (and it probably will be necessary), you might also schedule some filming for after school or during a prep period. Before filming on location, be sure to make appropriate arrangements, ask for permission, and explain the project to anyone who might need to know. As shots are filmed, they can be imported to iMovie, where they will be stored as clips.

Session 3

Continue brainstorming ideas and filming. As a class, watch and discuss the clips that have been filmed so far.

At this point, you might also discuss how simile and metaphor can influence the selection and arrangement of shots. In figurative language, objects and images that don't seem literally connected are juxtaposed. The same thing can be done in film and video—two or more seemingly unrelated shots can be juxtaposed to create new and surprising layers of meaning. This is called montage editing and can be illustrated with the simple formula $A + B = C$.

Begin to select and arrange the clips into a rough cut. The text and rhythm of the poem will help guide these decisions. Trim the clips. Most of the time, less is better. As with some of the filming, some of the editing might be done outside of class by a small group. This group should receive directions from the class.

Session 4

Watch and critique what has been done so far. Make final decisions about editing and any additional sound or sound effects. You might use just the voice-over or decide to add text to the screen. Make sure you have a title for the production (most likely, the title of the poem) and a complete list of credits, including the name of the poet, names of students in the class (or at least the title of the class) and anyone else who helped with the production, the name of your school, and the year. Between now and session 5, complete the video poem.

Session 5

View and critique the video poem. What do you like about the production? What works well? What doesn't work well? What would you change? This critique might be done as a short essay or as a class discussion. You might even do a final edit based on the critiques. Then show the video poem to other classes, to parents, to other audiences. If possible, show it on a wide screen in an auditorium with a good sound system. If possible, send a DVD copy of the video poem to the poet.

Individual and Small-Group Projects

For a number of years, I began all five of my classes by reading "Today's Poem," a poem that I selected, perhaps because I really liked the poem, because the poet would be visiting our school, because the poet was from Minnesota or a nearby state, or because the poem spoke to a current issue or something we were discussing in class. My intention was to read the poem, not to study or analyze it, and introduce to students as many poems and poets as possible. I punched three holes in the handouts so students could collect them in Today's Poem notebooks.

By the end of a semester or school year, students had a large collection from which they could choose a poem for their own video poem project. Also, I am always looking for poems that I think might make interesting videos, and I have compiled these in a separate collection that is available to students.

For a first project, to maintain some objective distance, you might suggest that students not use an original poem. For my students—living in a small, rural, Midwestern community—many of Ted Kooser's poems resonated with their experience and were used for video poems. In a letter sent to me after he had watched a collection of these projects, he wrote, "Of course, I have no objection to your using my work in this way, or in any way you choose. . . . And thanks for introducing my poems to your students. I got interested in writing by what my high school teachers showed me, and it's nice to give some small part back."

It seems best to limit small groups to no more than three students. To follow the progress of individual students and small groups, here's a list of steps for a video poem:

- Choose a poem.
- Brainstorm ideas.
- Write a treatment or a proposal.
- Write a script and/or storyboard.
- Shoot video.
- Record audio.
- Log shots.
- Design the title and credits.
- Develop an editing plan.
- Edit.
- Reedit, if necessary.
- Show the final project for critiquing by the class and teacher.
- Write a final report, including an evaluation of the project and, if working with a group, your contribution to the project. Hand in a paper trail for the entire production process.

As with any project of this nature, students should be given the opportunity to screen their work at various stages in the production process to receive constructive feedback from both their teacher and their peers. The term of the project could then culminate with a gala screening of both the class and group or individual video poems.

When screening and assessing works-in-progress and completed video poems, students should keep in mind the basic ingredients of an effective production. A steady camera, in-focus shots, a variety of shots and angles, minimal panning and zooming, good lighting, crisp editing, and clean sound are all important. Of course, every rule can also be broken in a successful production. That's why a rubric should allow for creative flexibility.

A question that can be used to guide the assessment is "Does the production, in its entirety, honor the poem?" Look at the title, video poem, and credits with this question in mind. Then, if necessary, get down to the difficult and rewarding work of revising.

Assessment

In addition to the steps mentioned above, assessment for individual and small-group projects should be based on the entire production process as well as on the final product. You might require that students keep production journals. You can create a rubric that emphasizes both the technical and the creative aspects of the video poem. The steps for a video poem listed in the previous section can be used as a checklist and as a basis for the rubric.

Connections and Adaptations

This activity can be adapted for use in other language arts classes at the elementary, middle school, and high school levels.

Works Cited

Bengtson, David. *Broken Lines: Prose Poems*. St. Paul, MN: Juniper, 2003.

National Poetry Association. "What is Cin(E)-Poetry?" 7 Feb. 2007 <http://www.nationalpoetry.org/npa/cinepoetry.html>.

Rezmerski, John Calvin. "Second Childhood." *Held for Questioning: Poems*. Columbia: U of Missouri P, 1969.

The United States of Poetry. Prod. Joshua Blumand and Bob Holman. Dir. Mark Pellington. Videorecording. Washington Square Films and Independent Television Service, 1996 <http://www.itvs.org/shows/ataglance.htm?showID=307>.

Suggested Resources

Print

Sponder, Barry, and Catherine Kurkjian. "Using Digital Video to Teach Reading and Language Arts." *The New England Reading Association Journal* 37.2. (2001): 19–24.

Websites

George Aguilar.com. <http://www.george.aguilar.com/>.

George Aguilar is a freelance multimedia director and producer of high-quality short films and cinepoems.

The Center for International Education. <http://www.thecie.org/>.

The Center for International Education (CIE) is a media arts micro-organization that makes poetic media. Mike Hazard, a.k.a. Media Mike, is artist-in-residence.

13 Turning Text into Movie Trailers: The *Romeo and Juliet* iMovie Experience

Scott Williams
Adlai E. Stevenson High School
Lincolnshire, Illinois

Context

Located in the northwest suburbs of Chicago, Adlai E. Stevenson High School educates about 4,500 students. The following activity has been used in Freshmen English College Prep with standard-level students. As in most standard-level classes, student ability and performance levels vary from excellent to poor. Overall, the effort of the students and the results they achieve on this project exceed those of traditional writing assignments on Shakespeare.

Rationale

At times, maximizing student engagement can seem like chasing the Grail. Add Shakespeare and first-year students into the mix and that student engagement can feel like chasing the Grail blindfolded with snow skis on . . . backward. But tell students that they will be making a movie trailer, and as the blindfold and skis evanesce, the Grail blooms into view. Not only are we constantly seeking to maximize student engagement, but we are also looking to further their movement through the zone of proximal development. Having students create movie trailers that are focused on theme, and not plot, is a way to combine creativity and rigor. This lesson is intended to have students demonstrate understanding of thematic components of a literary work through synthesizing elements of vision, sound, and text while providing a written evaluation of their creative choices.

Objectives

Students will be able to:

- Analyze text for thematic connections
- Synthesize audio, visual, and text components that converge on to a unified theme
- Evaluate the merits of the material they choose to use

NCTE/IRA standards addressed: 3, 6, 8

Materials/Preactivity Preparation

In addition to the text to be used for this assignment, computers with an iMovie application are required in addition to digital video recorders. The iMovie program is part of the Macintosh system, and comparable programs can be found for PCs. To transfer the information from the video recorder to the computer, FireWire (or iLink or IEEE1394) is necessary. You will need to provide students a detailed prompt that explains the requirements of the project (see Figure 13.1 on the companion disk), a blank storyboard worksheet (see Figures 7.1 and 7.2), and a detailed outline (see Figure 13.2).

When my former colleague Jason Block and I developed the idea to have students create trailers, we started asking ourselves questions: How long will this take? How should we proceed? How do we make sure this is not an exercise in plot summary? We thought the best way for us to answer all of these questions was to create the same product we would be asking our students to produce, and so that's what we did. Instead of beaches and boats, we spent one spring break at El stations and on the gray streets of Chicago filming our live footage. We used the theme of fate for our model. (I assign each group of three or four students one of the other major themes we have been following throughout our study of *Romeo and Juliet*: lack of communication, impulsive action, and excessive family pride.) In addition to making the actual iMovie model, I also completed the written portion of the assignment; I wrote the entire analysis paper that explained all of the choices I made for my movie trailer (which you can view on the companion disk in Figure 13.3).

I recommend completing both of these tasks before you embark on this project. Going through both the creative and the analytical process will not only serve as a guide and model for the students, but it will also help you more effectively navigate some of the potential frustrations. Obviously, using the technology will educate you on the iMovie program. If you have little experience using iMovie, refer to the tutorial available at apple.com/support/imovie. When students panic because they are unfamiliar with the iMovie program, it is easy for me to calm them down because I have probably encountered a similar situation. Providing students with a teacher-generated model for the creative and analytical portions of this project serves as an invaluable guide. Consider the following student question: "Mr. Williams, I understand how to explain the connection between my song lyrics and my theme, but how do I explain how the actual music contributes to my theme?" If you have worked through the process, you will be better able to anticipate and answer that question.

I have my model iMovie cued up every day during this project. We watch a segment of my movie trailer, and we turn to my written analysis and discuss the connections. Simply put, a teacher model provides much structure and clarity for teacher and students alike.

Time Frame

Ten consecutive classroom days (50 minutes per period) should be scheduled for this project. Give students a calendar when you introduce the project. I typically do not give students additional homework during these two weeks, and they must make arrangements outside of class for any work they do not complete during class. If ten consecutive classroom days is not a reality in your classroom, I would suggest eliminating some components of the assignment. For example, live footage could be eliminated, or the number of shots could be reduced from four to three.

Description of Activity

The first step is to assign the groups their theme. Make it clear to students that their movie trailer is to be billed as a story of _____ (they fill in the blank with their assigned or selected theme). I used the theme of fate for my model. For my students, I assign each group one of the other major themes we have been following throughout *Romeo and Juliet*: lack of communication, impulsive action, or excessive family pride.

Briefly explain the project by going over the handout in Figure 13.1, included on the companion disk, which explains all of the project requirements. Before students start working, show them the model iMovie that I have created and included on the companion disk. Showing the model before going into any great depth on the written prompt

saves much unnecessary stress. It is best to give students a quick overview and then get them working.

Now it is time for groups to gather quotes that support their
theme. Students should be required to compile a list of ten quotes that
support their theme. They certainly will not use all of these, but it is
important that they have a sizable list. For a variety of reasons, I found
myself changing my mind about which quotes I would use for my trailer,
and I expect some of your students will have a similar experience. Ultimately, students choose three quotes from three different acts to incorporate into their trailer. I give them about 20 minutes to compile their
list of quotes and then it is on to creating the storyboard.

So what exactly is a storyboard? A storyboard is a series of drawings (picture the frames of a cartoon in the newspaper) that is used to
outline the components of a movie: the images, the text, the music, location for any live footage, any special effects (for further information
about storyboarding, refer to Chapter 7).

The next step is developing the outline (a template is included in
Figure 13.2). Although the storyboard serves as an outline for *what* is
going into the trailer, the outline requires students to explain *why* they
have chosen the images/text/music and *how* these elements connect to
their theme. The project requires four separate shots, along with a detailed written explanation for each shot. Since there are four members
to a group, give them about two days to complete the outline. Two days
would not be enough time for one student, considering the detailed
analysis expected. With four shots to analyze and four students to a
group, group members can split up the workload so that each student
is writing an analysis of one frame. Because they are so invested in this
project, the students give one another ample support in crafting their
written analyses, and overall, these are the best-written products I receive all year. While introducing the project, be explicit about the outline requirement: the group does *not* get a camera or a computer until
they have my stamp of approval on a completed outline.

Once the outline is approved, the technology part of the process
begins. I dedicate seven full class periods to the technology. I show students eight separate skills over the course of these seven days: (1) importing still images from the Internet, (2) importing video footage, (3)
importing music, (4) editing the video footage, (5) sequencing the video
and stills, (6) inserting text, (7) inserting transitions, and (8) editing
music. Instead of showing the students these skills all at once, I proceed in the aforementioned order one day at a time. I take about eight
minutes to show them a skill, and then they get to work while I assist

as needed. You can provide students with an iMovie flow chart (Figure 13.4 on the companion disk) to help them remember the steps you've modeled. Remember, if you do not have this kind of time in class to devote to this project, in addition to removing some of the technological components (e.g., switch from four shots to three shots, eliminate the live footage requirement), you can require that all of the portions of the project that are not technology related be completed outside of class.

During this project, the energy in the room is abundant and positive. The sounds I hear as I walk the room range from laughter at humorous ways to synthesize material to involved discussions about the best use of textual evidence; questions range from an ebullient, "Do you think this song will work with this quote?" to "Mr. Williams, this is awesome, can we do more projects like this?" When I speak to former students, the iMovie project inevitably enters the conversation. The comment that resonates the most with me is from a former student who said, "That project was so much fun, but it looked like you worked way harder than we did." Maybe I did and maybe I didn't—but that is not the point. The students are engaged in all of the skills and activities that we want them to be engaged in—knowledge building, comprehension, analysis, application, synthesis, and evaluation—and their perception is that they are not working that hard. What more can we ask for?

This lesson plan is time consuming; this lesson is intense; this lesson is exciting; and above all, this lesson is both valuable and entertaining for the students. As with most assignments, the products vary in quality. What does not vary is the process. Every student of mine who has been involved in this lesson has been completely engaged in the process. A vision and then a product—and what happens in between is oh, so much more.

Assessment

Group members get the same grade on 90 percent of this project. They are assessed on their storyboard (10 percent), their written outline (40 percent), and their completed iMovie (40 percent). The other 10 percent of their grade is determined by their group members; I assure them that this part of the grade will remain completely anonymous. The grade for the storyboard is more of a grade for time management. If students have all of their images, quotes, and music chosen and logically sequenced, I give them full credit. As long as they are diligent, I want to give them some confidence in the beginning stage. Also, having gone through all of these stages myself, I know that most groups will make revisions along the way. The written outline is scored as any other literary analysis paper would be scored: analysis, support, organization, and mechanics. Grading the iMovie itself is based on three main components: Does the movie trailer fit within the required time limit (1–3 minutes)? Are all of the required components present? How much effort did the group put forth? For an example of a student-made video, see Figure 13.5 on the companion disk.

Since it is easy for most groups to complete the preliminary steps, the 40 percent for the iMovie product really becomes a grade based on effort. This is something I struggled with in formulating this project. So how exactly do I assess these iMovies? I reminded myself that much like other forms of alternative assessment such as in-class performances and creative projects involving posters and signs, it is difficult to implement a rigid rubric. I live this project with the students for two intense weeks, so I am keenly aware of how much effort they give it, and at the end of the project, the assessment on this portion is quite intuitive. But I still wasn't satisfied with the intuitive way of assessing the iMovie, so I went a step further. Before I handed out final project grades to each of my students, I asked them to write down and hand in what grade they thought they had earned; there was *very* little variation between what they thought they had earned and the grade they received. Incidentally, this is a practice I continue to use with most large assignments.

Connections and Adaptations

This project can be implemented with any literary text. Any Shakespeare play would work, as well as novels, including *To Kill a Mockingbird*, *Fahrenheit 451*, and *A Tale of Two Cities*. Also, if the two- or three-week project seems daunting, starting out with a scaled-down version would be a valuable experience. The film footage could be eliminated, so students would be combining still images and music (both can be obtained from the Internet) with text and transitions. If an even more incremental process is desired, you could use only the storyboard portion of the assignment with texts earlier in the school year. Also, if no computers are available, this project could be adapted to a live performance. This project, in part or in its entirety, could be implemented with students ranging from grades 6–12; of course, the caveat here is to have expectations and allotted time appropriate to both students' developmental level and age.

III Media and Popular Culture

Watching *The Simpsons* Can Make Me Smarter?

Mary T. Christel
Adlai E. Stevenson High School
Lincolnshire, Illinois

When the McCormick Tribune Freedom Museum opened in Chicago in the spring of 2006, a news release reported that "one in five Americans could name" the five members of the Simpson family but they could not necessarily name all five freedoms guaranteed by the first amendment to the U.S. Constitution. Frankly, that claim seems to make sense considering that popular culture has become the center of most Americans' lives. We certainly spend more time watching television, listening to music, and reading about celebrities than we spend studying the essential documents of American democracy.

In the spring of 2005, Steven Johnson published *Everything Bad Is Good for You: How Today's Popular Culture Is Actually Making Us Smarter*. Now, Johnson wouldn't necessarily support our ignorance of basic civics, but he would support viewing a "rich" popular culture text like *The Simpsons*, which is rife with social, political, and cultural satire as well as loaded with sly intertextuality. A full appreciation of a popular culture text can require a sophisticated understanding of the genre it represents, the social context that produces it, and the economic realities that depend on its success and legacy in the cultural landscape (in the form of reprints, reruns, downloads, DVDs).

This section begins with two particularly rich lessons that focus on the study of film text apart from its connection to a literary text. In

"Reflections of Society in Film: From *Citizen Kane* to *Erin Brockovich*," Jane Freiburg Nickerson uses those two controversial and acclaimed films as vehicles to examine important themes and social issues that film can present powerfully through the use of narrative and cinematic techniques. This is an ideal lesson to help teachers select and integrate film texts as important elements of a unit of study that may bring together a range of canonical and nontraditional texts to examine themes like the American dream or social responsibility that are endemic to existing English language arts curricula. In "Teaching Nontraditional Film Narrative: *Reversal of Fortune*'s Reversal of Convention," Cynthia Lucia examines how *Reversal of Fortune* develops a provocative series of events and complex points of view in an unconventional manner to challenge its viewers to uncover the "truth" or essence of a sensational "true crime" trial. Whereas Freiburg Nickerson provides an introductory range of cinematic techniques to explore how themes are presented in a film text, Lucia expands on how to examine a film that doesn't follow the simple, linear conventions of a typical, mainstream Hollywood narrative. The two complementary lessons allow both teachers and students, who may be new to the study of film, to develop a growing sense of sophistication in analyzing a cinematic text.

Since music seems to be the most pervasive form of popular culture among students of all ages, this medium, properly integrated into a unit of study, should stimulate a high level of interest among students and hopefully yield fruitful results. The two lessons that focus on the music industry, Karen Ambrosh's "Unpacking the Popular Music Package: Analyzing the Production, Impact, and Potential of the Music Industry" and Kate Glass and Rich Clark's "So, You Want to Be a Pop Star? Examining Corporate Control in the Music Industry," explore aspects of music's cultural history, production, marketing, and media icons by giving students the opportunity to conduct research, apply analytical strategies, and create their own music industry products. Either of these two lessons would facilitate students working collaboratively in a context that demands the refinement of their research skills as well as their ability to synthesize that research into analytical and creative expressions.

Film and music routinely find their way into ELA classrooms, but some teachers might find it harder to rationalize the use of television, and the integration of reality television might be the hardest form of all to justify. But Kevin Howley focuses effectively on a controversial television genre as means to examine media literacy. In "Reading Reality Television: Cultivating Critical Media Literacy," Howley presents an

analytical approach targeting not only the narrative and aesthetic properties of a television program but also its commercial goals of generating revenue through sales of advertising time and appealing to specifically targeted audiences to garner high ratings. These concepts are at
the core of media literacy instruction. Howley's approach also can be
adapted easily to the gamut of television genres and coordinated with
other lessons, both in this section of the text as well as in others, to explore the impact of entertainment media on the cultural landscape, of
which traditional literature in the ELA curriculum is only a part.

The final two lessons examine the potentially violent content of
video games, film, and television aimed at middle school audiences.
Angela Paradise's "Video Game Vigilance: Applying Critical Thinking
to Video Games" encourages the careful analysis of the images found
in popular video games, with special attention to representation of gender, stereotypes, and violent behavior. This lesson isn't limited to the
games themselves but includes examining the magazines that target
gamers and promote messages embedded in the games in a different
medium. Students are also asked to consider the effectiveness of the
ratings established by the video game industry and to create proposals
for video games that address the issues of violence and representation
revealed by classroom activities. To complement Paradise's lesson, Erica
Scharrer, Leda Cooks, and Mari Castañeda Paredes, in "Viewing Violence Critically: Examining Conflict in Media and Day-to-Day Life,"
offer an approach that facilitates having students confront how consuming media with violent content shapes individual behavior in subtle and
dramatic ways through the use of role-playing and creating public service announcements that focus on the effects of violent media messages.
Again, these might not seem to be typical topics for the ELA classroom,
but they are issues that can stimulate research, analysis, collaboration,
synthesis, and production (of a variety of texts), all practical and necessary skills for the developing thinker and communicator.

Using popular culture texts in the ELA classroom has the potential to capture students' attention and interests as well as provide a context to examine what makes some of these media products rich and
deserving of close scrutiny. It also offers the opportunity to explore why
some highly popular media texts don't provide much challenge to the
consumer yet dominate the cultural landscape. It becomes the responsibility of the instructor to orchestrate the integration of a variety of
"high" and "low" culture texts to serve the mission of any sound ELA
curriculum: to provide rich experiences in reading, writing, viewing,
thinking, and speaking. We also must be reminded that Shakespeare got

his start in the popular culture realm and that his plays weren't widely regarded as "high art" in his time. So when might a film or screenplay be widely enshrined as "required" viewing or reading? When it happens, Steven Johnson, and maybe Bart Simpson, would support that move.

Works Cited

Johnson, Steven. *Everything Bad Is Good for You: How Today's Popular Culture Is Actually Making Us Smarter*. New York: Riverhead, 2005.

McCormick Tribune Freedom Museum. "Characters from 'The Simpsons' More Well Known to Americans Than Their First Amendment Freedoms." News release. 1 Mar. 2006. 7 Feb. 2007 <http://www.rrmtf.org/mtf/pressroom/2006/pr030106.htm>.

Recommended Resources

Alvermann, Donna E., Jennifer S. Moon, and Margaret C. Hagood. *Popular Culture in the Classroom: Teaching and Researching Critical Media Literacy*. Newark, DE: International Reading Association, 1999.

de Zengotita, Thomas. *Mediated: How the Media Shapes Your World and the Way You Live in It*. New York: Bloomsbury, 2005.

Gitlin, Todd. *Media Unlimited: How the Torrent of Images and Sounds Overwhelms Our Lives*. New York: Metropolitan/Henry Holt, 2001.

Hiebert, Ray Eldon. *Impact of Mass Media: Current Issues*. 4th ed. New York: Longman, 1999.

Lusted, David, ed. *The Media Studies Book: A Guide for Teachers*. New York: Routledge, 1991.

O'Sullivan, Tim, and Yvonne Jewkes, eds. *The Media Studies Reader*. London: Arnold, 1997.

Rushkoff, Douglas. *Media Virus! Hidden Agendas in Popular Culture*. New York: Ballantine, 1994.

14 Reflections of Society in Film: From *Citizen Kane* to *Erin Brockovich*

Jane Freiburg Nickerson
Gallaudet University
Washington, D.C.

Context

Gallaudet University is a liberal arts university for students who are deaf or hard-of-hearing. It is located in Washington, D.C. and has 1,600 students. The following lesson can easily be adapted for high school students since these films present themes that younger students can easily identify with.

Rationale

Both students and teachers appreciate the use of films because they make their classes more visually oriented. Literature becomes more interesting and more immediate for students if they can develop their own ideas about the themes being presented. As they view films, students may not fully realize that the movies they watch contain important themes that provide insight into their society and culture. This lesson focuses on two films, *Citizen Kane* and *Erin Brockovich*, that provide perspectives on society that our students can relate to, and the lesson challenges them to think critically about the content and structure of the films. *Citizen Kane* highlights themes such as loneliness, family issues, hope, wealth, and politics. In *Erin Brockovich*, which focuses on how one woman fought a huge company to right a wrong, Erin Brockovich is determined to show that each person can make a difference and help change the world for the better.

Films can bring ideas into focus for students as they analyze, discuss, and write about what they watch. Films provide a different way for students to learn, and at times students can easily determine the themes and moral values expressed in a film. This leads to an improvement in students' abilities to find similar themes and values in print literature, an important goal for high school students. Students can learn how to analyze and discuss films, explore film techniques, and write film critiques. They have an easier time relating what they see in modern films such as *Erin Brockovich* to their own society but have a more difficult time when they view films set in the past such as *Citizen Kane*. I offer suggestions on how to help students make connections between contemporary society and films such as *Citizen Kane*. If you decide to watch a different film, please note the "all purpose" questions presented in the "Connections and Adaptations" section, since you can apply them to most films.

Objectives

Students will be able to:

- Analyze scenes from various films and relate ideas presented in the films to contemporary society
- Compare and contrast scenes in films and analyze how directors portray social issues
- Demonstrate writing abilities by writing film critiques
- Demonstrate the ability to discuss film techniques that emphasize elements, especially thematic ideas, in the films

NCTE/IRA standards addressed: 1, 3, 5, 6, 9, 11, 12

Materials/Preactivity Preparation

Copies of the following videos/DVDs will need to be secured:

- *Citizen Kane*. Dir. Orson Welles. RKO, 1941.
- *Erin Brockovich*. Dir. Steven Soderbergh. Universal, 2000.

You may want to read professionally written film critiques because they often provide significant background information. You can find these online at the Internet Movie Database (www.imdb.com) or at Rottentomatoes.com. Numerous print resources provide a wealth of information as well. For example, in his review of *Citizen Kane*, published in *The Great Movies* (109–17), Roger Ebert explains why this film was important in 1941 and how it has influenced films ever since. Ebert provides readers with details they need to be aware of when they watch the film and explains in detail the film techniques that director Orson Welles used.

You may also want to read information on various websites that focus on specific films. For *Erin Brockovich*, check the following website, which provides background on the film: www.lawbuzz.com/famous_trials/erin_brockovich/erin_brockovich_ch1.htm.

Time Frame

This unit can be implemented in different ways depending on the time you can allot for it. Here are two scenarios that have worked well:

> Scenario 1: Approximately three to four standard class periods. You might choose to view only one film, watch it in class incrementally over several days, and discuss it in depth. You can then have students watch the second film on their own, using guiding questions to focus their viewing, and then come back to the classroom to discuss it.

> Scenario 2: Approximately six to seven class periods. Teachers and students can watch both films incrementally and discuss them.

Description of Activity

Citizen Kane

Citizen Kane is an important film because many of its techniques have been copied in many films since. A true appreciation of *Citizen Kane* requires some background information in film techniques, so before showing the movie, I define the following film terms: *low-key lighting, camera angle, deep-focus photography, flashback, montage,* and *newsreel footage.* After students learn these basic film terms and techniques, they can explain what happens in different scenes. Since these techniques are universal in film, as students learn to discuss and analyze film techniques they become better film critics.

Ideas for Previewing Citizen Kane

Before my students watch *Citizen Kane,* I summarize the plot, which explains one man's life story and how reporters want to characterize him in a newsreel after his death. This is the first film in history to start with the main character's death and then show his life through flashbacks. Previewing enables students to more easily understand the film as they watch for the various techniques. To set the stage for analyzing how the film reflects modern society, previewing possible themes such as "money cannot buy happiness or love" often helps students focus on deeper meanings in the film. Social issues are important throughout the film, so students can watch for ways to compare today's society with society in the 1940s.

Although the focus is thematic analysis of the film, ideas are expressed and emphasized in film through cinematic techniques. I provide a list of key film techniques used by Welles and his cinematographer, Gregg Toland. I include here examples from the film for teacher reference, but I would not recommend providing them to the students; let them discover these examples for themselves:

- Low-key lighting creates light and dark contrasts between images, which often leave the principal subjects in the dark. Example: Mr. Thompson, the reporter who searches for Rosebud, is always in the dark, both literally and figuratively.

- Camera angles can vary from eye level (most natural), to high-angle shots, to low-angle shots. Angles can be tilted or rolled for different effects. Example: Welles uses camera angles to show Kane's power when the camera looks up at him and looks down on the weak Susan.

- A montage sequence is created by editing a series of seemingly unrelated frames together through the use of dissolves or panning shots. These fast shots typically show the passage of time. Example: Welles creates a remarkable segment (the breakfast table scene) in which the ten-year story of Kane's first marriage is told in two minutes of film.

- Through deep-focus photography, objects are in sharp focus in the background as well as the foreground. Example: This technique was used before *Citizen Kane*, but Welles does a superb job of implementing deep focus, which emphasizes perspective. One scene that employs deep-focus photography well is when Kane is a young boy playing in the snow behind his house. While Mr. Thatcher, the banker who becomes Charles's guardian, is shown speaking to Mrs. Kane, viewers can see Charles clearly in the background through a window.

- Newsreel footage was exhibited in theatres before television was invented to cover news events both nationally and internationally. Example: The newsreel provides the catalyst for Mr. Thompson as he searches for information to write Kane's story. An interesting note is that Welles scratched the newsreel to make it look old.

- Flashbacks change the order of the story being told. We see characters in the past, which often explains events in the present. Example: Flashbacks are used to piece together information about Kane's life after he is dead. Mr. Thompson asks people who knew Kane to describe their experiences with him, which leads to several flashbacks in the film.

As students watch the film, they should focus on themes related to social issues and concepts related to attaining the American dream. They will quickly discover that the film includes ideas about marriage, power, money, politics, loneliness, and childhood. With close viewing, students should be able to understand how the visual techniques as well as the dialogue emphasize these thematic ideas.

Questions for Analysis and Discussion

- Welles was the first director to have the major character die at the beginning of the film and then have other characters describe his life through the use of flashbacks. What makes this an effective way to open the film and develop the narrative? How does this strategy change the viewers' focus and complicate their ability to understand Kane as a man?

- How does the newsreel, *News on the March,* develop character and set tone? How does the newsreel set the stage for examining or critiquing certain aspects of Kane's life and ambitions?

- What are some of the general themes portrayed in this film? How does dialogue, key images, or editing emphasize these ideas? Examples of themes: money doesn't buy happiness or love, depression, loneliness, obsession, power, and the inability to love others.

- Which scenes present the "money doesn't buy happiness" theme in Kane's life? Example: Compare the first scene, in which Kane has very few things as a young boy in Colorado, with later scenes, in which the adult Kane has many things in Xanadu. When the reporters are looking at Kane's possessions near the end of the film, viewers realize that Kane was a wealthy man who couldn't find the happiness he sought.

- How did Welles use different film techniques to present themes?
    - What does the flashback about Kane's childhood show? How is time effectively collapsed through editing?
    - How does the breakfast montage present the disintegration of Kane's marriage and the reasons behind it?
    - How do the camera angles and lighting reinforce Kane's power over Susan when they discuss Jed's review of her performance and the continuation of her opera career?
    - In the final sequence in the castle, how does the lighting of Mr. Thompson reflect the degree to which he and viewers are able to understand Kane and the meaning of his dying words, his life?

- How do the film's themes relate to post-Depression society? How are themes developed in this film still relevant today?

- Why is this film rated so highly by various organizations, including the American Film Institute (which ranked it number one in 1998)?

- What might have contributed to the lack of recognition the film garnered in 1941? (See Ebert's review in *The Great Movies* for details.)

- How have the techniques that Welles used in this film influenced films made after 1941? (See Ebert's review for details.)

Erin Brockovich

Erin Brockovich shows how a determined woman was able to stand up to a corporate giant and fight the injustice she uncovered. My students love the message in this film—that is, people who want to change something in their lives can work hard and succeed. Students also enjoy watching one woman bring down a company that contaminated water and subsequently be forced to pay millions of dollars to compensate the people who became ill.

Ideas for Previewing Erin Brockovich

Before watching *Erin Brockovich*, I briefly explain what the film is about. After summarizing the plot, I explain the film techniques that students should track. The list includes the following:

- *Mise-en-scène* is a French term for the whole composition of a shot, which includes the space actors inhabit, the movement within the shot, the lighting, and the set/décor.
- Décor includes the setting of the scene and the objects or actors in the scene. Décor often sets the mood of the film.
- Colors can reflect the moods of the characters or situations. Steven Soderbergh uses various colors for characters (blue), courtroom sessions (green), and the California desert (orange, brown).
- Makeup, costumes, and hairstyles create character traits in films. Erin is seen as someone who uses clothes, makeup, and hairstyles to show that she is strong and independent.

Questions for Analysis and Discussion

- How did Erin Brockovich fight the Pacific Gas and Electric Company? What evidence does Erin gather that enables her to start putting together pieces of the puzzle about how the company was contaminating water in the area? From whom does she gain additional information about the company's chromium use? How does Erin deal with the company lawyers? How does she gain confidence in her work as the story unfolds?
- Identify the scenes that suggest Erin's growing determination to win the case. Example: Starting with Chapter 37 on the DVD, Erin shows that she will not give up. She continues to discuss the case with Hinkley residents, and later Charles Embry gives her a "smoking gun" document that supports the idea that executives at the company's headquarters knew about the poisonous chromium much earlier than they admitted.
- Which scenes present the difficulties of being a working mother? Why is this an essential aspect in developing Erin's character? Examples:

Chapter 25 on the DVD is the scene in which Erin finds out that she was not home when her youngest daughter spoke her first word. Chapter 30 is when George asks her to quit her job because it is consuming most of her time and energy.

- How do Erin's clothes, makeup, and hairstyles express her self-concept? To what extent does her look change over the course of the film and how does that reflect the dynamic nature of her character?

- How does the décor in this film reflect the social status of individuals and organizations? Example: The film includes scenes in various lawyers' offices. When viewers first see Mr. Masry's office, they notice that it is run-of-the-mill, whereas after the lawsuit, his new offices are well appointed and show his rise in status. Kurt Potter's offices are fancy, an indication of his status.

- How did Steven Soderbergh use color in this film? What is his purpose for using blues and oranges? What do they tend to emphasize?

- What is a "whistle-blower"? What other companies have produced whistle-blowers in the last few years? Would you become a whistle-blower if you found out that a company was hurting people or unethically or illegally taking their money?

- How does the film develop themes related to contemporary American society? Are some of the themes (e.g., marriage, power, relationships, roles of women) similar to those you saw in *Citizen Kane*? Which ones are different? What accounts for those differences? How typical is Erin's success as a "whistle-blower"?

Assessment

Students can be assessed in many ways. Class discussion enables them to explore in more depth what they saw and to bounce ideas off of their classmates. Students make connections when they discuss themes. They can make connections to their own lives as well as to society in general.

Students should write film critiques for each film. When writing critiques, students should follow guidelines that include the following:

- Describe the film briefly.

- Write your reactions about the film and rate it based on a five-star scale.

- Discuss the techniques that made the film more interesting, such as flashbacks, camera angles, lighting, makeup, costumes, and others.

- Describe any parts of the movie that were puzzling or repeated and how that affects the viewer's reception and understanding of the film.

- Explain important themes in the film and relate them to issues found in contemporary society.

Another assignment can focus on essays that compare the two films by examining the American dream and what that meant to people in the 1940s and to people in the 1990s. What are some similarities and differences between the themes presented in these films? How are the characters similar and different? What scenes in these films show that characters are pursuing the American dream? How did characters in these films achieve the American dream?

Connections and Adaptations

When you present films that reflect social values and issues, you can ask your students to think about these generic questions:

- What themes can you find in this film that are issues found in contemporary society, such as family life, economic situations, and others?
- What ideas presented in these films can you relate to? Why?
- What other films have you seen that represent issues related to society?
- What films have you seen that represent issues that might be seen in future society?
- What cinematic techniques in the film made it unique? How did the aspects of mise-en-scène play a role in the film to evoke a particular time period?

This approach to analyzing themes from films and relating them to issues found in our society can be easily connected to other films and texts. Other films can be used to show past or contemporary society depending on what your students are studying. Many high school students read a variety of texts that include social issues. If your students are reading any of the following novels, you may want to include the film version(s) as well so that students can compare and contrast them:

- *The Grapes of Wrath* by John Steinbeck
- *The Manchurian Candidate* by Richard Condon
- *Cool Hand Luke* by Donn Pearce
- *To Kill a Mockingbird* by Harper Lee
- *Ordinary People* by Judith Guest
- *Kramer versus Kramer* by Avery Corman

You may also want to have your students watch *On the Waterfront, Rebel without a Cause,* or *Guess Who's Coming to Dinner?*, as all of these films include themes that focus on issues common in our society. Information about these films can be found in the Internet Movie Database (www.imdb.com) and in the works cited and supplementary reading for this chapter.

Works Cited

Citizen Kane. Dir. Orson Welles. RKO, 1941.

Ebert, Roger. "Citizen Kane." *The Great Movies*. New York: Broadway, 2002: 109–117.

Erin Brockovich. Dir. Steven Soderbergh. Universal, 2000.

Supplemental Reading

Bordwell, David, and Kristin Thompson. *Film Art: An Introduction*. 7th ed. Boston: McGraw-Hill, 2004.

Brockovich, Erin, with Marc Eliot. *Take it from Me: Life's a Struggle but You Can Win*. New York: McGraw-Hill, 2002.

Estrin, Mark W., ed. *Orson Welles Interviews*. Jackson: UP of Mississippi, 2002.

Kael, Pauline. *The Citizen Kane Book: Raising Kane*. Boston: Little, Brown, 1971.

15 Teaching Nontraditional Film Narrative: *Reversal of Fortune*'s Reversal of Convention

Cynthia Lucia
Rider University

Context

For many years at Horace Greeley High School in suburban Chappaqua, New York, I taught a semester-long film study course offered for English credit to juniors and seniors of widely ranging abilities. I found that the study of film *as film*, along with frequent writing assignments to ensure active viewing, worked to level the playing field by challenging talented students while making material accessible to students with more limited abilities.

Rationale

For most of our students, exposure to film begins and ends at the multiplex or on rental shelves featuring relatively recent Hollywood fare. While certainly entertaining, such films seldom challenge students to assume the intellectually active viewing positions more common to international cinema, which tends to embrace delicious ambiguities of character and situation. And although films such as *Eternal Sunshine of the Spotless Mind*, *Memento*, *Magnolia*, and *Pulp Fiction* are structurally complex, that complexity tends to emerge from plot-based manipulations rather than from character intricacies and ethical or ideological dilemmas. *Reversal of Fortune* (1990) is a good place to begin broadening our students' exposure to and appreciation of nontraditional narrative approaches and can be used in a film or literature class after students have studied several conventional film or literary narratives.

Reversal of Fortune is a fiction film based on the nonfiction book by attorney Alan Dershowitz chronicling his attempt to win an appeal for the wealthy Claus von Bülow, who, in 1982, was convicted of attempting to murder his wife Sunny. *Reversal of Fortune* is really two narratives in one—a straightforward, conventional Hollywood narrative and an unconventional narrative reflecting the European roots of its director, Barbet Schroeder. The law-centered narrative, with Dershowitz as its protagonist, self-consciously follows Hollywood conventions, drawing attention to its parallels with the legal process. The relationship-centered narrative, with Claus and Sunny as its protagonists, departs from Hollywood (and legal) convention, revealing the inadequacies of both systems in their attempt to "contain" contradictions of the human heart and mind within resolutions, or verdicts, that neatly line up with truth. Through voice-over narration performed by a comatose Sunny, the interplay of sometimes conflicting versions of events, and the infusion of sly dark humor, the film defies the notion of a single or discernable "truth."

Objectives

Students will be able to:

- Define and identify basic film terms and concepts such as *voice-over narration, Steadicam movement, shot composition, lens filters*
- Define and identify elements of conventional Hollywood narrative
- Define and identify departures from conventional Hollywood narrative
- Analyze the thematic impact of the film's juxtaposing conventional and unconventional elements

NCTE/IRA standards addressed: 6, 11, 12

Materials/Preactivity Preparation

You will need to secure a copy of the film: *Reversal of Fortune* (Dir. Barbet Schroeder, Warner, 1990) in either VHS or DVD format.

Although the questions below and the synopsis on the companion disk (Figure 15.1) are designed to illuminate film terms and concepts through viewing the film itself, William H. Phillips provides a useful illustrated glossary of film terms and concepts in his book *Film: An Introduction*.

Supplemental readings I've given to students include a review and two interviews—one with director Barbet Schroeder and the other with attorney Alan Dershowitz—published by *Cineaste* (Jacobson; Sklar, "Justice," "Saint Alan").

I've sometimes also shown the A&E network's treatment of the case in their 1995 *American Justice* episode, "Von Bulow: A Wealth of Evidence." This should be viewed *after* students have seen *Reversal of Fortune*. Students will recognize the sensational nature of the *American Justice* version and, by comparison, will appreciate the value of ambiguity as it enriches the Schroeder film.

Time Frame

In 45-minute teaching periods, viewing of the film (112 minutes), interspersed with discussion and activities, will take four class periods. A fifth period, though not essential, will provide greater time for rescreening and analysis.

Description of Activity

The following daily breakdown is based on 45-minute class periods. Discussion time is built in to encourage active viewing. Feel free to pick and choose among the questions, which are written to help students define terms through viewing the film. You may want to ask students to create their own lists of film terms and definitions, based on the questions and their observations. This is a very effective way of actively engaging students in learning these concepts while simultaneously recognizing their application and effect. It's best to provide questions before viewing (see Figure 15.2 on the companion disk) so that students will actively attend to specific details, and it's helpful to rescreen scenes that will become the basis for longer writing assignments. Some questions can elicit written responses of a paragraph or two, whereas others, marked with an asterisk (*), are designed for essay responses of 400–1,000 words, depending on your framing of the assignment. DVD counter entries are included for convenience.

Day 1

Rather than establishing the ideas of conventional narrative and departures from convention before students watch the film, it is best to allow them to discover these concepts through the very process of watching the film (see day 4 activities connected with question 5). You may want to begin by providing brief background into the von Bülow case, citing some of the information presented above. Most of what students need, however, is presented within the film itself, so perhaps 5 to 10 minutes is all you'll need. If you view through the scene in which Alan and his son discuss the case over Chinese takeout (18:54) (about 23 minutes), you will have ample discussion time.

1. Describe details of setting during the title sequence. What is implied about the characters and events to follow?

2. What mood(s) does the blue lens filter evoke in Sunny's hospital room?

3. In what ways does the Steadicam movement become associated with Sunny? What does this movement imply about Sunny's "consciousness"?

4. When actress Glenn Close speaks as Sunny in voice-over narration, how does she speak? What feeling or mood does her style of narration establish? Does Sunny seem to feel her situation is tragic, oddly amusing, or a combination of both?

5. Summarize the factual information Sunny provides concerning her two comas and the legal activity surrounding these events.

6. How does the film use details of setting or nuances of acting style to characterize Alan?

7. How does the film use details of setting or nuances of acting style to characterize Claus?

8. Quote or paraphrase lines that strike you as darkly humorous. What purpose do they serve in shaping our response to character or in establishing mood?

9. Describe the order of actions and events as Alan and his son discuss the trial transcript. How does Maria's narration and the flashbacks that accompany it serve both to answer certain questions and to raise additional questions? Make a list of questions answered and new questions raised.

Day 2

Since students are now well grounded in the film, more time can be spent viewing with less discussion. This is a good time to have students write about the film—either short responses to a series of questions or longer responses to a few key questions. You may also want to divide the class in assigning questions. Begin with the scene in which Alan gathers his legal assistants (18:55) and end after Claus discusses Sunny's first coma at the Dershowitz house (59:19)—about 40 minutes of viewing. It's important not to interrupt the flow of this last scene; if you think you're running out of time, it is best to end when the characters exit the Chinese restaurant, leaving the next scene for the following day.

1. What reasons does Alan give for taking the von Bülow case?

2. Marriott is given a private moment in which the camera remains with him after Alan exits. Describe what Marriott does as the camera remains with him. (The seemingly insignificant gesture of adjusting his tie will take on a larger significance later in the film.)

3. In what ways does the film hint at darkly perverse aspects of Claus's character during his meeting with Alan? To what degree do these details strike you as creepy? To what degree do they strike you as oddly amusing? Explain.

4. How is Sunny made to appear when we see her from a high camera angle as her arms are being manipulated and her body is being washed?

5. How do Sunny's words, detailing her daily routine and her consumption of drugs, work in connection with the image we see? What impressions are we given of Sunny?

6. How does the blue lens filter contribute to the mood of this short scene?

7. We frequently see Claus from a low angle looking down at Sunny in bed, as in the flashback to her aspirin overdose. How is he made to appear? How do you interpret his watchful stillness?

*8. In the sequence in which Claus discusses Sunny's first coma, analyze the ways in which the structure or order of events enriches our knowledge of characters and, at the same time, raises further questions about Sunny, Claus, and their relationship. Describe the ordering of events within the several flashbacks. How does this structure present us with contradictory impressions? What questions are raised that remain unanswered or unanswerable? As you think about this sequence, also consider the impact of elements such as costuming, Sunny's movement and behavior, and contrasting uses of lighting.

Day 3

Viewing begins with a legal-strategy scene involving the needle allegedly used to inject Sunny (59:20) and ends during the hearing when the prosecutor nibbles at the "bait" Alan presents (137:11)—38 minutes of viewing.

1. Dialogue between Claus and Sunny as she frantically searches for drugs sometimes gives rise to chuckles. Are there amusing lines that also further define the relationship?

2. This flashback narrated by Claus raises further questions concerning Sunny's current comatose state. Discuss some of those questions and how details of the flashback help to raise them.

3. Consider the effect of placing Sunny's third narration so close to the scene narrated by Claus. How does Sunny's vision of herself, of Claus, and of their relationship coincide with or contradict what we see in Claus's version of Sunny and their marriage?

*4. Analyze the overall effect of Sunny's narration. Discuss where we are taken in time and place from beginning to end of the narration. Comment on the visual style of this narration, paying particular attention to the contrasting tones of color from sequence to sequence, the use of the blue filter in the two bedroom settings, and soft focus during the outdoor wedding party. Consider the significance of these details in relation to what Sunny is telling us. What do we learn? What new questions are posed? What is the overall tone and mood of this sequence? What are we left feeling as the narration ends?

*5. In the sequence in which Claus discusses Sunny's second coma, analyze the ways in which the structure or order of events enriches our knowledge of characters and, at the same time, raises further questions about Sunny, Claus, and their relationship. Consider the effect of shot compositions echoing those of the earlier flashback to Sunny's first coma, as well as incongruities or gaps between what Claus tells us in voice-over and what we actually see in the image. What questions are raised that remain unanswered or unanswerable? As you think about this sequence, also consider the impact of visual elements such as costuming, Sunny's movement and behavior versus Claus's movement and behavior, and contrasting uses of lighting.

6. How does repetition of the aspirin overdose sequence force you to revise impressions of both Sunny and Claus you may have formed the first time you saw this scene? Examine how the visual details and the placement of the scene at this particular point may contribute to your revised impressions.

*7. How does Sunny's fourth narration comment on various aspects of the legal process? How do the aspects of the legal process involving time, chains of cause and effect, and chronology line up with the film's approach to presenting its law-centered story in which Alan is the protagonist?

*8. Compare and contrast the film's approach to the law-centered story with its approach to the relationship-centered story. In what ways does the film depart from convention in its use and arrangement of flashbacks and in its use and placement of Sunny's voice-over narration? How do these departures complicate or enrich the narrative?

Day 4

Viewing begins as Sarah and Alan present their versions of what may have happened to Sunny (1.37:12) and continues to the end of the film (1.49.08)—about 15 minutes of viewing. Following viewing, there will be ample time to discuss and to rescreen selected scenes that will be useful for students writing longer essays.

*1. Describe the ways in which lighting, pacing, and the musical sound track establish mood during sequences in which Alan and Sarah present their versions of events leading to Sunny's second coma. How do actions repeated from earlier flashbacks narrated by Claus take on new meanings and shape our attitudes differently toward Sunny, toward Claus, and toward their relationship?

2. As the elevator door closes on Claus, consider the effect of image composition and lighting combined with Alan's words. What do those words suggest about the nature of Claus's legal victory?

*3. Sunny's voice-over ultimately asserts that we cannot know the truth, in a singular, legal sense. Discuss the possible multiple, sometimes contradictory truths that do emerge in this film. For instance, consider the extent to which Claus may be legally innocent but morally guilty of twice attempting to murder his wife. Use key moments in the film, considering structure and visual style to support your conclusions.

4. Dark humor asserts itself once again as the film closes. Define black humor based on its presence in this film. Provide examples throughout the film and in the closing moments. How do these moments add to your viewing experience as a whole?

*5. After seeing the entire film, return to questions 7 and 8 under day 3 viewing, considering further how this movie, with its parallel narratives, comments on storytelling methods in movies. How does the film use unconventional elements to comment on a more conventional approach to storytelling? What approach does filmmaker Barbet Schroeder—a director who has worked both in Europe and in Hollywood—appear to champion or prefer? Use direct reference to specific moments in the film to support your discussion.

For students to construct a definition of conventional narrative and to consider ways in which departure from convention operates and adds texture to the film, an extended discussion of question 5 (day 4) is essential. Conventional Hollywood and literary narrative (like narratives constructed by lawyers presenting their cases in the courtroom) generally consists of a chronologically ordered series of events, linked by chains of cause and effect. These events are initiated by a character driven by some sort of desire (termed *motive* in the courtroom). Obstacles confronted in attempting to reach the desired goal result in conflict that ultimately finds unambiguous resolution or closure, often aligning closely with a revelation of "truth"—not unlike a legal verdict declaring innocence or guilt. When films depart from convention, motivation may not always be entirely clear; conflict may be expressed in ambiguous or unconventional ways; chronological ordering often breaks down, with flashbacks nested within flashbacks, with repetition of single narrative events, or with the construction of parallel or "competing" narratives; cause-and-effect chains are not necessarily clear or even present; and the narrative may be open-ended, lacking a firm sense of closure.

Before discussing question 5 (day 4), you may want to ask students to divide a sheet of paper in half, with the left side labeled "Dershowitz/legal narrative" and the right labeled "Claus and Sunny/ relationship narrative." Together as a class, in small groups, or as individuals, students should list the events in the Dershowitz narrative as they occur within the film. Stop to discuss how these events line up with conventional narrative, helping students to arrive at a definition that accounts for the elements above. Then ask students to fill in the right half of the page. This will be difficult—and the difficulty alone will reveal the degree of departure from convention. Students will find, for instance, that before we even hear about the first coma, we are told about the aspirin overdose, which happened several weeks prior to the second coma. They will also, of course, recognize that there is no real narrative "flow" here, and that Sunny's voice-over sequences interrupt the flow of even the Dershowitz narrative. As students work on this part of the activity, you may want to forward scan through the film at a moderate pace, perhaps with several students saying what they see as others record notes. Students will now be ready to approach question 5 with a clear sense of how departures from convention complexify character and our own position as viewers.

Assessment

Student assessment can range from short written responses of a paragraph each to longer essays ranging from 400–1,000 words each, based on selected viewing questions. To facilitate in-depth responses and attention to detail, you can rescreen key sequences during the postviewing discussion, making certain that students take careful notes. You might also place the film on reserve in the library or AV area so that students can drop by to rescreen scenes they will analyze. I've often made my own room available for this purpose at specific times during, before, and after the school day.

Instead of or in addition to written responses, group discussions or individual/group student presentations might center on a single question, with the rescreening of a particular scene as part of the activity.

Connections and Adaptations

Concepts learned in the study of *Reversal of Fortune* might be applied to other unconventional American film narratives such as *Citizen Kane, The Conversation, Vertigo, Annie Hall, Mystery Train, Memento, Eternal Sunshine of the Spotless Mind,* and *American Splendor,* or to international films such as *Breathless, Run Lola Run, Suzhou River,* and *In the Mood for Love.*

In the context of a literature course, the study of narrative structure in *Reversal of Fortune* might help to illuminate and make more accessible the study of complex works of fiction that take a nonlinear approach to storytelling—from William Faulkner, to James Joyce, to Toni Morrison.

One might also use the film in the context of a literary work(s) focused on law—something like *Twelve Angry Men,* for instance—in which the notion of legal truth appears far more definitive than it does in the case of *Reversal of Fortune.*

Works Cited

Phillips, William H. *Film: An Introduction*. 3rd ed. Boston: Bedford/St. Martin's, 2005.

Reversal of Fortune. Dir. Barbet Schroeder. Warner, 1990.

Supplemental Reading and Viewing

Jacobson, Harlan. "Revisionist of Fortune: An Interview with Alan Dershowitz." *Cineaste* 18.2 (1991): 8–11, 16.

Sklar, Robert. "Justice, Irony, and *Reversal of Fortune*: An Interview with Barbet Schroeder." *Cineaste* 18:2 (1991): 6–7.

Sklar, Robert. "Saint Alan and the Prince of Perversion." *Cineaste* 18.2 (1991): 11.

"Von Bulow: A Wealth of Evidence." *American Justice*. [Television program]. Narr. Bill Kurtis. Videocassette. A & E Home Video, 1995.

16 Unpacking the Popular Music Package: Analyzing the Production, Impact, and Potential of the Music Industry

Karen Ambrosh
Audubon Technology and Communication Center
Milwaukee, Wisconsin

Context

Audubon is a Milwaukee public charter middle school with approximately 875 students in grades 6, 7, and 8. This unit on the music industry is part of a semester-long media design class for eighth graders in which students study a variety of media such as film, television, newspapers, and magazines. It is easily adaptable to different age groups, ability levels, and classroom settings.

Rationale

Media literacy requires a balance of both media analysis and production, so students need to engage in both. Through activities such as studying the development of musical genres, the business elements of the music business, and marketing strategies that affect the reception of popular music today, along with the technological changes, copyright issues, and stereotyping found in lyrics and videos, students develop important media analysis skills. They also are immersed in media production by brainstorming what the future of music might hold, producing their own bands or artists, writing lyrics, and creating packaging for a debut CD, all focused on a social issue they care deeply about.

This unit capitalizes on middle school students' passion for music, raising their level of interest and engagement. The topic of the music industry allows students of English to read and analyze a variety of print and nonprint texts, develop research and presentation skills, and practice creative writing in multimedia formats. Popular culture and music offer many connections to the study of poetry, literature, and the social construction of language. These lessons offer students an expanded view of communication that integrates mass media, the arts, technology, and so much more.

Objectives

Students will be able to:

- Read and respond to a variety of print and nonprint texts
- Analyze the power of music to reflect the human experience
- Evaluate the effects that business has on the production and distribution of "creativity" in society
- Communicate about socially conscious issues through multimedia formats

NCTE/IRA standards addressed: 1, 6, 7, 8, 12

Materials/Preactivity Preparation

To keep this unit fresh and current, I have learned to collect resources in a folder whenever I find them in the media (newspaper clippings, websites, and curricular materials). It isn't crucial that I know every hot new artist the students like, because they are always willing to educate me. It *is* important to have a collection of samples of the following to share with students:

- Songs and lyrics from a variety of artists that focus on social issues
- CDs (or even "antique" album covers) to talk about the artwork and design elements that make up the package
- News articles related to musical issues (e.g., controversial lyrics, CD reviews, technology issues and copyright laws, stereotypical images in videos)
- Video documentaries: VH1's "Up from the Underground" in *The History of Rock 'n' Roll* and/or PBS *Frontline*'s "The Merchants of Cool"

Time Frame

With class periods of 60 minutes, I have implemented this unit in different formats from as short as two weeks to as long as six weeks. It is not necessary to address each activity in depth. Some of the topics can be covered in one to three class periods or simply introduced as journaling assignments, leaving the bulk of the time for the production phase. When I have used low-tech methods for the creation of the CD case, I have been able to keep that portion of the project to one week. Anytime I introduce technology into the project, I have learned to allow extra days for the students' learning curve and the inevitable technical glitches.

Description of Activity

Past: Tracing the Roots of Musical Genres

Duration: 3 to 5 days

While there are many rich resources surrounding the historical development of hip-hop music, I believe it is important to allow students to research the history of their own music because they will be so much more invested in the project. I begin with an exploration of genre and ask the students to work in groups to classify the different types of music. This usually causes a lot of energetic discussion as students argue over terminology and categories. Together as a class, we create a chart of generic headings with subcategories and crossovers, providing examples of artists next to each type of music. This one-day activity is a good introduction to the research project of tracing the roots of contemporary music.

The research project can be as simple or as elaborate as in-class time allows. I ask students to choose a contemporary musical artist/ group they admire. Through research, they need to find out who that artist/group modeled themselves after or find an artist/group from a previous generation that had some similarities with their artist/group. The two artists or musical groups they choose must be at least ten years apart. This condition pushes students to explore another time period of music and helps them make connections to common trends in music. Examples from some of my students' projects include a comparison of Alicia Keys to Ray Charles, Green Day to the Kinks, Usher to Luther Vandross, and Tupac to Elvis. Often students have a hard time finding an older example to compare their artist/group to because they think that their type of music is so unique it has never been done before. This project forces them to see the trend of marketing to a youth culture that rebels against the societal norms of older generations—a trend that has been well established since the 1950s.

The following questions constitute the framework for the research project, as well as the criteria for evaluation:

- Describe the history of how each artist/group broke into the music business, including some facts about the social, economic, or political climate of their time period.
- Describe the unique qualities of the artist/group that made them famous (e.g., style and content of music, performance, personalities, promotion, other talents).
- Compare the two artists/groups, highlighting their similarities and differences based on your research.

The research results can be presented orally with a slideshow presentation or in an essay format. The students enjoy sharing what they found and can include music samples, pictures, and video clips.

Present: How the Music Industry Impacts Today's Society

Duration: 2 to 3 days

As a transition from the historical project to the study of current issues in music, I use VH1's documentary *The History of Rock 'n' Roll*, Episode 10: "Up from the Underground." It is available for purchase and also airs on VH1 through Cable in the Classroom; lesson plans can be found online. Episode 10 (one hour) covers the eighties and the nineties, outlining the growth of hip-hop music, the impact of MTV and music videos on the music industry, social issues appearing in music of this period, and the introduction of alternative music in the early nineties. I have also used PBS's *Frontline* episode "The Merchants of Cool" (one hour), which explores the marketing of "cool" through music, television, and products.

These documentaries present many issues, and I have taken different directions with them, depending on the ability level of the students and the time available. Adapted from Peyton Paxson's *Media Literacy: Thinking Critically about Music and Media*, here is a sampling of possible topics to use for journaling, small- and large-group discussions, or further research:

Marketing

- Discuss how music videos and other technology have changed the emphasis from musical talent to good looks and packaging of an image.
- Discuss the impact of product placement in songs.
- Discuss the positive and negative effects of "cool hunting" marketing strategies.

Messages and Images

- Discuss the impact of a drug-related death of a musician on fans.
- Discuss the effectiveness of parental advisory labels on CDs.
- Discuss the images of women and other minority groups in music videos.

Technological Changes and Copyright Issues

- Discuss how technology changes will impact the medium of radio.
- Explore how licensing organizations like ASCAP and BMI protect the rights of musicians and producers.
- Discuss the positive and negative aspects of Internet file sharing and downloading of music.

Time could be made available for small groups to report back on the outcomes of their discussions.

Future: Designing the Future of Music

Duration: 3 to 5 days, depending on access to technology

Building on the knowledge they have gained from the previous activities, the students are now ready to design their own ideal music package focusing on a social issue they care about. We analyze songs that have had a social impact in the past (a quick Google search of "protest songs" will bring up many possibilities such as John Lennon, U2, Public Enemy, Black Eyed Peas, etc.). I ask the students to bring in examples from their own genres, always previewing the lyrics before sharing them with the whole class. YouTHink.org offers an inspiring CD of socially conscious songs from a variety of artists, along with a curriculum guide.

I have found that it is important to set the tone for this project. If students are given the freedom to copy their favorite artists, they usually do not stretch their creativity and choose simplistic or inappropriate topics for the classroom. I always have a discussion with them about the different level of "censorship" needed in the classroom compared to the free market. An example I share is when a student asked me if she could put pictures of aborted fetuses on her "Pro-Life" CD case. I had a discussion with her about the controversy over this practice, and after careful consideration and discussion with other teachers, I said no to her and asked her to find other ways to get her message across. This example provides a wonderful teachable moment to talk about my decision as the "producer" of this student's CD and how I wanted to protect the reputation of my company.

The students choose a social issue that is meaningful to them. It can be about personal choices, or about local, national, or international concerns. After doing a little research into the topic and looking at sample CDs to analyze the design elements, students can work individually or in small groups of two or three to create the following components of a music package:

- Describe the genre of music and personality of the artists involved in the project to establish the artist's or group's name and identity.

- Design a CD case front booklet and back page complete with a minimum of twelve song titles, production company logo, images, dedication page, letter to fans, history of artist or group, and any other creative text they would like to share with their fans about their topic.

- Write at least one complete song with a minimum of three verses and a chorus about their social issue.

- Design merchandise that can be sold or given away as incentives at concerts and radio promotions (T-shirts, other clothing items, bumper stickers, key chains, etc.).

- Plan a concert tour with a map of cities visited, cost considerations, and promotional events that will take place along with the concerts.

These activities have been implemented with low-tech options such as hand drawing and cutting and pasting pictures. When computers were available, I have also had the students design everything on computer using simple word-processing drawing tools, as well as professional design software such as Macromedia FreeHand and Fireworks. If students are interested, I have allowed them to perform their songs a cappella or with generic beats and tape-recording equipment. I have transferred the songs to the computer and created class CDs that are inexpensive to reproduce for everyone in the class. I have also had students produce music videos to accompany their CD. The creative possibilities are many depending on the availability of equipment and time in the classroom.

Assessment

This unit provides a range of assessments that can be tailored to the ability level of the students and the depth of each assignment. The following are standards I have adapted to the particular assignments.

Past: Tracing the Roots of Musical Genres

Research, writing, and formal oral presentation

- Conducts research and inquiry on self-selected artists/groups
- Organizes and evaluates information, taking notes and summarizing
- Produces an organized oral presentation with visual elements that explains each artist/group's history, makes comparisons between them, and cites sources

Present: How the Music Industry Impacts Today's Society

Reading, journaling, and responding in small- and large-group discussion

- Listens attentively, demonstrates respect for the opinions of others
- Evaluates the stated ideas and opinions of others
- Invites ideas and opinions of others into the discussion
- Summarizes the main points of a discussion, orally and in writing, specifying areas of agreement and disagreement and paraphrasing contributions

Future: Designing the Future of Music

Analyzing media messages and creating multimedia products

- Analyzes how songs may affect or be affected by economic, social, and political factors
- Creates a CD case, song lyrics, and promotional merchandise appropriate to a teen audience, for the purpose of promoting an opinion on a social issue
- Demonstrates a working knowledge of music production and distribution
- Plans a promotional campaign to sell a musical artist or group

Connections and Adaptations

English language arts as a discipline needs to help students transfer the skills of deconstruction of traditional literature to nontraditional texts in popular culture. Today's English classroom is still dominated by the printed word, not reflecting what is going on in the real world. To correct this imbalance, English teachers need to embrace visual and aural literacy as well. This is a crucial step in creating future media-wise and literate citizens and consumers who are capable of accessing, interpreting, evaluating, and responding to all types of media messages.

I have implemented versions of these lessons with sixth graders as well as tenth graders. I adjusted the content and the level of questions to fit each group's needs. I have also incorporated more math, geography, history, art, music, and scientific research methods when doing this as a collaborative cross-curricular unit with other teachers. My co-workers, students, and I have always found this topic to be flexible, expandable, and enjoyable to pursue. I hope you do too.

Work Cited

Paxson, Peyton. *Media Literacy: Thinking Critically about Music and Media.* Portland, ME: Walch, 2003.

Supplemental Resources

Print

Stansberry, Suzanne, and Sheree Sevilla. *Rock and Rap Middle School.* Fort Collins, CO: Cottonwood, 2004.

Video

"Up from the Underground." *The History of Rock 'n' Roll.* Episode 10. DVD. Warner Home Video, 2004.

"The Merchants of Cool." *Frontline.* Dir. Barak Goodman. Writ. Rachel Dretzin. WBGH, Boston, 27 Feb. 2001.

Online

"Flipping the Script: Critical Thinking in a Hip-Hop World." 2004. *Just Think Foundation.* 9 Feb. 2007 <http://www.justthink.org/flippingthescript/>.

"History of Rock 'n' Roll Lesson Plans." 26 Mar. 2004. *VH1 Cable in the Classroom Initiative.* 9 Feb. 2007 <http://www.vh1.com/partners/vh1_music_studio/lessons-history.jhtml>.

"Take Back the Music Campaign." *Essence.* 5 May 2005 <http://www.essence.com/essence/takebackthemusic/>.

"YouTHink: Music for Positive Change CD and Teacher's Guide." 2005. *Zimmer Children's Museum and the Center for American Studies and Culture.* 9 Feb. 2007 <http://www.youthink.org/yT_cd.html>.

17 So, You Want to Be a Pop Star? Examining Corporate Control in the Music Industry

Kate Glass and Rich Clark
Buffalo Grove High School
Buffalo Grove, Illinois

Context

Buffalo Grove High School is a suburban school of 2,400 students in the northwest suburbs of Chicago. This lesson is part of our semester-long humanities/fine arts curriculum, an elective course taken by seniors in which students are required to study visual, aural, and written texts from the Renaissance to the present day. Though we present this mini-unit in our Humanities/Fine Arts 1 course, it could easily be used as a springboard for researched-based writing, for persona projects, or in any course where contemporary text is scrutinized.

Rationale

The emergence of shared music networks (e.g., Kazaa), Internet-based music services (Rhapsody), satellite-based radio (Xfm), and portable music devices (iPod) creates the impression that consumers have unlimited freedom when it comes to choosing music. For instance, students have the ability to share songs via email, can amass thousands of songs on a portable player, and can even link sound bites to incoming calls on their cell phones. But do these "unlimited" bounds actually encourage students to develop a diversified musical palate? This unit prompts the following question: Does the emerging global marketplace foster a broadening of the musical discourse, or is it dictating our collective musical taste?

While this unit may strike some teachers as a detour from the traditional English curriculum, our curriculum is one that requires students to develop a critical understanding and a conventional vocabulary of the artistic paradigms that have shaped Western culture since the Middle Ages. That said, we often establish connections to the present in order to engage students in older texts. However, this mini-unit has been successfully adapted for a Popular Literature class (a senior remedial-level course), an American Studies class (an interdisciplinary junior/senior course), and even a ninth-grade college prep English class.

Objectives

Students will be able to:

- Recognize why current musical innovations have flourished
- Develop an understanding of the relationship between the musician, the market, and the listener
- Recognize and analyze marketing strategies used by artists and record companies to promote their product
- Actively listen to mainstream media to determine target audience, musical trends, and marketing strategies
- Create and market an original pop star

NCTE/IRA standards addressed: 1, 3, 4, 5, 6, 7, 8, 11, 12

Materials/Preactivity Preparation

The following articles are used:

- "Exploring the Right to Share, Mix and Burn" (Carr)
- "Who's That Girl?" (Hirschberg)

The following video clips are used:

- Episode from MTV's *Cribs* ("Season 11")
- *Gap* TV commercial featuring the band Aerosmith
- Cadillac commercial featuring the music of Led Zeppelin

The following AV equipment is used:

- Five radios
- Television monitor and VCR

Time Frame

This is a mini-unit, which should take approximately five to seven days of in-class time to cover. Although we provide daily lesson plans here, teachers should feel free to compress some of these activities, or broaden them, depending on the shape that class discussions take. We are assuming that these activities will take place in a classroom where students have experience journaling; if this is not the case, some additional writing instruction may be necessary before beginning this unit.

Description of Activity

Lesson 1: The Hypothesis

Begin by having students address the following question in their journals: What kinds of music do you have access to as compared to your parents when they were your age? At this point, students may address technological innovations (CD players, iPods, Napster, etc.), or they may talk more specifically about a perceived change in the quality of music. In the past, students have noted that contemporary music often contains coarse language and "sounds better" (in other words, reflects technological advances, i.e., "production"). Once they have finished journaling, put them in groups and have them compile a list of all these innovations that now make up the world of music.

Next, challenge the students to think about the following question, either in their journals or in class discussion: What are the advantages to all these musical innovations? Are there any disadvantages? Responses may vary here; while it is easy to list the obvious advantages of these technological innovations (increased access to music, for example), coming up with disadvantages can be more challenging. If the students are stumped, the following discussion questions may be helpful:

- How diverse is the music we listen to?
- Could the iPod's limited storage capacity contribute to this? How?
- How are you exposed to new music as compared to the way your parents were?
- Does downloading music allow for *more* exposure to musical genres or *less*?

Finally, before students leave the classroom, pose this question: Do we really have unlimited access to music?

Lesson 2: Napster and Friends

As a prereading activity, ask students what they know about Napster, the downloadable music program (especially if this didn't come up in the previous day's discussion). Then pass out the article "Exploring the Right to Share, Mix and Burn" (Carr). Read this aloud and then have students either independently or in pairs take on the persona of a pop musician. For homework, have the students craft a letter to the editor in response to the article.

Lesson 3: Selling Out

Begin by sharing the letters to the editor from the previous day's activity. Then ask the class to name any musicians or bands that market products (Britney Spears selling Pepsi, for example, or U2's iPod campaign). Next, show clips from commercials in which we see this phenomenon at play. iPod commercial trailers featuring famous musicians, for example, are available online at Apple's website, http://www.apple.com/itunes/ads, as well as on YouTube at http://www.youtube.com/results?search_query=ipod+commercials&search=Search. Also, see the ads on YouTube for Gap and Cadillac. Show each ad once, then a second time, asking the students to analyze the marketing strategies. For instance, in some cases, musicians offer direct testimonials about the product; in other cases, the musicians do not appear in the ad but their music is played in the background. Commercials like these can be recorded from TV channels such as VH1, MTV, or the major networks during prime-time hours.

For homework, have students bring in ads they have either printed out from the Internet or found in magazines in which we see musicians marketing products.

Lesson 4: Bling-Bling

First, create an impromptu gallery by having the students tape the ads they have collected around the room. Ask the class to study these images and note any trends they see.

Then ask the students to adopt the persona of an archaeologist in the future who is studying American culture at the turn of the millennium. The cultural artifact they will be examining today is an episode of MTV's *Cribs*, a modern-day *Lifestyles of the Rich and Famous* in which the homes of rappers and famous athletes are visited. The show itself is a half-hour long and is available on the Internet in DVD format. As an alternative, magazines such as *Cosmopolitan*, *Seventeen*, or *Glamour* run features where celebrities—often musicians—put their homes on display. Students can spend the remaining time in class commenting on the value systems embedded in such an artifact. Ultimately, the students should be asking themselves what impact such rampant materialism has on the music world.

Lesson 5: Learning by Ear

Start by dividing the class into groups of five or six and give each group a radio. Use the hallway or other resource areas if necessary as this activity may be a bit noisy for a small classroom. Each group is assigned a different radio station to which they should listen actively for 20 minutes. By "active listening," we mean they should be listening with the following purposes:

- To determine who the station's target audience is
- To ascertain which musical styles are dominating the airwaves
- To list what products are being marketed

A convenient method for note taking requires students to make two columns in their notebooks where song titles are listed and commercial descriptions are noted.

Next, have the groups examine the co-dependent nature of these three realms. For instance, why is a weight-loss ad found on a station that plays top-ten hits? Each group should appoint a representative to share their responses with the class.

Lesson 6: Who's That Girl?

Students should list on the board as many young female pop stars as they can. In pairs, they should determine what similarities can be found among these artists. Possible areas of scrutiny include physical body type, dress, ethnicity, demeanor, singing style, and lyrical content.

Hand out the article "Who's That Girl" (Hirschberg), which examines how a corporation manufactures and markets a female pop star. Since this article is lengthy, begin reading it aloud in class and have the students finish it for homework.

Lesson 7: The Making of an Artist

Discuss the Hirschberg article, ultimately asking students to articulate how corporate influence affects music.

The remainder of the period can be used to introduce the culminating project, "So, You Wanna Be a Pop Star?" This project consists of four written components—a biography, lyrics, a song description, and a letter to a recording company CEO—and allows students to choose their method of presenting their pop star to the class. Depending on the nature of the class and the type of students undertaking the project, presentations could range from performing an original song to writing a radio advertisement plugging an upcoming album. Figure 17.1 on the companion disk thoroughly outlines the components of the project.

Assessment

Figure 17.2, also on the disk, is a rubric we use to assess the culminating project. The project could be readily adapted for other courses. For example, a fine arts teacher might choose to put more emphasis on the presentation component, while a writing teacher might focus more on the written components. Typically, we have assigned 20 percent of the overall grade to each of the following elements: biography, written description, lyrics, letter, presentation.

Connections and Adaptations

"Reading" a text—that is, studying and critically evaluating it—is a skill that can be applied in a variety of contexts: to a poem in creative writing, an essay in biology, or a magazine advertisement in sociology. In addition, any class that uses authentic writing assignments or examines current events could be enriched by a lesson plan such as this.

To shorten this activity, start with lesson 5, where students listen to the radio to record trends. Use this as a discussion springboard for the culminating assignment, in which students create and market their own pop star. Students could also complete this project in class in groups of three or four.

Works Cited

Aerosmith Gap Commercial Full. *YouTube*. 16 July 2007 <http://youtube.com/watch?v=QMdIxGujcug>.

Cadillac Breakthrough Commercial. *YouTube*. 16 July 2007 <http://www.youtube.com/watch?v=SDe23UM6kjY>.

Carr, David. "Exploring the Right to Share, Mix and Burn." *New York Times* 9 Apr. 2005.

Hirschberg, Lynn. "Who's That Girl?" *New York Times* 4 August 2002.

"iPod Features." *The Apple Store Online*. Apple Computer, Inc., 2006. <http://www.apple.com/itunes/ads>.

"Season 11, Episode 10: LeAnn Rimes and Chad Reed." *Cribs*. Prod. Lauren Lazin. MTV, 2005.

Supplemental Reading

Berger, John. *Ways of Seeing*. London: Penguin, 1995.

18 Reading Reality Television: Cultivating Critical Media Literacy

Kevin Howley
DePauw University

Context

DePauw University is a private liberal arts institution in central Indiana, enrolling approximately 2,300 students. Variations in the following lesson are used in three courses: Media, Culture, and Society; Television Production and Televisual Literacy; and Media Criticism. Although these are college-level courses, this activity is easily adapted to meet the aptitudes, television viewing preferences, and media habits of middle and high school students.

Rationale

"It's only a movie." "It's just entertainment." "You're reading too much into it." For media educators, these are common refrains. Despite spending, or more accurately, perhaps, *because* they spend so much time with media technologies and texts—from cell phones and iPods to MTV and online chat rooms—many students underestimate the value, let alone the relevance, of critically informed media analysis. Student resistance to our efforts to "take seriously" media form and content represents a formidable obstacle to teaching goals and learning objectives.

The purpose of this lesson plan is to help educators overcome student resistance to critically informed media analysis through a discussion of so-called reality television programs such as *American Idol, The Bachelor, The Apprentice*, and *The Amazing Race*. Specifically, I want to demonstrate the value and utility of three distinct but related approaches to media studies: textual analysis, industry analysis, and audience analysis. Separately, each of these perspectives yields important insights into media form and content; together they represent a dynamic mechanism for overcoming student resistance to media studies and cultivating critical media literacy.

Reality television (RTV) is the object of study for several reasons. First, RTV is one of the most ubiquitous, successful, and profitable genres in the television industry today. Second, RTV holds considerable appeal for our students. Finally, RTV is as much a throwback to "traditional" broadcasting as it is indicative of emerging industrial practices in the neo-network era. As such, RTV lends itself to precisely the sort of multiperspectival analysis (Kellner) that is the hallmark of effective, engaging, and politically responsible media critique.

Objectives

Students will be able to:

- Perform a "close reading" of a scene from RTV and discuss the visual, auditory, and discursive techniques and conventions that help create meaning within that scene
- Identify media industry structures and practices at work in RTV
- Compare audience responses and reactions to RTV and discuss the ways in which audiences actively construct meaning from the text
- Analyze the relationship between media texts, industries, and audiences

NCTE/IRA standards addressed: 1, 3, 6, 11

Materials/Preactivity Preparation

Instructors are encouraged to record several RTV programs, including one installment of *Survivor*, as well as other examples based on student interests and preferences. In preparing for this activity, teachers are encouraged to acquaint themselves with television production techniques. For a comprehensive and accessible guide to television production, see Jeremy Butler's *Television: Critical Methods and Applications*.

Teachers should also familiarize themselves with trade publications such as *Broadcasting & Cable*, *Advertising Age*, and *Variety*. These materials are extremely helpful for keeping abreast of current trends in the television industry. Several reliable online resources likewise document current trends in media ownership. For instance, *Columbia Journalism Review*'s website (www.cjr.org/resources/) demonstrates the scale and scope of media consolidation at the local and national level. Media Channel (www.mediachannel.org/ownership) provides information related to global ownership patterns and television flows.

Further, teachers are encouraged to periodically consult news reports that discuss current industry trends and practices. *The New York Times*, *USA Today*, and *TV Guide* are but a few of the periodicals that routinely cover the television industry. These popular press accounts provide an excellent point of departure to discuss the prevalence of RTV and to gauge critical and popular reaction to these programs. Finally, teachers may find that my earlier discussion of RTV (Howley, "Reading *Survivor*: A Primer on Media Studies") provides useful background on the activities described below.

Time Frame

Instructors are advised to plan at least four to five class sessions to accommodate this learning unit. In the context of a media literacy course, this lesson can be expanded further.

Teachers should screen a brief (3–4 minutes) segment from an RTV program prior to engaging in the textual analysis proper. During this session, teachers discuss the basics of television analysis (picture composition, camera framing, editing, sound design, etc.). It is advisable to create a glossary of terms and techniques associated with television production that students can refer to often. This activity typically takes one class period. Having familiarized themselves with these terms, students are more comfortable moving on to the subsequent class session on textual analysis.

The central objective of this lesson can be accomplished by the end of the fourth class session. However, it is advisable—and often quite rewarding—to spend an additional class period bringing together the various strands of media studies. Doing so highlights the importance of considering a variety of perspectives on contemporary media culture.

Description of Activity

Textual Analysis

Screen an extended RTV segment (10–12 minutes) and ask students to recount the segment's narrative elements. That is, have students discuss the main "characters," their motivations, their actions and reactions. Have students identify the program segment's protagonists and antagonists. Likewise, have students consider how the characters' motivations and actions help propel the narrative forward.

Following this, have students divide sheets of paper into three columns, labeling them Image, Sound, and Editing. Then screen the segment at least twice more. Working in teams, students describe the visual and auditory elements of the segment.

For instance, encourage students, when describing images, to consider how camera framing (long shot, medium shot, close-up, extreme close-up) varies in relation to the segment's narrative development. Have students consider how framing functions to create a sense of intimacy, distance, or tension within a scene.

Similarly, students should attend to the use of sound (dialogue, voice-over narration, sound effects, and music) throughout the segment, keeping in mind the way in which audio is used to reinforce, supplement, and occasionally contradict visual information. In addition, ask students to consider how tones of voice—demanding, pleading, shouting, whispering—provide information about a character or situation.

Finally, students should note the relationship between two distinct images (editing). Encourage students to pay special attention to the use of reaction shots during conversations between two or more characters. Further, have students consider the way editing is used to construct a sense of space or, conversely, signal the passage of time.

To extend and sustain this exercise, have students analyze each of these categories in depth. For instance, students might address how foreground–background relationships between actors and objects help to create meaning for the viewer. Ask students to consider how the use of camera movement, color, and light and shadow work to communicate narrative or character information. Likewise, have students discuss the role that icons (flags, costuming, brand names, and products) play within and between images.

Questions for Analysis and Discussion

- In what ways does RTV resemble other television genres: soap operas, game shows, newscasts, infomercials, etc.?
- What visual or auditory cues do the producers use to align audience members' sympathies with a particular character?
- How do picture composition, camera framing, music, and editing work to create tension within a scene?
- How does this attention to narrative structure—the use of protagonists and antagonists, the cause-effect chain of action, the reliance on narrative climax and resolution—challenge implicit and explicit claims of authenticity in RTV?

Industry Analysis

This activity is designed to get students to think "beyond the text" and consider RTV in relation to current trends in media industry structures and practices. To that end, instructors lead students in an in-depth investigation of *Survivor*—arguably the industry standard for RTV.

One of the defining features of RTV is the way in which media conglomerates such as ABC/Disney, Fox, NBC/Universal, and CBS make use of these shows in an attempt to realize *synergies* within and between various media holdings. That is, media companies use RTV to create a "brand image," for cross-promotion purposes and as merchandising opportunities.

For instance, when it became clear that *Survivor* was a hit, CBS leveraged the program's popular appeal on both radio and television. Contestants from *Survivor* appeared regularly on CBS's *Early Show* and helped enhance that show's performance against its morning television competition: NBC's *Today Show* and ABC's *Good Morning America*. Likewise, programs aired on the CBS Radio Network, and its affiliate stations featured participants from *Survivor*. In turn, these cameo appearances helped CBS promote other network programs and media outlets.

With this in mind, have students use Internet resources—such as the Media Tracker tool on the Center for Public Integrity's website (www.publicintegrity.org/telecom/) —to find the local CBS affiliate that airs *Survivor*. Ask students to profile this local station, with special attention to the station's ownership and its relationship to other media outlets within and beyond the local market it serves.

Following this, have students visit the CBS corporate website. Have them divide sheets of paper into five columns, labeling them Television, Radio, Advertising, Publishing, and Digital Media. Then ask students to review each of CBS's corporate divisions and assign them to the appropriate category. Encourage students to discuss those media outlets, products, and services they are familiar with.

Another feature of the RTV genre is its penchant for product placement. Product placement is attractive for program producers inasmuch as it is an effective way to keep production costs down. For their part, broadcast networks please advertisers by integrating products directly into the sets and storylines of their programs.

Having alerted students to the strategic and tactical uses of product placement, instructors should screen an extended segment of *Survivor* and ask students to take note of the various products and services that are embedded within the program. Following this, have students visit the *Survivor* website and discuss the role of the Internet in extending and elaborating RTV's status as a multidimensional marketing platform.

Questions for Analysis and Discussion

- What are the relative advantages and disadvantages of the corporate consolidation of media ownership and control?
- To what extent does RTV reflect current trends and practices in the media industries?
- How might the practice of product placement influence media form and content?
- What do the products integrated into RTV tell us about the audience that program producers are trying to reach?

Audience Analysis

Nielsen ratings provide some indication of any given program's popularity. What's more, these numbers dictate whether a particular show will survive for another week, or another season. Assign students to research the ratings for two weeks of prime-time television programming. How well does RTV do in the ratings? How many of these programs are in the top twenty-five television shows?

While ratings are useful to the television industry, teachers should remind students that quantitative data of this sort—how many television sets were tuned in to a specific show at a particular time—elide a more difficult, but far more intriguing question: Why is *The Apprentice*, for example, so popular? Television critics provide some clues. Teachers should make several reviews of RTV available to students and encourage students to identify certain themes.

For instance, some critics claim that *Extreme Makeover: Home Edition*, *The Bachelor*, and *Fear Factor* are indicative of a society enamored with voyeurism, titillation, and spectacle. Others suggest that RTV programs that place "ordinary" people in extraordinary situations demonstrate the lengths to which some people will go to achieve even fleeting moments of celebrity. Still others suggest that RTV taps into deep-seated cultural anxieties related to fundamental issues of individual autonomy, privacy, security, and survival.

Like other forms of popular culture, *Amazing Race*, for instance, is *polysemic*—a text whose meanings are neither rigidly determined nor fixed but, rather, open to different interpretations. Have students write a short essay on their impression of a particularly dramatic moment from an RTV program. Then have students compare their responses to the segment, paying particularly close attention to individual impressions of the scene, the characters, and the nature of the narrative conflict.

Fan culture likewise provides a window into understanding the popularity of *The Bachelor*, for example. The proliferation of Web pages devoted to this and other "reality" shows demonstrates the level to which audiences invest meaning in the show's characters, its plot twists, and its resolution. Equally important, online chats and water cooler discussions illustrate that audiences take away different meanings from media texts, meanings that are determined, in part, by an individual's race, class, gender, ethnicity, and lifestyle. *The Bachelor*'s meaning, therefore, does not reside solely in its images, words, and sounds, but rather is produced by audience members.

Assign groups of students to review the fan sites for several RTV programs. Ask students to compare and contrast the content of these sites. Encourage students to consider how these sites reflect audience tastes and preferences.

Questions for Analysis and Discussion

- What aspects of RTV do audiences find most appealing? Why?
- To what extent do TV reviewers reflect the opinion of general audiences?
- What do electronic discussion boards and fan websites for RTV tell us about audience behaviors, tastes, and preferences?
- Why should we take RTV—as well as other forms of media culture—seriously?

Assessment

The exercises described in this chapter provide instructors with ample opportunity to assess class discussion, small-group work, and research, as well as written responses. As a final assignment, students might present their findings on a particular example of RTV. Students could use clips from the program to support a textual analysis; draw on industry-generated data and trade publications to support an industrial analysis; and open up their presentation to the class for an ad hoc audience analysis.

Alternatively, students can develop a formal essay organized along similar lines. Of course, instructors are encouraged to adapt these exercises for purposes of student assessment and evaluation.

Connections and Adaptations

This approach to "reading reality television" can be applied to any number of media texts: fictional television, Hollywood films, video games, books, and popular music. Taking media seriously in this fashion helps students to consider the profound role that media forms and practices play in constructing a *version* of reality. Thus, critical media literacy of the sort outlined here is equally relevant for courses in sociology, anthropology, political science, philosophy, and history.

Works Cited

Butler, Jeremy G. *Television: Critical Methods and Applications*. 3rd ed. Mahwah, NJ: Erlbaum, 2007.

Howley, Kevin. "Reading *Survivor*: A Primer on Media Studies." 4 May 2001. *M/C Reviews*. 12 Feb 2007 <http://reviews.media-culture.org.au/modules.php?name=News&file=article&sid=1802>.

Kellner, Douglas. "Overcoming the Divide: Cultural Studies and Political Economy." *Cultural Studies in Question*. Ed. Marjorie Ferguson and Peter Golding. London: Sage, 1997. 102–120.

Supplemental Reading

Murray, Susan, and Laurie Ouellette, eds. *Reality TV: Remaking Television Culture*. New York: New York UP, 2004.

19 Video Game Vigilance: Applying Critical Thinking to Video Games

Angela Paradise
University of Massachusetts

Context

As a doctoral student of communication at the University of Massachusetts, I have developed a passion for media literacy, particularly in the area of youth and video games. In an effort to extend my interest in and research on this topic beyond university walls, I developed and facilitated a media literacy lesson plan in approximately ten sixth- and seventh-grade language arts and social studies classrooms in eastern Massachusetts. Most of the classrooms were located in urban elementary schools with students from diverse racial backgrounds and lower socioeconomic neighborhoods. After speaking with several teachers and a guidance counselor about their concern over video games, I created this lesson plan with a focus on portrayals of violence and gender in video game content.

Rationale

The popularity of video game use among young people has soared to new heights in recent years. In fact, a 1999 report by the Kaiser Family Foundation (Roberts, Foehr, Rideout, and Brodie) indicates that 39 percent of eight- to eighteen-year-olds engage in video game use on any given day—and this figure continues to grow. While video games are a source of enjoyment for many young people, the content of these games is often a cause of concern for parents and educators because of the prevalence of violence and problematic gender portrayals featured in the games. Given the centrality of video games in the lives of young people, coupled with the issues that arise in video game content, the following lesson plan and activities are designed to inspire critical thinking about video games and foster responsible video game use among young players. This lesson plan is a strong fit with language arts and social studies curricula because the subject matter provides ample opportunity for critical thinking exercises, writing assignments, and other creative projects. Furthermore, based on my experience with facilitating this lesson plan, I have found that students are eager to express their thoughts on the positive and negative attributes of video games. Indeed, video games play a significant role in young people's lives, and this timely topic is sure to spark important conversations in any classroom.

The choice to use video game advertisements in magazines rather than actual video games is driven by a number of motivating factors. First, the sizable cost of a console and game cartridges may prohibit some teachers from doing a game analysis; video game magazines, which often feature still images drawn straight from video games themselves, are a useful alternative at a fraction of the cost. The second advantage of using video game advertisements is that students are able to engage in an in-depth analysis of still images rather than being distracted by the quick pace and competitive nature of playing a game. Third, an analysis of video game magazines allows students to gain a better understanding of the general content patterns of a wide range of video games currently on the market, especially since the average game magazine features dozens of game ads; meanwhile, due to financial considerations and time restraints, it is unlikely that most teachers will be able to have students examine several actual games. A final benefit to examining game advertisements is that teachers have the advantage of knowing the exact material to which their students will be exposed; this may not be the case with a video game, especially given the wealth of options and scenarios that modern games present to players.

Objectives

Students will be able to:

- Analyze violence and gender roles portrayed in video games and consider the implications of such images
- Consider the positive and negative aspects of video games
- Learn about the video game ratings system
- Use creativity to design an educational and/or pro-social video game

NCTE/IRA standards addressed: 1, 3, 6, 11, 12

Materials/Preactivity Preparation

Although the lesson plan focuses on video games, one easy way to analyze game content without setting up a gaming console in the classroom is to use video game magazines (e.g., *Game Informer*, *Electronic Gaming Monthly*, *GamePro*, etc.), which feature countless ads, stories, and pictures taken directly from video game content. These magazines are available at most bookstores and magazine shops. Four or five magazines for a class of twenty students is ideal.

If teachers are unfamiliar with video games, I recommend that they secure a copy of the educational video *Game Over: Gender, Race, and Violence in Video Games*. Produced by the Media Education Foundation, this 41-minute video provides a thorough account of the presence and potential implications of violence and gender-stereotyped images in video games. *Game Over* provides a useful lens through which teachers can learn more about video games prior to facilitating this lesson plan with students. Note: After previewing *Game Over*, teachers can decide if they want to show the video (or portions of it) in class; however, having students watch the video is not a prerequisite of the following lesson plan and activities.

Time Frame

This is a three-part lesson plan; accordingly, teachers should allow for three class periods (approximately 50- 60-minute time blocks) to facilitate the three parts.

Description of Activity

Day 1: Facts and Figures, Pros and Cons

The first session includes two main activities, Part A and Part B. Part A offers an overview of video games, introducing students to some key facts regarding the history of video games, as well as figures pertaining to the use and content of the games. I generally distribute to students a handout (see Figure 19.1, Part A on the companion disk) that offers five pertinent facts and figures and then poses a discussion question(s) relevant to the information. For instance, I inform students that video games were first created in the 1970s and that the first game on the market was called Pong. I then pose the question: "In what ways do you think video games have changed in the last thirty years?" I allot approximately 30 minutes for Part A. In Part B (also about 30 minutes long), I ask students to create a list (using Part B of Figure 19.1) of positive and negative aspects of video games. Students share their list with the class, and then I ask the class to consider why it is important to think about both the positive and the negative aspects of video games. I usually end class by reminding students that successful critical thinking requires us to consider both the negative and the positive aspects of media, and that we can indeed be critical of media that we engage in and enjoy.

Day 2: An Analysis of Video Game Images

The second session requires students to analyze the images found in video game magazines. As previously noted, these magazines are a good substitute for the games themselves, as many of the images found in the magazines are taken straight from game content. Teachers should divide their classroom into groups of four or five students. Each group is given a video game magazine to examine for 20 minutes. Generally, I ask students to pay special attention to the following:

1. The number of times they see acts of violence (punching, shooting, kicking, etc.) and weapons (guns, knives, etc.) in the magazines.

2. The way in which men are portrayed as "hypermasculine" (i.e., males featured as violent, dangerous, macho, and superior to women).

3. The way in which females are featured. For instance, in general, are the female characters seen as weak or strong, heroes or villains? Also, I ask students to note how the female characters are dressed.

Finally, ask each group to select one image from the magazine that they found particularly disturbing or offensive in regard to the manner in which violence or gender (or both) was depicted. (Each group will later share their selection with the class during the final 15–20 minutes of class.)

Once students have finished examining the magazines, teachers should initiate a class discussion. Following is a list of questions aimed at helping teachers facilitate class discussion. Teachers need not pose every question, instead asking those they feel are relevant to their particular class.

Discussion Questions

- In general, how are males portrayed in the magazines? How are females portrayed in the magazines? Are the differences between male and female portrayals significant?

- Do you consider video game characters to be stereotyped? Why do you think male and female characters are presented in such a manner? Do you think representations of gender in video games have changed over the years? Do you see any signs of improvement in how men and women are portrayed in the games you play?

- How often are images of violence found in the video game magazines? Are these images similar to those you see in the video games you play? Why do you think that video game designers include so much violence in video games?

- Do you think that the violence in video games teaches young players that aggression is acceptable? Do you think that excessive time spent with violent video games may desensitize players to real-world violence? Do you think that excessive exposure to violent video games may lead people to behave or think in an aggressive manner?

- How are violence and gender associated in video games? How might the connections between violence and gender be dangerous or problematic for those exposed to video games?

To expand and sustain this discussion, ask students during the last 15 to 20 minutes of class to present the image that their group selected while examining the video game magazines. Ask each group to discuss the image in relation to the factors listed earlier (violence, weapons, gender roles, etc.). What do the students find particularly problematic about the image they selected? What message does the image send to players? Finally, ask each group how they would change the image if they could do so.

Day 3: Video Game Ratings—Is "E" Really for Everyone?

The third session requires students to consider the Entertainment Software Rating Board (ESRB) system used to rate video game content. Teachers should distribute Figure 19.2 ("Video Game Ratings: Is "E" Really for Everyone?" on the companion disk) to students. I recommend spending 15 to 20 minutes discussing the various ratings (e.g., EC, E, T, M, A, and RP). I also ask students to offer examples of various games that correspond to each of the given ratings. Next, it is useful to delve into a discussion about the ratings. Below is a list of questions that teachers can draw from to facilitate fruitful discussion:

Discussion Questions

- When selecting video games to purchase and/or play, do you pay attention to the ratings? Why or why not? Do your parents pay attention?

- Do you think that the ESRB ratings are effective? Are they necessary?

- Do you think that E-rated games are for "everyone," as implied by the ESRB ratings system? Can you think of any E-rated games that might be inappropriate for a younger audience? If you could change anything about the ESRB ratings system, what would it be?

- Do you know of anyone under the age of seventeen who has been able to purchase an M-rated game? To what extent should stores be penalized for selling M-rated games to minors?

After the discussion, teachers might want to recap the most important points brought up during the three lesson plans. Teachers should also remind students that critically examining media messages is an important part of being "media literate" and that part of being a responsible and informed player of video games requires us to be critical consumers. I recommend ending the session by telling students that they represent the media makers of tomorrow. To prepare students for the future, and to inspire creative thinking, teachers might choose to assign a capstone project (see Figure 19.3 on the companion disk).

Capstone Activity

As a final activity, I recommend requiring students to create an educational and/or pro-social video game that addresses some of the problematic characteristics of most video games currently on the market. Students should "think outside of the box" to develop a game premise that is fun, innovative, and creative (see Figure 19.3, "Creating Your Own Video Game"). In the past, I have required students to write up their design in a booklet that offers a summary of their proposed game idea, descriptions and sketches of all main characters, a description of the game's setting(s), a detailed account of the game's rules and objectives, and a print advertisement for the proposed game. I suggest allowing students one week to complete this activity as a homework assignment; however, I do recommend allotting some time in class for brainstorming preliminary ideas in small groups. If time permits, have students pitch their ideas to the class. This activity is a fun, creative, and interesting way to complete a section on video games.

Assessment

Assessment of students' understanding and critique of video game content can be made through class discussion, group exercises, and written responses to the select questions (like those listed above). Students' performance on the capstone activity (the video game proposal booklet) should also be assessed; recommended grading criteria include the extent of creative thinking, strength of writing, and inclusion of all required components in the booklet (i.e., items 1–6, as described in Figure 19.3).

If time permits, teachers could also involve their classroom in a letter-writing activity in which students have the opportunity to voice their concerns and ideas to video game manufacturers. (Note: The names and addresses of video game manufacturers are easily obtainable online.)

Connections and Adaptations

This approach to examining and critiquing video games can be applied to different media (e.g., television, film, music lyrics). Also, these activities are easily adaptable to high school students. For instance, as an extension to this lesson plan and activities, high school students would be well equipped to take a closer look at attempts by legislators to regulate video games, as well as the implications of such regulatory actions. In addition, high school teachers could assign their students to examine and analyze various academic studies that have been published on video games. High school students could also examine the international nature of the video game industry and the role of video games in the global economy.

Works Cited

Entertainment Software Rating Board (ESRB). "Game Ratings and Descriptor Guide." 12 Feb. 2007 <http://www.esrb.org/ratings/ratings_guide.jsp>.

Game Over: Gender, Race, and Violence in Video Games. Dir. Nina Huntemann. Media Education Foundation, 2000.

Roberts, Donald F., Ulla G. Foehr, Victoria J. Rideout, and Mollyann Brodie. *Kids & Media @ the New Millennium.* Kaiser Family Foundation, 1999. 24 Aug. 2007 <http://www.kff.org/entmedia/upload/Kids-Media-The-New-Millennium-Report.pdf>.

Supplemental Reading

Anderson, Craig A., and Brad J. Bushman. "Effects of Violent Video Games on Aggressive Behavior, Aggressive Cognition, Aggressive Affect, Physiological Arousal, and Prosocial Behavior: A Meta-Analytic

Review of the Scientific Literature." *Psychological Science* 12.2 (2001): 353–359.

Potter, W. James. *On Media Violence.* Thousand Oaks, CA: Sage, 1999.

Roberts, Donald F., and Ulla G. Foehr. *Kids and Media in America.* Cambridge, UK: Cambridge UP, 2004.

Scharrer, Erica. "Virtual Violence: Gender and Aggression in Video Game Advertisements." *Mass Communication and Society* 7.4 (2004): 393–412.

Smith, Stacy L., Ken Lachlan, and Ron Tamborini. "Popular Video Games: Quantifying the Presentation of Violence and Its Context." *Journal of Broadcasting and Electronic Media* 47.1 (2003): 58–76.

"Video Gaming Hits 9.9 Billion in Record Sales Year (Newswire)." *Brandweek* 24 Jan. 2005: 15.

20 Viewing Violence Critically: Examining Conflict in Media and Day-to-Day Life

Erica Scharrer, Leda Cooks, and Mari Castañeda Paredes
University of Massachusetts

Context

Each year, our college students go to one or more of the following schools—Deerfield Elementary in South Deerfield, Michael E. Smith School in South Hadley, Wildwood Elementary School in Amherst, and John J. Lynch School in Holyoke—to offer this unit to sixth graders. We've typically worked with twenty-two students per classroom and visited six to ten classrooms each year. The schools vary in their geographic and demographic profiles from rural and predominately white to urban with large majorities of Latino students.

Rationale

The overall aim of this unit is to inspire critical thinking about the messages sent by popular media forms about violence and conflict and compare those messages with everyday experiences with conflict. In doing so, we seek to raise awareness that media texts are "constructions of reality" that reflect the particular points of view and values of their creators and of an industry that operates for commercial gain. We also invite students to consider how they respond to media messages about conflict and violence, as well as how others respond. Finally, we hope to introduce students to some basic conventions and terms used in the production of television programs and films, which show students that media texts are not inevitable forms but rather result from a series of conscious decisions. These aims stem from the general principles of media literacy as defined by the Center for Media Literacy (www.medialit.org), and the last aim—to help students see the constructed nature of media texts—speaks more broadly to author decisions in the English language arts.

The unit has connections to health (since conflict and violence are public health issues) and to anti-bullying and peer mediation curricula. One way to integrate our unit into existing English language arts curricula is to compare the representation of violence or conflict in the same story as presented in a print text compared to an electronic media text. For example, violence portrayed in Harper Lee's *To Kill a Mockingbird* could be compared to Robert Mulligan's 1962 film of the same name. Another way is to introduce basic video production elements (camera angles, editing styles, use of sound effects, etc.) at the same time that literary devices such as metaphor and simile are introduced, to make the point to students that both are tools that authors use for specific purposes and toward particular ends. Still another method of integration is to introduce the public-service-announcement (PSA)-creation exercise at the same time as other types of creative writing (such as poetry or essays) and point out the ways in which these two means of authoring texts are similar as well as different.

Objectives

Students will be able to:

- Define conflict, name a number of realistic nonviolent alternatives to managing a conflict situation, and understand the consequences of moves they make in conflict situations
- Compare and contrast the way conflict is shown on television, in films, and in video games with the reality of conflict in everyday life
- Identify types of "high-risk" violent portrayals in media and assess the implicit message those portrayals send about violence
- Learn about three major ways that media violence can influence viewers and consider whether they have ever experienced any of these

NCTE/IRA standards addressed: 4, 5, 6, 12

Material/Preactivity Preparation

- We have used a reading packet, called *Viewing Violence Critically: A Media Literacy and Violence Prevention Program*, which we created with our college-level students. We've included sample pages from the packet on the companion disk (see Fig-

ure 20.1). This packet is not necessary, however, in implementing this unit.

- A series of short (45-second to 3-minute) clips from age-appropriate and popular films and television programs, to be analyzed in class. We have used the films *The Lion King*, *Spy Kids*,
and *Shrek* in the past, as well as TV programs such as *The
Simpsons* and cartoons like *Dragon Ball Z*.
- A TV and VCR unit for showing the clips.
- At least one video camera for the video production exercise.

Time Frame

We have implemented this unit in both five 45-minute sessions and five
60-minute sessions. Depending on the preferences of the teachers, we
have conducted one session per week for five weeks or two per week
for two and a half weeks. Homework assignments are necessary to keep
to this schedule, and time management tips include limiting responses
to discussion questions, conducting short reviews of lessons learned in
previous sessions, and not allowing students multiple "takes" in which
they stop recording their video production projects. Experience has
taught us that it is difficult to fit in all of these elements in this time
frame, and more time allotted would be optimal. However, we recognize the crowded nature of the middle school curriculum and have
therefore attempted to keep our unit short and to the point.

Description of Activity

Day 1

We begin our sessions by communicating our overall goals for the unit
and introducing the concept of critical thinking (defined in terms of the
media literacy principles we have already discussed). We begin the section on real-life conflict and ways to mediate it with an open-ended
question, "What is conflict?," writing students' responses on the board.
Students tend to offer such definitions as "fighting," "an argument," and
even, occasionally, "a war." We then sum up these responses by providing the basic definition that conflict occurs when two or more people
don't agree on something, and we suggest that conflicts can be physical, verbal, or even nonverbal (like giving someone the "silent treatment"). We ask students the open-ended question "Why do conflicts
occur?" and they typically suggest fighting over some object or person,
having different ideas about how to go about something, and so on. We
introduce "incompatible goals" as a prime explanation for conflict (e.g.,

two individuals have divergent ideas about how to conduct their science project). An additional open-ended question is posed, "What are
some ways to resolve a conflict?" and students have mentioned such
strategies as compromising, seeking intervention from an adult, or, conversely, getting into a fight over the conflict to see who "wins." To make
a concrete connection to the traditional ELA curriculum, teachers can
discuss the central role of conflict in most forms of storytelling, including books, poetry, and plays. Once again, although we use college students to lead these discussions, classroom teachers could certainly do
this themselves or with teacher aides, or they could recruit their own
former students who have already participated in this lesson or train
high school students.

Day 2

We introduce two conflict mediation approaches, the LTA model (which
stands for *Listen* to the point of view of the other person; *Think* about
the consequences of how you respond, your goals in the situation as
well as the goals of the other person, and your relationship with the
person; and then *Act* only after considering these issues) and the lens
model (which involves thinking of the conflict from the other person's
perspective and acknowledging that there may not be a right or wrong
"reality" but rather different ways of seeing the same thing). The college students then role-play a conflict and explain how each of their
views of the situation had an effect on the conflict. The sixth graders
are assigned to groups in which they discuss their own recent conflicts
and decide on one to role-play to the class. We ask the other students in
the class to jump in to suggest how the conflict could have been averted
or resolved. For example, students have role-played how aggravating
it can be to be called out at home plate when you feel you were safe.
They acted out how the emotions in the heat of the moment can contribute to a verbal argument ("I was safe by a mile! What are you,
blind?"). Then their classmates reenacted the scenario, this time with
cooler heads prevailing ("I really think I was safe, but since you are the
umpire, what you say counts. Anyway, I'll try to remember that it's only
a game."), in order to demonstrate how potential conflicts can be dif-
fused by cooling down before responding and putting angry feelings
in check.

Day 3

We transition into the second major part of our unit on media violence
by asking students to discuss the responses they have written to an

open-ended question about how real-life conflicts differ from conflicts we see in the media. We ask students what makes something they see in the media "violent" and then write on the board their responses, which typically include "fighting," "guns," "punches," etc. Incorporating those responses, we provide a basic definition of media violence as "anytime a character in the media intentionally hurts or attempts to hurt another one, even with words." We then broach the topic of the potential effects of viewing violence by asking the students an open-ended discussion question about why people might be concerned about violence in the media. They usually say things like "because kids watching might copy what they see," and we acknowledge that possibility but suggest that is only part of the story. We introduce and define three effects of media violence that have been documented in research: *learning aggression* (i.e., television and other media forms can affect our attitudes about aggression [like thinking that it's a good way to solve problems] as well as our behavior [as when you watch something that is action packed and exciting and you can't sit still]; *desensitization* (the more violence we see in the media, the less sensitive we'll be to violence, so that we come to think of it as no big deal); and *"the mean world syndrome"* (heavy television viewing can make us think of the world around us as violent and dangerous) (Gerbner). In the past, we have asked students to volunteer to the class whether they have ever experienced any one of these effects, and once we had a student speak of breaking his arm while trying out a wrestling move on a backyard trampoline, trying to emulate wrestlers on television.

Day 4

The next lesson involves discussing ways of portraying violence in the media that increase the likelihood of one of those three effects. We call these "high-risk portrayals" and we adapt them from the 1998 *National Television Violence Study* (Center for Communication and Social Policy). We introduce the concepts of *rewarded violence, justified violence, violence without consequences, violence done by likeable characters,* and *realistic violence* as negative ways in which violence can be shown in the media. We ask for examples of each type to ensure comprehension, and students have observed, for example, that rewarded violence happens when a video game has characters rescuing the damsel in distress; that superheroes fighting against "bad guys" are committing justified violence (also an example of violence done by likeable characters); that cartoons often gloss over consequences like pain, grief, and harm; and that animated shows are less realistic than live action shows with more plausible characters and plots. Then we watch the clips we have brought in (e.g., from *Shrek*, *Spy Kids*, cartoons, etc.) and ask students to complete the Media Violence Scorecard (see Figure 20.2 on the companion disk) to tabulate the presence or absence of the high-risk ways of showing violence. Any age-appropriate clip will do, actually, and a teacher interested in this unit could pop almost any tape into the VCR and likely get something showing conflict and violence that can be "deconstructed" in class. We bridge back to the conflict mediation part of our unit by asking students why the conflicts seen in the clips occurred and, when appropriate, how they could have been resolved in a more productive manner. This is typically a very productive conversation, and we use the students' responses to ask further about *why* conflict is sometimes not resolved peacefully in a movie or TV program, which can spawn discussion of the economics of the media industry and media creators' presumptions about what will sell. A connection to the traditional curriculum can be made here as well, since students can be asked if these same pressures about what audiences want are experienced by book authors in addition to movie or TV creators, and why and why not.

We assign the Media Violence Scorecard as a homework activity to promote discussion of the lessons with parents or caregivers and so that students can apply the critical viewing principles to their own viewing. Students have said of this exercise: "I learned to look closer at most shows," and "I did not know the types of violence and learned to use a critical eye." We follow up on this homework exercise on day 4 by choosing a few students to report back on what TV programs they watched and how rewarded violence, justified violence, violence without consequences, violence done by likeable characters, and realistic violence were depicted in those programs.

At the end of day 4, we introduce the final exercise, a creative video production project in which students script, act out, and videotape a public service announcement designed for young children, covering one of the main topics from the unit (see Figure 20.3 on the companion disk). We define a PSA, encourage students to put themselves in the role of media creators by deciding what to put in and what to leave out of the PSA, and give them an opportunity to learn the basics of scriptwriting and video production. We give them some time on day 4 to work in groups on writing their scripts, but we often need to assign the rest of the scriptwriting as homework in order to keep on schedule.

Day 5

Our final session is devoted to the fine-tuning of the PSA scripts and the acting out and videotaping of the PSAs. Once again, tie-ins with the authorship of print texts can be made here, as creativity and self-expression in writing are sparked, and discussions take place about the definition and targeting of an audience. The additional consideration for the TV texts (as opposed to print texts) that the students create is the role of visuals in how audiences will respond. Last year, students said, "I think the skits [PSAs] we did helped us to recognize better ways to solve problems," and "The part where we made skits was the most useful and enjoyable part of the program."

For a further definition of PSAs and an expanded approach to production, see Chapter 27, "Creating a Public Service Announcement: Powerful Persuasion in 60 Seconds."

Assessment

We evaluate the students' class participation (informally through observation), homework assignments, and writing to look for *vocabulary* (do the students use the terms discussed in appropriate situations?), *application of ideas* (can they apply critical thinking skills to television content? can they apply conflict theories to their observations of conflict and attempts at resolution?), and *making connections* between the portrayals of conflict and violence on television and conflict behaviors in everyday life. We also give students closed-ended and open-ended items on a questionnaire (see Figure 20.4 on the companion disk) to respond to before the unit has begun and again after it has ended in order to measure change. Examples of items include "What are some ways to deal with a conflict?" and a series of items for which students indicate their agreement, such as "The people who make TV shows use violence as a way to attract an audience for advertisers," and "People who watch a lot of TV may get the idea that the real world is a mean and scary place." We have also videotaped our sessions to analyze the interactions between the college students and the sixth graders, as well as to observe the physical ways in which students responded to the media clips that ran counter to what they said (e.g., They said, "I'm not affected by the media at all," but a fast-paced clip had them squirming in their seats and even punching the air in excitement).

Connections and Adaptations

To extend this lesson, students can compare the representation of violence in an electronic media text to a printed text. For example, S. E. Hinton's *The Outsiders* could be analyzed for how conflict is discussed and resolved in comparison to the Francis Ford Coppola movie of the same name. Similarly, any piece of literature students are reading can be analyzed for how it depicts conflict, and students can be asked how that conflict might be different if a movie or TV show were made from the book or essay. To extend this lesson plan to other students, the media violence and conflict mediation lessons can be used in middle school and high school, with more advanced questions posed about the structure of the media industry and a more thorough application of video production techniques (such as sound effects, camera angles, editing, etc.) and how they shape audiences' interpretations of media texts.

Works Cited

Center for Communication and Social Policy, University of California, Santa Barbara. *National Television Violence Study.* Vol. 3. Thousand Oaks, CA: Sage, 1998.

Gerbner, George. "Cultural Indicators: The Case of Violence in Television Drama." *Political Intelligence for America's Future.* Ed. Betram M. Gross and Michael Springer. Vol. 388 of *The Annals of the American Academy of Political and Social Science.* Philadelphia: American Academy of Political and Social Science, 1970. 69–81.

Supplemental Reading and Viewing

The annotated bibliography by Alita Zurav Letwin located at http://www.civiced.org/index.php?page=bioviol is an excellent resource for print literature for children and young adults that deals with violence and conflict resolution.

A website created by Laura L. Brown, a contributor to this text, on how to lead students in a PSA creation exercise is located at http://www6.district125.k12.il.us/~lbrown/default.html.

The website for Adobe Digital Kids Club (http://www.adobe.com/education/digkids/lessons/storyboards.html) contains instructions and forms for creating a television storyboard, which can be very useful in scripting the PSAs called for in our unit.

For other violence-related media literacy curriculum ideas and materials, as well as for other information pertaining to media literacy, the Center for Media Literacy website can be consulted: http://www.medialit.org/.

Links to data about and school programs on violence and conflict that include many lesson plan ideas around conflict resolution include http://www.keystosaferschools.com/about_keys.htm and the Teachnology listing, http://teach-nology.com/teachers/lesson_plans/health/conflict/.

IV Media and Persuasion

Techniques, Forms, and Construction

Scott Sullivan
National-Louis University

Most people, if pressed, would never admit to being influenced by advertising, yet billions of dollars are spent on advertising every year in the United States. Children recognize characters on cereal boxes more easily than they do the president of the United States. Teenagers develop identities through the purchase of brand-specific clothing and accessories. Who we are is becoming increasingly defined by what we consume. Which begs the question: How does an ELA teacher use advertising, the news, and an understanding of a profit-based media system as teaching tools for understanding persuasion?

Persuasion has become a matter of economics. It is also a matter of the media and message composition. Few truly public outlets for media exist any more. Public space is slowly disappearing, as formerly ad-free spaces such as school hallways and restaurant restrooms become sites of ad placement. Students need to be able to navigate this sea of competing messages and understand its underlying codes and principles of persuasion for two purposes: to become informed and conscientious citizens and to communicate clearly.

Understanding the underlying issue of profit in advertising gives students a lens through which to begin examining a variety of persuasive techniques, many of which can be used by students to compose their own messages for a variety of audiences. If students can begin to see how ads are constructed to get a message out to a specific audience, they can begin to understand how to construct their own messages to convey the meanings they intend and to evoke the responses they desire, in a variety of formats.

In this section, we explore persuasion and how it operates in the world of our students. The initial lesson, by Stephanie A. Flores-Koulish, deals with the economics of our media system and how money helps drive all aspects of the creation of media. Understanding that the underlying principle of the media system is profit is the first step toward developing students' abilities to understand and utilize the powers of persuasion. Typically, ELA teachers would use the persuasive essay to address these issues, but the NCTE Resolution on Composing with Nonprint Media also recognizes that composition takes a variety of formats, primarily visual, and encourages teachers to explore ways to have students create meaning in a wide range of formats.

Advertising is the primary economic focus of most forms of mass media. But one particularly pertinent form of advertising that affects students is fast-food advertising. Frank W. Baker's lesson on media literacy and junk food helps students to use fast-food advertising as a tool for understanding the basic principles of persuasion as applied to the realm of marketing. Brian Turnbaugh's lesson on deconstructing the photographs that appear on the covers of magazines is a logical extension of the principles outlined in Baker's chapter. Examining magazine covers gives students the opportunity to study advertising in more depth by looking at how people define standards of beauty, acceptance, and social norms based on our shared visual culture.

Having developed an understanding of the profit-driven media system, students can begin to explore how various media formats use their particular strengths to maximize their ability to capture attention and relate a message. Newspapers are a resource that most classroom teachers have access to, and they provide a safe jumping off point for teachers who are still learning media literacy themselves to begin discussions, but Jason Block's lesson on how to "read" the newspaper will allow students to begin deconstructing their own hometown paper and exploring the subtle, but myriad, ways that editorial choices influence the way readers perceive the importance of the news. Editorial processes are often very similar to those we hope to teach our students: What stands out in your argument? How can you present these points most effectively? How do you determine the most important elements of the piece? What is the overall tone you are trying to achieve? These are all questions we hope our students are considering while they create their own persuasive pieces.

Once students have a grasp on the intricacies of the front page, they can begin to critique the local news broadcast—the place where many people go to find out what is going on in the world. Charles F.

Trafford's lessons on deconstructing the network news picks up where the newspaper lesson left off, examining the objectivity of TV news, the construction of the daily newscast, and the editorial decisions necessary to get a thirty-minute newscast on the air, but most important, to make it marketable by attracting and retaining viewers and generating profits for the corporate ownership.

By exploring the intrinsic relationships between content, product, and profit, students can begin to see that what may once have seemed an objective enterprise is, in fact, subject to a variety of influences, some subtle, some not. One of the tools currently used in many local news broadcasts, thanks to budget cuts and a drive to maximize profits, is the video news release (VNR). Produced by public relations firms to market a product, inform an audience, or promote a concept, VNRs are packaged and sent to local broadcast outlets ready for broadcast. Local news organizations, when faced with lack of staff due to budgetary constraints, or needing a story they know will bring in viewers, then use the VNR in their own local broadcast, usually without crediting the source of the VNR. To help decode these messages, Denise Sevick Bortree's lesson helps students notice the telltale signs of VNR use: what to look for, how to determine whether the news is accurate, and whether there is any actual value to the information presented.

A final, more involved project involving the intersection of persuasive skill, understanding of media systems, ability to use visual codes, and create meaning for a prescribed audience culminates in Laura L. Brown's lesson on creating public service announcements, or PSAs. Before the Telecommunications Act of 1996, which deregulated the public broadcast spectrum over which television stations broadcast, station owners were required to produce and air a variety of public service announcements as part of their agreement to broadcast over the publicly held airwaves. The passage of the act, though, removed that requirement for broadcast corporations. As a result, there has been a precipitous decline in the production of PSAs, as any airtime used to show a PSA would, by definition, be time that isn't being sold at a profit to an advertiser. Brown's lesson allows students to explore an issue that many will feel passionately about, walking them through the steps of production, revision, and editing, which will eventually lead them to create a series of PSAs. Students compose, edit, revise, and receive assessment by an authentic audience for their work—just what every ELA teacher hopes for!

By focusing not on the "evil nature" of a profit-driven media system but instead asking students to think about, analyze, and create their own media, ELA teachers help students become more active and critical consumers, not just through their purchasing power, which is substantial, but also through the choices they make. The world is becoming increasingly more packaged, processed, or "spun" by a variety of sources; by making students aware of some of the ways in which information is used and manipulated, we allow them to begin making wiser, more informed choices. We also help them to create messages of their own so that they can communicate clearly, effectively, and purposefully. Not teaching students how to interact with their world does them a great disservice. The teachers with chapters in this section are doing their best to make sure their students will thrive in the media-saturated world they inhabit.

Recommended Resources

Bollier, David. *Brand Name Bullies: The Quest to Own and Control Culture.* Hoboken,NJ: Wiley, 2005.

Kilbourne, Jean. *Deadly Persuasion: Why Women and Girls Must Fight the Addictive Power of Advertising.* New York: Free Press, 1999.

Klein, Naomi. *No Logo: Taking Aim at the Brand Bullies.* New York: Picador, 1999.

McChesney, Robert W. *Rich Media, Poor Democracy: Communication Politics in Dubious Times.* New York: New Press, 2000.

Postman, Neil, and Steve Powers. *How to Watch TV News.* New York: Penguin, 1992.

Pratkanis, Anthony R., and Elliot Aronson. *Age of Propaganda: The Everyday Use and Abuse of Persuasion.* Rev. ed. New York: Freeman, 2001.

Quart, Alissa. *Branded: The Buying and Selling of Teenagers.* Cambridge, MA: Perseus, 2003.

Sanford, Bruce W. *Don't Shoot the Messenger: How Our Growing Hatred of the Media Threatens Free Speech for All of Us.* Lanham, MD: Rowan and Littlefied, 1999.

Schechter, Danny. *The More You Watch, the Less You Know: News Wars/ [Sub]merged Hopes/Media Adventures.* New York: Seven Stories, 1998.

Twitchell, James B. *Adcult USA: The Triumph of Advertising in American Culture.* New York: Columbia UP, 1996.

21 Filling in the Big Picture: Understanding Media Economics

Stephanie A. Flores-Koulish
Loyola College in Maryland

Context

This lesson is intended for secondary education students. It was originally developed for use with current elementary and secondary teachers in a master's degree course on media literacy education, and most of these teachers have expressed the possibility for this lesson's adaptability to their settings, especially at the secondary level. Additionally, teachers have felt that this is an engaging, yet practical way for students to understand what otherwise might be considered a dry facet of media literacy education.

Rationale

The business of media is complicated and convoluted. Media economics is an important and misunderstood concept underlying media litereracy. If students understand that the popular culture they experience is really a thriving business, and if they understand at least in general how that business operates, they will better understand how to judge the value of popular versus alternative media.

Creative writers exist and no doubt bombard the media industry with high-quality work. But the realities of the media dictate that a business model prevails, which positions viewers as the commodity for the advertisers chased by the media corporations. Much of what ultimately gets produced for mass consumption, then, is that which will attract the most viewers in relation to the lowest possible production costs. In film, for example, slapstick, violence, and sexually explicit material are most likely to be produced because each of these aspects translates well to international audiences. That is, dialogue and cultural nuances are virtually irrelevant. If a film can attain audiences worldwide, mass consumption can be achieved. What emerges from the study of media economics is an understanding that creative quality is certainly not *the* primary consideration in how an idea (or "pitch") makes it to our living rooms.

In the English language arts classroom, this lesson enables students to move beyond simply a text-based analysis to consider broader sociopolitical issues surrounding the media they are exposed to, which in turn develops students' critical thinking skills. Additionally, this lesson promotes collaborative learning, a skill needed across the curriculum. Given the collaborative nature of this lesson, modifications might be necessary depending on particular behavior concerns of individual classrooms.

Objectives

Students will be able to:

- Map ownership patterns of mass media outlets
- Understand that media productions depend on advertising
- Understand that the audience is the product for advertisers
- Understand that advertising dictates content and on-air placement

NCTE/IRA standards addressed: 4, 6, 9

Materials/Preactivity Preparation

Materials include two scenario handouts with the following instructions (Figures 21.1 and 21.2 are available on the companion disk):

> Group 1 (X Network Executives): The X network, which owns an abundance of cable channels, has been approached by Company Y [name a company and their product]. Choose a channel, time slot, and day for a program the network will produce that will expose a large audience to this product's advertisements. Your job is to choose the type of television program (i.e., genre) you will produce that will attract the desired audience for Company Y's product(s).

> Group 2 (Creative Media Productions Team): As a group, come up with the title, concept, and tagline (*TV Guide*–type short description) for three brand-new television programs. Be creative with your ideas.

> **Vocabulary List**
>
> Genre   A type or class; in this case, television media, such as a situation comedy, a reality show, a talk show, etc.

Tagline	The brief description (one to three sentences max) of a television show that appears in the television guide.
Target Audience	The group that a show is being aimed toward, such as the elderly, African American youth, working professional women, etc.
Demographics	The characteristics of human populations and population segments that define a particular consumer group (or grouping of consumers).

These terms should be placed on an overhead projector or written on the chalkboard for students' reference.

Time Frame

This activity can be accomplished, as is, within one class period (50 to 60 minutes), though it can also be extended to two class periods with a longer preactivity preparation discussion and individualized adaptations.

Description of Activity

Begin by sharing the following statistics with the students:

- Teens are exposed to an estimated 3,000 ads a day (Rogow, Bracciale, Kane, and Smith 2).
- 81 percent of eight- to eighteen-year-olds watch television every day (Roberts, Foehr, and Rideout 7).
- The average amount of time eight- to eighteen-year-olds spend watching TV per day is 3.04 hours (Roberts, Foehr, and Rideout 7).
- In 2001, U.S. teens spent an estimated $172 billion ("Teens Spend" 1).
- In 1998, U.S. companies spent nearly $200 billion on advertising. Worldwide ad spending is estimated at $435 billion (Rogow, Bracciale, Kane, and Smith 2).
- Thirty seconds of advertising during the Super Bowl costs $2.4 million (Strasburger and Wilson 53).

Next, to provide reinforcement of the terms and their definitions, distribute to the students a word search puzzle using these vocabulary words (see Figure 21.3 on the companion disk). Then engage students in a general discussion related to the new words. In this discussion, all answers to questions are acceptable, because the subsequent activity will show students that some of their ideas are accurate, while other ideas need refining. Specifically, first, discuss how rare it is that we stop to think about how certain programs make it to television and survive for an extended period of time and others do not. Ask students, "Do you ever stop to think about how what you watch on television makes it to television and then either stays on for years or quickly gets cancelled?" The general assumption is that quality television succeeds while poor-quality television does not. For this reason, ask students "Why do you think that certain television shows succeed?" and list their answers on the board. Undoubtedly they will respond in the following ways, and again, all answers are "correct" at this point:

- "People watch it."
- "It's funny."
- "People talk about it."

When we stop to think about the types of television shows that do succeed, we discover contradictions. Ask the students to name some of their all-time favorite television shows and list them on another part of the board. Ask, "How long have these shows been on the air? Are they still on the air? Have they been cancelled?" Mark each show with an asterisk if it is still on the air (and indicate how long) and cross out shows that have been cancelled. Next, have students revisit their list of why certain shows succeed and ask them if the shows that have been cancelled met their criteria (e.g., people watched it, it was funny, people talked about it, etc.). Then ask the rhetorical question "Why do you think the shows that were cancelled were chosen for cancellation?"

Also, ask students if they have ever had an idea for a television show, what the concept was, and why it would appeal to a specific audience. From there, tell them that they are about to experience a simulation in the television production process, and that some of them will get a chance to share their ideas for new TV shows.

Start the television "pitch" exercise by dividing the class into groups, depending on the size of the class, but you should have both a "pitch" group and a group that represents "the network" and is deciding whether the show should be produced. Group size should be four students for each team, though larger groups would most likely work, and the usual group logistics roles (recorder, reporter, idea person, etc.) could be assigned if needed. You may have several pitch groups and network groups in one class.

The next step is to distribute the scenario handouts that describe each group's task (Figures 21.1 and 21.2) and allow 20 to 30 minutes for preparation. The times for preparation can vary depending on the level of student involvement, whether you are requiring a written component to this process, or whether the time just doesn't seem long enough. The pitch and network groups should be kept apart from each other so that each group's work isn't influenced by overhearing the discussions of the opposite group. Some groups might need more structure by receiving expanded details and directions (use your discretion based on your knowledge of your groups' behavior and academic skills). For example, you might need to give the pitch group a specific product, such as a preschool toy, instead of having them name a product on their own. From there, they can more easily identify the genre of programming that would be appropriate given the target audience for this type of product (e.g., young children, mothers). As an adaptation, they might be asked to approach two other companies who also might be interested in advertising during this time slot (e.g., the group might want to approach a snack company and a cereal company). Essentially, the goal for this group is to understand target markets—that particular products are targeted to specific consumers. Once they have defined the consumer group, they should then be able to identify the type of programming that appeals to this demographic. Using the same illustration, network executives (group 1) would choose a program like *Barney* or *Sesame Street*—a program that appeals to the preschool-age demographic. Group 1 needs to understand that this is the genre (or type) of program they will need to buy, regardless of the quality of the program presented to them by group 2 (the Creative Media Productions team).

Group 2 might need assistance in writing their taglines. It is best to describe the taglines as the short paragraph descriptions that are listed in the television guides. If needed, bring in authentic examples for the students to use as models. Encourage this group to be as creative as possible in coming up with new shows that they think would be successful on television and/or that they themselves would like to see. Stress creativity. Ask students to think outside the box to create new shows that break out of the formulas currently on television (e.g., *Fred, the Dog* [Genre: cartoon]. Tagline: Disguised as an ordinary pet, when his family is at work, Fred sets off on adventures saving other pets before they are captured by the city's pound. He narrowly returns home by 5 o'clock each day to excitedly greet his family; his cat friend, Coco, is jealous and always tries to reveal his secret to the family. Or *The Social Worker* [Genre: Drama]. Tagline: Set in a busy city school, social worker Lydia McFallen encounters a different family problem each episode and dedicates herself to positive change and a return to family values, albeit in new ways, while navigating the urban social services agencies.) Also, inform students that their "pitch" will also be important, so they should think about how they can convince the network to purchase their pilot episode (e.g., make up a poster, sing a song, bring in the "actors," etc.).

If this lesson will take up more than one class period, this is the place to continue the lesson the next day.

Reconvene in X Network's "board room" for a formal presentation/pitch of the creative shows to the network executives. Encourage group 2 to creatively present their ideas. Group 1 should take notes, listing the shows' titles. They should also attempt to list the genre and then the target audience. At this time, group 1 should not make any comments.

Take a short break for X Network (group 1) to discuss the options and possible negotiations with Creative Media Productions (group 2). For each of the three shows, group 1 should list the genre and the target audience as intended by group 2. If possible, group 1 should alter each show's idea so that it can fit within their intended target market.

Meanwhile, group 2 should self-assess their presentations, answering the following questions: What did we do effectively? What would we change if we could do this again? What piece of information do we wish we had before we began this process?

Reconvene for X Network to negotiate with the Creative Media Production team. Group 1 should make their suggestions and ask group 2 if they are willing to compromise on their original ideas. Group 2 can respond by discussing the proposed changes in an orderly manner. X Network has the power to accept or reject the original proposals. The Creative Media Production team can only consider compromise of their original creative ideas, unless they happened to have created a show that fits perfectly with X Network's target market. Therefore, a "sale" may or may not take place.

Wrap up by discussing broader media economic issues. Begin by reviewing the students' original list of criteria for television success. Ask them which elements they feel no longer belong and what new elements are needed given what they have learned from their simulation. Discuss the role that advertising plays in a media production. Discuss the role of the audience. Ask the students how they feel about the fact that quality is not the primary consideration in whether a television show actually gets produced. Ask them how they think this applies to other media (e.g., music, movies, etc.). Finally, ask students if they think that the model could be any different. And ask what they think happens to all the creative ideas that never make it into wide distribution. This last question would ideally lead to a discussion on alternative media outlets.

Assessment

To assess the students' understanding of the original objectives, the class discussion wrap-up will initially suffice. Then add in a reflection time after this class discussion whereby students freewrite their personal responses to the lesson objective of developing a basic understanding of media economics. Specifically, ask students this question again: "Why do you think that certain television shows succeed?" Given basic prompts (i.e., the terms *audience, advertising, media production*, etc.), they should be able to articulate that media productions depend on advertising, that the audience is the product for advertisers, and that advertising dictates content and on-air placement. Finally, it is also important for students to realize that whether a show is funny, well acted, well written, and so forth is essentially irrelevant if massive viewers do not tune in to the show.

Connections and Adaptations

As stated earlier, this lesson can be adapted for middle school and high school levels given the subject matter and the basic ideas presented. Within the English language arts curricula, this lesson can easily be implemented in a creative writing or journalism class. Since creative writing is an element within various courses, this lesson could be an introduction to the literary concepts of "audience" or "genre," or it could be an important activity during a unit on media literacy because it reaches beyond just a textual analysis approach toward broader political, economic understandings.

Works Cited

Roberts, Donald F., Ulla G. Foehr, and Victoria Rideout. *Generation M: Media in the Lives of 8–18 Year-Olds*. Menlo Park, CA: Kaiser Family Foundation, 2005.

Rogow, Faith, Jim Bracciale, Erin Martin Kane, and Jessica Smith. "*The Merchants of Cool*: Teachers Guide." *Frontline*. 15 Feb. 2007 <http://www.pbs.org/wgbh/pages/frontline/teach/cool/>.

Strasburger, Victor C., and Barbara J. Wilson. *Children, Adolescents, and the Media*. Thousand Oaks, CA: Sage, 2002.

"Teens Spend $172 Billion in 2001." 25 Jan. 2002. *Teenage Research Unlimited*. 15 Feb. 2007 <http://www.teenresearch.com/ PRview.cfm?edit_id=120>.

Supplemental Reading and Viewing

Frontline: The Merchants of Cool. 2001. WGBH Educational Foundation. 15 Feb. 2007 <http://www.pbs.org/wgbh/pages/frontline/shows/cool/>.

"The Merchants of Cool." *Frontline*. Dir. Barak Goodman. Writ. Rachel Dretzin. WBGH, Boston, 27 Feb. 2001.

22 I Ate the Ad: Media Literacy and the Marketing of Junk Food

Frank W. Baker
Media Consultant
Columbia, South Carolina

Context

As a media educator and consultant, I travel throughout the United States into classrooms and professional development inservice workshops, showcasing simple ways of integrating media literacy into the curriculum, ways that meet specific state standards.

The following lesson has been conducted many times with middle and high school students and teachers. A typical reaction is from a high school teacher:

> Our kids are being bombarded with food marketing and most of it is for the wrong kind of food. They worship the actors and athletes they see promoting these products. The result is an epidemic of teenage obesity and overweight-related health factors. Your media literacy training is the only antidote they have. I believe it will start them thinking and hopefully start to change their behavior.

Rationale

Advertising is ripe for deconstruction, and this activity is designed to fully engage students in the study of print ads and the techniques of persuasion in advertising and marketing.

In 2006 the issue of junk food marketing was at the forefront of the news. In December 2005, for example, an Institute of Medicine report concluded: "There is strong evidence that marketing of food and beverages to children influences their preferences, requests, purchases, and diets" (McGinnis, Gootman, and Kraak). Shortly thereafter, two consumer groups sued Kellogg's and Viacom (parent of the kid-popular Nickelodeon cable network). The Center for Science in the Public Interest and the Campaign for a Commercial-Free Childhood claim that the two corporations are harming children's health since most of the products they push to youngsters are loaded with salt, sugar, and/or fat or are "almost devoid of nutrients" ("Parents and Advocates").

As media educators, here is an opportunity to link both media literacy and nutrition literacy by introducing junk food marketing to students. Even though junk food targeted to younger students is in the news, junk food manufacturers also target those in middle and high school. This lesson also gives the English language arts teacher an opportunity to create an experience that could be linked to activities in a health education class since this lesson would address the following National Health Education standard: Students will analyze the influence of family, peers, culture, media, technology and other factors on health behaviors (Standard 2, National Health Education Standards).

Objectives

Students will be able to:

- Understand the written and visual methods (codes) all ads utilize
- Identify common "techniques of persuasion"
- Apply critical thinking/critical viewing skills to print ads
- Apply media literacy concepts to print advertisements

NCTE/IRA standards addressed: 1, 3, 4, 5, 6

Materials/Preactivity Preparation

The teacher should have access to *Advertising Age* (www.adage.com) or *Brand Week* (www.brandweek.com) magazines; both are online. These periodicals regularly cover the business of advertising. Additionally, the *New York Times* Business section and the *Wall Street Journal* report daily on advertising developments. In these publications, teachers will find relevant essays on topics of interest to young people, including food advertising.

In preparation for teaching this lesson, here are some suggested resources. Several of these websites offer reproducible handouts for student use:

- *Why Analyze Ads?*
  webserve.govst.edu/pa/Advertising/Pitch/why_analyze_ads.htm
- Specific Tools for Media Analysis
  www.mda.gov.sg/wms.ftp/specifictools.pdf

- *Media Investigations: Specific Tools for Analysis*
  reta.nmsu.edu/traincd/media/tools.html
- *Checklist for Analyzing Print Advertisements*
  medialit.med.sc.edu/checklist.htm

To execute the activity, the teacher should have on hand a large number of magazines targeted to middle and high school students, including *Sports Illustrated, Rolling Stone, Ebony, Seventeen, Cosmopolitan, ESPN The Magazine, Latina, People, Entertainment Weekly, Us Weekly, Teen People, CosmoGIRL, Sports Illustrated for Kids, Nick Magazine*, etc.

Time Frame

This activity is designed for a 45-minute to one-hour class period. Extensions, such as having students create a counter ad and parody, can be assigned as homework or extend the lesson for one or two more periods.

Description of Activity

The teacher begins by asking students to recall any particular ads (on television, radio, etc.) they have seen or heard. Students should be prompted to be as specific as possible about words, slogans, or images they remember. Attention should be drawn to the types of traditional and nontraditional advertising that might exist in the school or classroom as well (drink vending machines, logos on clothing, school supplies, posters in classroom sponsored by corporations, etc.). The teacher then can help students recognize that advertising surrounds us, yet we spend little if any time in classrooms understanding how it works. A prevailing belief, for example, is that advertising appeals to our emotions, turning off that part of the brain that deals with questioning and analysis, so that these messages slip into our subconscious.

The students, seated in groups around tables, receive the handout "Common Techniques of Persuasion" (the URL is listed in the Materials/Preactivity Preparation section under *Media Investigations*), and the teacher then reviews the list with the class, asking students if they remember any particular ads that use any of the specific techniques. Anticipate which strategies are going to require more time to explain.

The teacher then explains that the class will examine magazines whose target audience is middle or high school students. Set up the activity this way: Distribute magazines to each table so that each group can quickly identify any and all ads for "junk food," food generally understood to be of questionable nutritional value. In some instances, teachers may feel the need to engage students in a longer discussion about which types of snack and fast food have low nutritional values. When that common understanding is established, students carefully remove these ads, placing them in the center of the table for further analysis.

Once this task is completed, each table should have several junk food ads to examine. The products may be fast food (e.g., McDonald's, Wendy's, Burger King), candy, fruit drinks, dessert, chips, and other snack foods. The teacher provides the following information, which briefly describes the core concepts of media literacy adapted from the "Five Core Concepts" at www.medialit.org/reading_room/gifs/ MML_405.jpg (see the expanded version in Figure 22.1 on the companion disk):

Core Concept	Questions to Consider
1. All media are constructed.	In what ways is an ad a constructed message?
2. Media utilize unique languages with their own sets of rules.	In ads, there are slogans, the rule-of-thirds—all important concepts for students to understand.
3. Media convey values and points of view.	What is the food maker communicating through its ads—e.g., eating is fun; eating makes us happy?
4. Audiences negotiate meanings.	How might people different from me see this ad differently?
5. Media are about power and profit.	Who owns the company that creates this product/ad; why is this ad in this magazine; what does the producer of the message hope to accomplish by promoting this product to this audience?

The teacher then explains how to deconstruct, or take apart, an ad. She or he might say that literally hundreds of hours are spent creating these ads and testing them through focus groups. To deconstruct the ad, students look for three things:

- The words used in the ad (even those in the smallest font)
- The images (the pictures)
- The layout (position of words and images on the page and in relationship to one another)

The teacher might also provide students with a series of questions for each group to work through in deconstructing their ads:

- Who produced/created the ad?
- What is the name of the product? How many times do you see its name in the ad?
- What is dramatized or emphasized by the picture(s)?
- What do the expressions on people's faces tell you about how they feel about the product?
- Is there a slogan? If so, what does it emphasize about the product?
- Is there any reference to nutritional content? What information is provided?
- Is there any pertinent information *not* included in the ad?
- Is there a website? If not, where might you go to get additional information not contained in the ad?

Students should answer these questions on paper. Assign one student to be a "recorder" who writes down responses generated by the small-group discussion.

Students should explore answers to the core concept questions and the deconstruction questions for about 10 to 15 minutes, again using the group's recorder to write down their responses. After groups complete this part of the task, the teacher invites each group (time permitting) to display their ad and report to the entire class.

To extend these discussion activities, students could create a one-page (8 1/2 × 11) counteradvertisment for a junk food product. This ad should be designed to tell the "truth"—in other words , it will include vital and pertinent information omitted from the original ad. To prepare for this assignment, students may need to become more familiar with the concept of counteradvertising. To this end, a follow-up class period could focus on the identification and analysis of counteradvertising. Students can research the concept of counteradvertising and look for examples using a search engine like Google or Ask.com.

The counterad should include elements similar to, but in a context distinctly different from, the original ad, including:

- A clearly articulated target audience
- A slogan that is not currently used
- An image of the packaging
- An image of the product (though not an idealized or "beautiful food" shot)
- Nutritional information
- Responsible testimony
- The inclusion of parody (this is an option for older students)

Students can assemble their ads in a number of different ways. Certainly, they can use computer software to create their prototypes. Effective ads also can be created using the tried-and-true cut-and-paste method in which students clip images from existing ads or from their Google search. Students should type up their copy, slogans, and headlines rather than hand-lettering them to give the prototype a neat, professional look. If the cut-and-paste ad is photocopied on a color machine, it can look every bit as good as a computer-generated ad.

Assessment

In evaluating the counterads, the teacher should use a checklist to determine what elements are included effectively in the prototype:

- Is the name of the product clear on the ad? What makes it clear?
- Is there a slogan? If there is, what does it emphasize about the product?
- Is the design or layout similar to that of the original ad?
- What relevant information did the student include that was omitted from the original?
- Is it clear who (target audience) the ad is trying to reach?
- How was parody used, if at all?
- How effective is the overall execution (neatness, etc.)?

Connections and Adaptations

This activity can also be used at the elementary level. Teachers should have access to magazines such as *Nick Magazine*, *Sports Illustrated for Kids*, *Disney Adventures*, etc. Many of these magazines carry ads for junk food and other unhealthy consumer choices. It may be necessary for students in this age group to identify any cartoon characters or TV stars used in the ads promoting the foods (e.g., Sponge Bob Squarepants on Kellogg's cereals).

Older students can examine not only print advertising but also broadcast and Internet advertising, examining programs and Web pages targeted at them. Students could be encouraged to video-record TV ads and bring them into class for analysis and discussion. Companion food product websites might also be perused for contests and other attractive features.

Works Cited

"Five Core Concepts." *Center for Media Literacy*. 15 Feb. 2007 <http://www.medialit.org/reading_room/gifs/MML_405.jpg>.

McGinnis, J. Michael, Jennifer Appleton Gootman, Vivica I. Kraak, eds. *Food Marketing to Children and Youth: Threat or Opportunity*? Washington, DC: National Academies Press, 2006. 15 Feb. 2007 <http://www.nap.edu/catalog/11514.html>.

National Health Education Standards. December 2005–August 2006. 30 May 2007 <http://www.aahperd.org/aahe.pdf_files/standards.pdf>.

"Parents and Advocates Will Sue Viacom & Kellogg: Lawsuit Aimed at Stopping Junk-Food Marketing to Children by Kellogg and Viacom's Nickelodeon." 18 Jan. 2005. *Campaign for a Commercial-Free Childhood*. 15 Feb. 2007 <http://www.commercialexploitation.org/pressreleases/nickkellogglawsuit.htm>.

Supplemental Reading and Viewing

Print

Linn, Susan. *Consuming Kids: Protecting Our Children from the Onslaught of Marketing and Advertising*. New York: Anchor, 2005.

Schlosser, Eric, and Charles Wilson. *Chew On This: Everything You Don't Want to Know About Fast Food*. Boston: Houghton Mifflin, 2006.

Schor, Juliet B. *Born to Buy: The Commercialized Child and the New Consumer Culture*. New York: Scribner, 2004.

Spurlock, Morgan. *Don't Eat This Book: Fast Food and the Supersizing of America*. New York: Putnam, 2005.

Video

Super Size Me: A Film of Epic Proportions. Dir. Morgan Spurlock. Hart Sharp Video, 2004.

Online

"Advertising, Marketing and the Media: Improving Messages." Fact Sheet. September 2004. *Institute of Medicine of the National Academies.* 15 Feb. 2007 <http://www.iom.edu/Object.File/Master/22/609/0.pdf>.

Campaign for a Commercial-Free Childhood. <http://www.commercial exploitation.org/>.

Center for Science in the Public Interest. <http://www.cspinet.org/>.

Federal Trade Commission. <http://www.ftc.gov/>. (Search for junk food advertising).

Ippolito, Pauline M., and Janis K. Pappalardo. *Advertising Nutrition and Health: Evidence from Food Advertising, 1977–1997.* Washington, DC: Bureau of Economics, Federal Trade Commission, 2002. 15 Feb. 2007 <http://www.ftc.gov/opa/2002/10/advertisingfinal.pdf>.

Schlosser, Eric. "Fast-Food Nation: The True Cost of America's Diet." *Rolling Stone* 3 Sept. 1998. 15 Feb. 2007 <http://www.mcspotlight.org/media/press/rollingstone1.html>.

23 Inadequacy Illustrated: Decoding Teen Magazine Covers

Brian Turnbaugh
Community High School District 94
West Chicago, Illinois

Context

West Chicago High School houses 2,000 students in the western suburbs of Chicago. The following activity was developed for use in Modern Media, a senior elective, during a unit linking the messages embedded in advertising to the content of the media it supports, such as mainstream magazines. While this activity fits into a media literacy course, it can be adapted to fit any unit in which students investigate the influence of gender, consumerism, and the methods of persuasion in media texts.

Rationale

As English teachers, we ask our students to uncover meaning in fiction and nonfiction texts. Hopefully, our teaching of the literature introduces our students to the wisdom of a variety of writers. Yet we rarely take time to prepare students to read critically their texts of choice—specifically, how do they read the genre of popular teen lifestyle magazines? These texts continue to fly under the radar of critical examination in high schools. The popularity of teen lifestyle magazines and the stocking of these periodicals in our school's library warrant the guided analysis of the values represented in the magazines. The narrative blurbs and images on the covers reveal how corporate culture attempts to mold teens' consumer attitudes and beliefs to fit the magazine advertisers' need to promote and sell products.

In examining headlines on covers of magazines like *TV Guide* and *Teen People*, we can peel back the layers of the lifestyle magazine and find that the texts are overtly selling narrowly defined concepts of gender, body image, consumerism, and relationships to their readers. They snare readers by exploiting anxieties of inadequacies in body image, relationships, and wealth. This activity demonstrates how media messages are constructed and how specific values become embedded in the text of the covers. Several important questions emerge as we break down these values: Is materialism a means to personal happiness and peer acceptance? Are relationships defined by sensuality? Is exploitation of body image fair game to sell more issues? Are these stories an accurate reflection of their readers' values? Do we feel better about ourselves after reading the covers or are the seeds of inadequacy planted? In other words, are these magazines "educating" their readers or tearing down their self-esteem?

Objectives

Students will be able to:

- Analyze and evaluate effectiveness of image and text on magazine cover
- Recognize the language of persuasion within the text
- Produce a satirical cover exhibiting similar methods of persuasion
- Demonstrate an understanding of typical persuasive tools utilized by magazine cover designers

NCTE/IRA standards addressed: 3, 6, 9, 11, 12

Materials/ Preactivity Preparation

High Tech

- Selection of covers from teen lifestyle magazines saved in digital format (*Teen People, CosmoGIRL!, Teen Vogue,* and *ELLEgirl*)
- Computer lab with access to shared folders on school server
- Digital camera and access to equipment for uploading images to shared folder on school server

Low or "No" Tech

- Photocopies or actual covers from teen lifestyle magazines
- Scissors, colored paper, tape, and markers

Suggested Viewing

- "The Merchants of Cool" from PBS's *Frontline* series

Of course, you can walk down to the newsstand and pick up copies of any of the teen lifestyle magazines or invite students to bring in their own. I select covers from either Yahoo! or Google image searches using the terms "Cosmo Girl," "Seventeen," and "Teen Vogue." From the queue of images, you will have no problem selecting a current cover featuring a young celebrity. Click on the image and save it into the format you feel most comfortable with (e.g., PowerPoint, Word). Image sizes over 40kB are large enough to be formatted and stretched into various formats.

Our students also read publications such as *Vogue*, *Glamour*, and *Cosmopolitan*, so covers from these magazines can be used as examples as well. However, as these magazines are intended for a more mature demographic, the sexuality depicted visually and verbally on the covers is more overt and amplified. A comparison of the degree or amplification of themes from teen to adult covers is powerful but must be predicated on the maturity level of the class and the comfort level of the teacher to guide the discussion.

While I have used a folder on the school server to share images with students in a computer lab, the effectiveness of this activity does not hinge on access to such technology. Students can use photocopies and magazine cutouts, and the final product can retain the same level of sophistication.

Time Frame

Analysis of magazine covers as text takes no more than a class period. The follow-up production of student parody covers may take up to a period and a half if photos are taken within school and uploaded to school computers. If students wish to complete their covers outside of class, they should finish for the next day's class.

Description of Activity

Day 1

The PBS series *Frontline* episode "The Merchants of Cool" is a valuable documentary that exposes the aggressive tactics corporations use to court the teen consumer. Since the film first aired in February of 2001, the mercurial nature of "cool" has changed, thus dating the film somewhat; but the rich commentary of industry insiders and media critics provides essential perspectives that reveal the foundation of how media exploit teen culture for profit.

A good place to stop the film and begin discussion is with the analogy made by Professor Robert McChesney (17.22) when he compares corporations to colonial powers and identifies their weaponry as "music, books, CDs, Internet access, clothing, amusement parks, sports teams." At this point, you can test his analogy by listing on the board the "weaponry" and dating students' most recent "purchases" of these commodities (movies, music, video games, fast food, frequently visited websites, and visits to the mall). For example, on the chalkboard under movies seen in the past month, students might list purchased tickets for *V for Vendetta* and *Scary Movie 4* and the rental of *Jarhead*. Through such illustration of their purchasing power over the past month, the class can visualize McChesney's claim that corporations are aggressively targeting teens. It is a smooth transition to extend the analogy to show how teen lifestyle magazines serve as a "weapon" for corporations. This comparison builds a bridge from these basic ideas to the activity described on the first handout, which begins the next day's lesson.

Day 2

By taking a quick survey of the "weaponry" that has been used against students since yesterday, you can do a quick recap of the first day's theme. This discussion will remind students that they are the targets of persuasion that demands their consumerism. The "weaponry" in focus today is the teen lifestyle magazine.

The first handout (Figure 23.1 on the companion disk) prepares students to think about the text of the covers removed from the colors and imagery. The handout lists consistent themes from typical texts such as peer acceptance, celebrity worship, health scare, romantic promise, body anxiety, and materialism. From this list, students must match these themes to actual margin text from back issues of *CosmoGIRL!*, *Teen Vogue*, and *ELLEgirl*. This initial analysis strips the text away from the glossy distractions of the cover and allows students to view the text separately so that they can see the persuasion more clearly.

While the themes are fresh in students' minds, the second handout (Figure 23.2 on the companion disk) asks students to evaluate covers by examining how text and image work together in persuasion. Use a variety of covers so students can evaluate how the patterns are similar. The steps of analysis and students' observations will carry students to the idea that underneath the gloss of the cover, the real themes promote an inadequate sense of self.

Deconstructing the covers will promote a lively discussion. The most important questions to emerge from the handouts and subsequent analysis may be:

- What are the demographics of the person who is expected to read this magazine? Race? Class? Body type?
- Why is the discovery of self-inadequacy an effective persuader?
- Do these magazines begin with the assumption that their readers have positive self-esteem?
- Do these magazines begin with the assumption that their readers are inadequate (i.e., not matching beauty, economic, or social standards)?
- Do the themes inherent in advertising, as discussed in the "The Merchants of Cool" and represented on magazine covers, appear to resonate within the content of these magazines? If so, what purpose might this serve?

Students will need time to process these questions, be it in small-group discussions or, depending on how much class time you have, a reflective journal assignment. I have found that both male and female students are animated during deconstruction, each sharing similar observations as they pick apart the methods magazines use to instill inadequacy in the reader.

Another level of examination compares the teen covers with the covers of the adult counterparts such as *ELLE, Glamour,* and *Cosmopolitan.* As mentioned previously, this may expand the time spent with the lesson by a day. As students contrast the two magazines, they will probably observe that the themes remain the same while attention to body and sex amplifies sharply. Another important comparison can be made with the covers of male-targeted magazines such as *Men's Health, Maxim,* and *Men's Fitness.* Again, this comparison raises another set of questions about the increase of attention to sexuality and body anxiety. While this evaluation of the teen and adult magazines is important, it may not fit the maturity of the classroom. I have held very mature and insightful conversations with seniors about the comparisons, yet I might not attempt this with a sophomore class. Adapt this to your level of comfort and available time.

Day 3

A host of emotions will be raised as a result of the analysis of the covers. Some students will be angry and feel betrayed while others will feel validated, as their suspicions of magazines' methods of persuasion prove true. It is essential to show that such media are not monolithic and can be changed for the better. The students spend the second day of this activity creating their own covers to satirize the absurdity of the published magazines.

I ask students to think of a ridiculous concept for a lifestyle magazine, such as *Burritos Illustrated* or *Thumb Wrestlers Weekly* (see Figure 23.3 on the companion disk as well as other student examples at www.d94.org/english/turnbaughweb/magindex.htm). Once students have an idea, take a digital photograph of students in some pose for their idea. I upload the image so students can access the photo on the computer and begin to create their cover by inserting the image into a Word or PowerPoint document. From this point, students create text to demonstrate the methods of instilling a sense of inadequacy in their readers. Students use the manipulators of fear of physical danger, social alienation, and body image while also promoting consumerism and romantic promise. Sample texts from *Burritos Illustrated* reflect such themes: "Are your peppers zesty enough?" "Survivor Story: How a chili pepper lodged in my nasal cavity," and "Spicy, Hot, and Saucy: A burrito's case for the 1st date meal." Students will need to use loaded language to capture the persuasion of the genuine covers. At least five to six teasers will provide a range of persuasive techniques on the covers.

Students become completely engaged in the production of their own satirical magazine covers. I advise students to make the covers appropriate for school as I may publish them to the class Web page or hang them in class. This parameter is helpful because students may try to model too closely the more risqué texts of real covers. Upon completion of the covers, we create a gallery to share our work. I feel that this last step of creating and sharing the covers is empowering for students because it lets them reclaim the space of the magazine by exposing its ploys. Whether the students know it or not, this activity taps into their rebellious nature while reflecting their understanding of persuasion.

If digital cameras and computer labs are not an option for you, this part of the activity is easily adaptable. Students can cut and paste photos of magazine covers from home or use existing photos of celebrities to anchor the image of their original cover.

The success of this activity is measured by the students' ability to articulate how the persuasive manipulators on these covers serve as the "weaponry" for sponsoring corporations, as McChesney stated in "The Merchants of Cool." From this point, you can delve into deeper issues of media and ethics: Can teen lifestyle magazines foster truly positive self-esteem with their content while still needing readers to consume the products advertised within its pages? Or is this conflict of interest impossible to resolve when corporations depend on teen consumerism to meet their profit expectations?

Assessment

Assessment of student understanding of the magazine cover texts can be made through student participation during class discussion and through their responses in reflective journals at the end of the first day. As an alternative day 1 assignment, students could find a magazine cover from home or from an image search and evaluate the methods of persuasion on their own.

Assessment of students' satirical covers should focus on three core areas: image, exploitation of the inadequacy of the original magazine cover, and word choice. The images must be appropriate while also modeling postures similar to those on the cover models. The text should also apply the methods of persuasion reviewed in class. Special attention must be given to word choice. Before students create the covers, it might be helpful to generate a list on the chalkboard of words associated with fear, guilt, shame, wealth, and fashion to serve as a primer for students' word choices on their satirical covers.

Connections and Adaptations

This activity can fit into a wide range of English language arts classes. In a media literacy course, this activity will provide strategies for how to read other media texts while demonstrating how both image and text work in conjunction to catch reader attention. This activity also can be implemented as a means to introduce the topic of gender and the "mirror" projection of values offered by these magazines. This activity could also be connected with any literary work that discusses the powerful reach of media into contemporary society, such as *Fahrenheit 451, 1984,* or a graphic novel like *V for Vendetta*.

Although the core of this activity is the analysis of persuasive techniques in teen lifestyle magazines, this approach can be easily adapted to magazines targeted to other demographics. Whether we look at *AARP* or *Parenting*, similar methods of persuasion through anxiety are implemented.

Work Cited

"The Merchants of Cool." *Frontline.* Dir. Barak Goodman. Writ. Rachel Dretzin. WBGH, Boston, 27 Feb. 2001.

Supplemental Reading

Gibbons, Sheila. "Wanted: Sexy Virgins." *AlterNet* 4 November 2003. <http://
www.alternet.org/story/17124/>.

Higginbotham, Anastasia. "Teen Mags: How to Get a Guy, Drop 20 Pounds,
and Lose Your Self-Esteem" *Ms.* 6.5 (1996): 84–87.

Websites

The following website features examples of students' past work creating
their covers: <http://www.d94.org/english/turnbaughweb/
magindex.htm>.

This website offers free tool to upload your photos and create a magazine
cover: <http://bighugelabs.com/flickr/magazine.php>.

See how *Cosmopolitan* covers have changed over the years: <http://
gono.com/adart/Cosmopolitan/cosmopolitan_magazine_
covers.htm>.

24 From Sammy Sosa to City Hall: Detecting Bias in Print News

Jason Block
Prospect High School
Mount Prospect, Illinois

Context

The following lesson has been used effectively at Prospect High School, a school of 2,000 students located in Chicago's northwest suburbs. The lesson was taught in a Journalistic Writing course to students of all ages and ability levels. The lesson fit into the larger unit of detecting bias in the media, specifically the print media.

Rationale

When our students venture outside of our classrooms, we all hope—perhaps wish, pray, and beg, as well—that they will continue reading after their formal education is complete. If our wish does come true, it will most likely take the form of reading the newspaper, as research shows newspaper readership increases with age. With this in mind, we as teachers need to prepare our students to be active consumers of the news media, not passive receivers of these messages—virtual media sponges soaking up every last drop. It is important that we make them aware of the bias inherent in all news media outlets, as well as the various forms this bias takes. If we do not arm our students with the tools necessary to detect bias in the news media, we are sending them into the world unprepared to be active, responsible, independent-thinking members of a democracy. The following lesson is intended to provide students a glimpse into the ways in which the print news media express bias, while at the same time allowing them to analyze the hot news topics of the day.

Objectives

Students will be able to:

- Identify the various techniques for expressing bias in a newspaper
- Compare and contrast competing newspapers to detect bias
- Analyze their own biases and the reasons they exist
- Understand how their own biases influence the way in which they respond to news coverage

NCTE/IRA standards addressed: 1, 3, 5, 6, 7, 11, 12

Materials/Preactivity Preparation

Before jumping into the activity, teachers must decide which news item they want their students to follow in order to complete this project. It can be a breaking story about which new pieces are running nearly every day, or it can be an older story about which students will have to go into archives to locate copies. The example I used, the Sammy Sosa corked bat incident from the summer of 2003, was an old story by the time I taught the lesson in October of that year, but it made the lesson no less interesting and engaging. Students can follow a local story, like corruption at City Hall, or a national story, like a presidential election, and learn just as much about bias regardless of story choice.

For this activity to be most effective, students should have at least two consecutive days of coverage in two newspapers. While I followed the Sosa story through the week after the event and provided students with copies of many of those pages, the lesson can be equally effective when stories are followed for two or three days. The Sosa story proved ideal because it was of enormous local interest, thus ensuring plenty of coverage in all local newspapers. Also, controversy followed this story from start to finish, which lends itself to greater opportunities for bias to be present.

It is important that students do not get only text versions of the stories that ran; they must have the entire newspaper pages on which the stories appeared, as they will be analyzing visual elements as well as diction and story structure.

Students also need to be presented with a list of key terms they can use when discussing bias in a newspaper. Without these terms, students will be left guessing why the newspaper made certain decisions and what the significance of those decisions was. The list of terms (see

Figure 24.1 on the companion disk) can either be copied and distributed or put on an overhead.

Time Frame

This lesson was implemented in two 50-minute class periods, not including the reflections the students wrote at home.

Description of Activity

Day 1

Once students have acquired—either on their own or from you—copies of the coverage of their selected news story in each of their publications for the number of days assigned, the teacher presents students with the list of key terms to be used when discussing newspaper design. This should take no more than 10 to 15 minutes and proved most effective for me when I held up the front page of that day's newspaper and pointed out each of the elements. With the visual reinforcement to go with the notes on the overhead, students seemed to more easily internalize the terms. Another option is to photocopy the front page of a newspaper, shrink its size, and then have the students label the elements as part of their note taking.

The only other term students need to understand is *bias*, which some might be familiar with, but they will probably need a formal definition. More important than identifying what bias means is figuring out why bias happens and how it is revealed. I find this discussion to be a very beneficial one that should not be rushed through. I first have the students list in their notes ideas or items they are biased toward (e.g., a baseball team, a type of food, a style of clothing). Once they are done, we share them as a class. Most answers will be relatively safe, but be careful: warn students about sharing any biases that might be considered racially insensitive or otherwise offensive to anyone in the class. I have never encountered this problem but can see how it is a remote possibility.

With this list generated, students must now return to their notes to try to identify why they are biased toward these ideas or items. This might stump students for a second or two, but be patient: they can do this. Perhaps give them a personal example such as, "I am biased toward chocolate ice cream because I grew up eating it every day as a child," and that should send them on their way. Now the class will be

able to generate a list of reasons for bias. More important than the specific reasons, such as "my dad owned a chocolate shop," are the categories in which these reasons fall. The standard categories into which
you are likely to be able to fit nearly all of their responses are:

- Family tradition (the way you were raised)
- Gender
- Culture
- Age
- Religion
- Race

Now that students have been introduced to the reasons why *all*
people have biases, they are ready to search for bias in real newspapers.
At this point, ask them to look for the headline that runs with the story
in each newspaper and read each carefully. Is there bias contained in
either the headline or the subhead, through diction, punctuation, figurative language, etc.? In the case of the Sosa coverage, students were
able to easily identify bias in both publications through simple analysis of diction. The *Tribune* used the word *apologetic*, while the *Sun-Times*
said "caught cheating" below the headline "SAY IT AIN'T SO-SA!" in
all capitals. Students saw the implications of word choice in each case:
the *Tribune* was implying that Sosa felt remorse, while the *Sun-Times* was
screaming that Sosa was trying to get away with it but was "caught."
Also, a handful of historically aware students caught the obvious allu-
sion to the most infamous scandal in Chicago sports history (the 1919
"Black Sox"), which causes a "guilt-by-association" reaction in many
readers, putting Sosa right alongside the White Sox players accused of
throwing the World Series.

Before allowing students to jump into the actual stories, where
bias can oftentimes be difficult to detect, I find it helpful to look at the
design of the page. Without reading a single word, students should look
at where the story is on the page. Is it above or below the fold? If above,
that shows that the newspaper believes this story is more important than
other news, as described in the terminology handout. Also, students can
be looking for the size of the headline, since typically there is one main
headline on each page in the largest point size; the rest of the headlines
descend in size from there. Obviously, the largest headline garners the
most reader attention. In the Sosa case, students quickly saw that "SAY
IT AIN'T SO-SA!" was in very large capital letters and located at the
top of the *Sun-Times* page, while the *Tribune* headline was much smaller

and located off to the left, below the main headline of the day about the Middle East peace talks. Students understood that the *Sun-Times* was trying to attract readers to the story, while the *Tribune* was attempting to do the opposite.

Here are some sample questions that can be used to analyze headlines in any news story. As with all of the questions contained in this lesson, these are most effective while students are comparing and contrasting two different newspapers. Looking at a single story in isolation makes the project more difficult.

- Are there any "loaded" words contained in the headline, words that carry implications with them, either positive or negative? Pay special attention to verb choice here.
- What punctuation, if any, is contained in the headline? How does this punctuation change the way you read the "sentence"?
- Are there any allusions contained in the headline? If so, are the allusions to positive events or people or to negative ones? What are the implications of these allusions?
- Where on the page does the headline appear, above or below the fold?
- Is the headline advertising this story as the main story of the day? How do you know?

This is typically the point at which you must end the first period of this unit, picking up with the visual elements the next class period. As closure for this lesson, students should complete an "exit slip" upon which they identify which publication is guiltier of bias and why.

Day 2

Students will thoroughly enjoy the next step, as it allows them to do a lot of creative thinking. Ask them to look at the photos that accompany each story. If the photos are of people, what are the facial expressions? What angle are they shot at? How tight of a close-up is the photo? While students might not have an understanding of the technical aspects of photography, that's okay, because all you have to ask them is how the photo makes them feel. They love this because it gives them total freedom. Does the photo make the person look intelligent, stupid, innocent, guilty, attractive, ugly—the list is endless. Always ask students *why* the photo makes them feel a certain way; that is the most important part. In the Sosa case, we looked at the photos that appeared on the sports page, and students found themselves feeling sorry for Sosa in the *Tribune*, and they weren't exactly sure why. When I prompted them with questions, such as those listed above, they quickly identified the tight close-up on Sammy's face as making him look sympathetic. You could see the remorse in those big brown eyes. Conversely, students laughed out loud when they looked at the *Sun-Times* photo, which has Sammy situated in the lower right-hand corner, eyes peering out of the dugout while the umpire approaches with the illegal bat. Students quickly made the comparison of Sosa to a child caught with his hand in the cookie jar and the umpire as the angry parent. Sosa looks like he is hiding, and only a guilty man hides from the authorities, right?

Students need to understand that literally hundreds of photos are taken at any event, whether it be a presidential news conference or a baseball game, and the decision makers at the newspaper choose the one or maybe two they are going to use that day. Basically, these editors get to decide how they are going to make the subject look. Put it to the kids in this context: if I shot a hundred pictures of you while you were listening to me blabber on for the past five minutes, I bet I could find at least one that makes you look mature and intelligent, and at least one more that makes you look goofy and unintelligent. Hence, the power of the media, as they get to decide which one runs, oftentimes expressing their own biases through this choice.

Finally, students are ready to look at the actual writing contained in the story. More so than diction, the most important element is the "stacking" of the story; students should be looking for the order in which the story is told. Rather than simply discussing the structure of the story, I find it helpful to have students complete a basic outline sequencing the items in each story. Once they have done this, their job is simple: look at what parts of the story (facts and quotations) are told first. These are the ones that will be read by the most readers; with each successive paragraph, more and more readers move on to the next story. Depending on what facts and quotes are presented first, stories can take on completely different tones and angles. In the Sosa case, the fact that he apologized appeared in the third paragraph of the *Tribune* story, followed by a quote from Sosa reiterating the apology. As for the *Sun-Times*, the apology was not in the story, replaced by the purpose of corking a bat and the idea that this raises doubts as to the legitimacy of Sosa's career. Very different stories, aren't they? At this point, students will be able to write a brief analysis identifying the angle each story takes and impression it gives them as readers. Ask them: How does the story make you feel about the subject or event? Why? (Figure 24.2 on the companion disk lists the sample questions I provided students for their analysis of the Sosa stories.)

Here are some sample questions that can be used to analyze the content of any news story:

- What facts are placed earliest in the story? Which are saved until later? Which come before the story "jumps" to another page and which come after the jump?
- What effect do these choices have on the meaning of the story?
- What loaded words are contained in the story? Look for any diction that generates emotion in the reader.
- What quotations are used in the story and in what order? What sources are being allowed to have their voices heard and which are being silenced?

If you feel as though students have not had enough time to perform a thorough analysis of the actual writing of the stories, the questions can always be assigned as homework to be turned in at the next class period.

At the end of the activity, discuss with students the motivation behind bias. Why did the decision makers at the respective newspapers take the stances they did? In cases like Sosa's, the motive was simple: the Tribune Company owns the Cubs and had a vested interest in protecting its prized commodity, Sammy Sosa, while the *Sun-Times* wanted to chop off the head of the golden goose of its main competition. Two useful resources for examining the impact of corporate influence on media production and selection include the video *Fear and Favor in the Newsroom* and Kristina Borjesson's book *Into the Buzzsaw: Leading Journalists Expose the Myth of a Free Press*. To balance this view of big business and media bias, students should also consider that bias may not be inserted into newspaper reporting maliciously or to further an agenda; rather, it is there simply as a result of the different backgrounds and prejudices we all have. Bias in the news media is not necessarily a conspiracy, as many of my students initially claim it to be; it is an expected result of having human beings writing about other human beings. This might lead to an investigation of codes of ethics and conduct among professional journalists. Once students understand that many different factors contribute to bias in news reporting, they will be ready to critically read a newspaper.

Assessment

In addition to constantly assessing students through their contribution to the discussion, I have found it helpful to distribute a worksheet at the start of the activity on which they can record their answers. I give them time to write down their individual answers to the prompts I listed above, which allows them to formulate their thoughts before being asked to participate. They then have the opportunity to add to their responses during the discussion. To avoid students becoming overwhelmed and lost, be sure to have them analyze only one aspect of the newspaper at a time before stopping to discuss. To this end, break up the lesson into smaller, more digestible chunks: headlines, page design, photos, articles. Students should also have numerous opportunities to complete written reflections on what they have learned.

To incorporate formal writing into the assessment, I provide students with a list of facts and quotations on a subject, and they put it all together into a newspaper article. Students then compare and contrast the choices they made with the choices of their peers in terms of stacking the story and which information they included and which they cut. They also can analyze how very different each story turned out, all as a result of these personal decisions. This activity allows them to see both the dangers of bias and the fact that it is virtually unavoidable in our writing (see the extension activity in Figure 24.3 on the companion disk).

Connections and Adaptations

This lesson can be used with any news story at any time, so long as multiple newspapers are covering it.

To adapt this lesson to an English classroom, teachers need to set aside only a few days during a larger writing unit in which the class is already discussing the choices writers make. Why did your students choose the thesis they did? How does it reflect any personal biases? Why did they opt to include certain details in a creative writing assignment and eliminate others? By looking at the decisions professional writers make, students can more easily understand that each and every choice they make influences the message they are sending to their readers.

Works Cited

Borjesson, Kristina, ed. *Into the Buzzsaw: Leading Journalists Expose the Myth of a Free Press*. Amherst, NY: Prometheus, 2002.

Fear and Favor in the Newsroom. Dir. Beth Sanders. California Newsreel, 1996.

Recommended Resources

Goodyear-Smith, Felicity. "Victim-Oriented Law Reforms: Advantages and Pitfalls." *Issues in Child Abuse Accusations* 8.2 (Spring 1996): 87–93.

Kiley, Mike. "A Tarnished Triumph." *Chicago Sun-Times* 4 June 2003: 135.

Morrissey, Rick. "Sammy's Act a Lot Harder to Buy Now." *Chicago Tribune* 4 June 2003: 1.

Sullivan, Paul. "Apologetic Sosa: I Picked the Wrong Bat." *Chicago Tribune* 4 June 2003: 1.

Telander, Rick. "Sosa Legend Reaches Cork in the Road." *Chicago Sun-Times* 4 June 2003: 142.

25 Deconstructing Broadcast News

Charles F. Trafford
Inglemoor High School
Bothell, Washington

Context

Inglemoor High School is a suburban school of approximately 1,850 students in the northeast suburbs of Seattle. Academically, the students at Inglemoor excel—over 85 percent go on to college. The following lesson is used in an eleventh-grade English class as part of a comprehensive unit on media literacy. The activity could easily be adapted to other grade and ability levels or used within other disciplines by modifying questions appropriately.

Rationale

The impact that broadcast news has on our lives is indisputable. The news defines which issues in our society are perceived as important and colors the way that we understand those issues. It plays a critical role in whom we elect and how we run our democracy. One valuable skill that is taught in English classes is critical analysis of a literary text: the ability to delve into a text beyond the obvious to extract a deeper meaning. Critical analysis is the capacity to define what is really being said through careful deconstruction. One of the goals of education is for students to apply the skills they learn in the classroom to the world outside. This lesson does just this. As students break down a broadcast into its discrete parts, influences shading the news become apparent. Biases and value judgments are brought to the forefront. In the end, students become more discerning consumers of the media system.

Objectives

Students will be able to:

- Apply (literary) critical analysis skills to the world outside of the classroom
- Analyze a television news broadcast for content
- Determine the distinction between hard and soft news
- Identify bias in the news
- Identify the influence of advertising on television news broadcasts

NCTE/IRA standards addressed: 1, 3, 6, 7, 8, 12

Materials/Preactivity Preparation

- A prerecorded copy of a 30-minute local television news broadcast
- A television and VCR
- A stopwatch
- A copy of a local newspaper for each student. Most newspapers will provide a set of papers free of charge if given a few weeks' notice.
- A dictionary

Time Frame

I teach this lesson in three 60-minute classes. The first class period is spent defining news terms, learning to identify bias, distinguishing between hard and soft news, and looking at influences on broadcast news. The second day students deconstruct a local newscast. The last day is used for analysis of the results and an in-class essay.

Description of Activity

Broadcast news undoubtedly has a profound effect on students' interpretation of the world. Unfortunately, the news does not necessarily give an unbiased and balanced picture of the world. By deconstructing a newscast and analyzing its content, this lesson effectively shows students the influence that broadcast news has on them. After students complete this activity, they have a far better understanding of bias, how content is chosen, and how a newscast is structured and why.

If this activity is used in combination with Jason Block's lesson that focuses on the analysis of bias in newspaper reporting (see Chapter 24), you may find that some of the attention placed in this lesson on analysis of bias in print news could be reduced or eliminated.

Day 1

The first day of the lesson begins with an explanation of hard news and soft news. Read to the class the dictionary definition of *hard news*, which consists of stories that deal with significant topics and events such as politics and foreign affairs. Hard news is information people need to know to better understand the world; soft news is simply the opposite. Soft news focuses on people's accomplishments, problems, and concerns. Many soft news stories are human interest stories. Their goal is to elicit sympathy, interest, or fear from the viewer—in other words, to keep the viewer's attention.

Then create a list with two columns on the board, one for hard news and one for soft news. Prompt students by giving them examples of stories and asking if a story falls under the category of hard or soft news. Students continue to brainstorm what types of news stories or news broadcast content fall under each list. This part of the activity usually takes between 10 to 15 minutes. Ultimately, the class creates two lists that look like something like this:

Hard News	Soft News
<ul><li>politics</li><li>economic issues</li><li>foreign affairs</li><li>issues relating to the public interest such as public works infrastructure, communications, etc.</li><li>natural disaster events of widespread and *direct significance to the public* such as an earthquake, flood, or storm</li></ul>	<ul><li>human interest stories</li><li>local petty crimes</li><li>accidents</li><li>sports</li><li>weather (unless a significant event, in which case it is handled as a separate story)</li><li>entertainment stories such as new movies, celebrities</li><li>reviews of new products such as cars, stereos, and computers</li></ul>

After discussing hard and soft news, move to the issue of bias. Although you will deconstruct broadcast news, start with a newspaper because it is easier to illustrate how to deconstruct news content with a print medium and then transfer those skills to the fast-paced newscast. For this part of the lesson, use the front page of a local newspaper. This activity takes approximately 30 minutes, although it can be expanded depending on the depth of discussion questions used. Before beginning to investigate possible instances of bias, again turn to the dictionary and read the definition. *Bias* in a story is a preference or a partiality that inhibits objective and unprejudiced judgment by unfairly guiding the readers' opinion or skewing their view of an issue.

Hold up the front page of the paper and tell students that this page contains a number of things that could possibly be biased. Students usually don't pick up on the possibilities right away, so guide them with examples. Pick a story and read it. Put particular emphasis on subjective language that could sway a reader one way or another. An example might be identifying combatants as "freedom fighters" or "insurgents" depending on the newspaper's stance toward the conflict. Also draw attention to omission of opposing points of view such as covering only one political party's view of a public issue.

After examining a couple of stories for language bias, look at possible bias in photographs. Choose a photograph and ask what it shows. What does the photographer want you to see? Does the photograph imply anything that may support the bias in the text?

Ask students what else is happening in the scene that was not captured in the photo:

- What is on either side of the subject of the photograph? What has been cropped out?
- Do the people in the picture know they are being photographed?
- How does that influence their behavior in the shot?
- Is there anything not being shown that could affect the nature of the photograph?

Point to the inherent problem with pictures. They show only a very narrow slice of an issue.

Then look at the possibility of bias through story proximity:

- What stories are near each other?
- Is there a theme to the selection of stories on the front page?
- Are most of the stories about one news event? Is there an association between the selection and the coordination of stories on the front page?

Finally, look at the impact of advertising:

- What kind of stories are near the advertising?

- What kind of stories are not?
- For example, if there is a story about rising gas prices, is there an advertisement for a truck next to it? Why?
- If there is a story about drought and starvation in Africa, is there an ad for a fast-food restaurant near it? Why?

Students then find ten examples of possible bias in a newspaper of their own. On a separate piece of paper, students list each instance, including the title of the story and where it appears, and explain what type of bias it is and why. This activity can be used as an individual in-class activity, a small-group activity, or homework, depending on the time available. One note: students must use a different edition of the newspaper than the one you used as an example.

Day 2

The second day of the lesson involves watching a half-hour prerecorded local television newscast. Record a newscast well in advance on an average day when there is no major news event dominating the headlines, such as the tsunami in Indonesia. This gives students the best representation of the average pace of a broadcast and the types of stories that are routinely covered. I also find that recording a newscast two or three weeks ahead of time forces students to look more critically at the structure of the broadcast since the news presented is stale.

Before viewing the newscast, have a 10-minute discussion. Open by posing this question to students: "What elements does a television newscast rely on?" Let students brainstorm until someone says, "A picture." Then discuss the tools that television stations use to obtain that picture, such as radar for weather, mobile vans, helicopters, etc. Finally, focus on the question of how that reliance on a picture could bias the news. Since television relies so heavily on dramatic pictures to maintain viewer attention, talk about how that could affect story choice. For the most part, if there is no picture, there is no story. Or, as said in the news business, "If it bleeds, it leads."

Pass out a copy of the handout on television news analysis (see Figure 25.1 on the companion disk). The handout I have provided has spots for only six stories, but make certain that your handout has space for at least twenty-six stories, a typical number for a half-hour newscast. Tell students that they will deconstruct the news by analyzing the content of specific stories, filling out the handout as they watch the prerecorded broadcast. Then start the tape. You should keep track of the duration of each story and the commercial breaks, while students are responsible for recording what the story is about: if it is hard or soft news; if it is local, national, or international; what types of news tools are used to obtain a picture; and what the content of the commercial breaks is. After each story, pause the tape and tell the class how long the story lasted in minutes and seconds. Give them a few moments to fill out the information they need. Because you have run though the broadcast yourself prior to viewing it in class, you will have an idea of the structure ahead of time.

With the first few stories, walk the class through the process and talk about whether a story is hard or soft; local, national, or international; and so on. Continue the process all the way though the broadcast. From my experience, viewing a half-hour broadcast in this way takes about 45 minutes. If you run out of time, finish the following day. When timing, count any time that stations use to promote the broadcast itself as commercial time. This includes teasers before a commercial break as well as leaders or bumps coming back from a commercial break. Also, since broadcast time is typically divided into half hours and hours with long commercial breaks at those points, it is fair to include the last commercial break with the half-hour broadcast so you get an accurate ratio of news to commercials.

Day 3

Begin class by breaking down the numbers from the broadcast. How much of the broadcast was soft news? How much was hard news? How much total advertising was there? What was the ratio of local to national news? This usually takes about 10 minutes. Once students are done, have a brief discussion of the findings in preparation for the essay they will write either in class or as homework. Most students have plenty to say about the content and structure of what they have seen. Some of my students' responses have included: "I was shocked by how the news seems to revolve around the advertising breaks"; "There was almost as much advertising as there was news"; "I can't believe how little of the news is actually anything that you need to know"; and "Sports took up far more time than significant events."

Since it's a local newscast, around 90 percent of the news will be local in nature. Most of the news is soft, usually 75 or 80 percent, but I have seen broadcasts for which that number is higher. Weather and sports combined generally take 20 to 25 percent of the total newscast. You will notice that because television relies on pictures, often stories are chosen because of the station's ability to obtain dramatic footage that keeps the viewer's attention rather than for actual story relevance.

The ratio of advertising to news time is staggering. I have never seen a newscast in which less than 25 percent of the half hour was devoted to advertising. Usually the time spent on advertising approaches 50 percent. Frequently, a greater number of products are advertised than there are news stories aired. You will notice that the newscast is structured around advertising breaks. Hard news is at the beginning of the broadcast. The amount of advertising increases as the half hour moves on. To avoid potential conflict of a story with a product, there is almost never a hard news story before a commercial break. For instance, a station certainly would not want to have a story about rising gas prices followed by an advertisement for a Ford Expedition, or a story about obesity followed by a McDonald's ad. Ad placement is intentional and biases the news.

Finally, suggest that students take the assignment home and view a newscast with their family to show them what they have learned. I have had many students come to class the following day and tell me that their parents were amazed, and often disturbed, by their observations.

Assessment

Assessment of students' understanding of the structure of and biases and influences in a newscast can be made through class discussion, through the bias list compiled on day 1, or through addressing questions in a formal essay. The handout for the prompt is Figure 25.2 on the companion disk.

Sample Prompt

Now that you have scrutinized a television newscast, it is time to analyze the data. In a one-and-one-half- to two-page single-spaced paper, discuss the following questions:

a. News. Discuss the most dominant type of news (i.e., local, national, or international; hard or soft) and what this tells you about the information you receive from local news broadcasts. Discuss the relationship between story length and story content, between story placement and advertising.

b. Advertising. Discuss the influence of advertising on the newscast. Include comments on the products advertised, advertisement length, number of advertisements, and proximity to specific news stories. Be sure to examine the pace and timing of the advertisements in relation to the overall broadcast.

    c. Finally, discuss your conclusions. What in your analysis jumps out at you or surprises you? Explain what your findings tell you about the information you receive in the news.

Connections and Adaptations

This is a flexible lesson with many applications. It can be easily transformed into a critical analysis of a national newscast. For advanced students, the lesson can be modified further to include critical analysis of the content of the advertisements within the news segment. Although this lesson is designed for high school, it can certainly be used at the middle school level by modifying the guiding questions used for discussions and essays.

Supplemental Reading

Bagdikian, Ben H. *The Media Monopoly*. 6th ed. Boston: Beacon, 2000.

Harris, Richard Jackson. *A Cognitive Psychology of Mass Communication*. 3rd. ed. Mahwah, NJ: Erlbaum, 1999.

26 Video News Releases: When Is News Really News?

Denise Sevick Bortree
University of Florida

Context

Parts of the following lesson plan are adapted from a college-level media literacy class taught at the University of Florida. Discussions of public relations and video news releases (VNRs) play a critical part in understanding the way decisions are made about the creation and dissemination of news. This lesson can also be used to develop and practice persuasive writing techniques.

Rationale

Video news releases are video clips produced by organizations and distributed to the media. The clips include footage that could be used by the media in news stories. For example, an organization that builds and sells automobiles might include footage of a new model that was just released. The clip might show how the car was assembled, what the interior and exterior look like, and what accessories and options the car offers. Some VNRs are produced to look exactly like news stories, with a "reporter" speaking from behind a desk and another "reporter" covering the story in the field. Organizations provide VNRs to the media so the media can supplement their own video clips. Many newsrooms don't have the resources to send someone to the organization's facilities to cover these new announcements, so the organizations feel they are assisting the media by providing video clips. However, using clips provided by organizations does create an ethical dilemma for journalists.

When the *Washington Post* broke the story in March 2005 about television stations' unedited use of White House VNRs on the topics of Medicare reform and the Iraq war, many in the public became aware of VNRs for the first time. Though VNRs had been in use for over ten years, this was the first reported documentation of broad use by television stations. News articles revealed that many stations in both large and small markets had run VNRs produced by the White House and other government organizations, including the Transportation Security Administration, the Department of Agriculture, the Department of Defense, and the Census Bureau, to name a few. The public responded with outrage, and 40,000 people signed a petition asking for an investigation into the issue, according to the Center for Media and Democracy (www. prwatch.org). The outrage was due in part to the fact that members of the media are charged with questioning authority and giving the public the "true" story, but in these instances, that was not the case. Instead, they allowed what some term *political propaganda* to be aired as valid news stories.

There is an ongoing debate surrounding this issue. On the one side, public relations firms believe that the VNR is simply the broadcast form of a press release. On the other side, organizations like the Center for Media and Democracy claim that it is "covert propaganda" intentionally designed to be run without source attribution, allowing organizations to circumvent the typical gatekeeping process traditionally performed by journalists.

The goal of this lesson plan is to encourage students to think critically about the media they consume. Students will be asked to take a position on this issue and defend it. They will also have the opportunity to use persuasive writing techniques by creating a video news release.

Objectives

Students will be able to:

- Understand the purpose of a VNR and the process of producing and distributing them
- Identify potential VNRs in news broadcasts
- Form their own opinion about when VNRs may be used ethically
- Present an argument for or against the use of VNRs

NCTE/IRA standards addressed: 4, 5, 6, 12

Material/Preactivity Preparation

Teachers will need to locate a few examples of video news releases to show to the class. Ideally, you will be able to find examples from corporations, government agencies, health organizations, and nonprofit/ charity organizations. Good sources for video news releases include:

- *PR Newswire* <http://www.prnewswire.com>
- U.S. military video news releases <http://www.dvidshub.net>
- *The World Bank* <http://www.worldbank.org>
- *American Dental Association* <http://www.ada.org/public/ media/videos/vnr/index.asp>
- *U.S. Department of Agriculture* <http://www.fsis.usda.gov/ News_&_Events/Video_Releases/index.asp>

You will need AV equipment that allows you to project the video news releases onto a screen, or, if your class is equipped with computers, you can have the students access the video news releases online.

Tape the 6 p.m. or 11 p.m. news (or whenever the news airs in your time zone). Be prepared to play it back and fast-forward through the commercials. You may want to tape a few nights and choose to play one broadcast in class that has a good example of a probable video news release. You'll likely have more luck with the local broadcast rather than national network news. However, you may have some luck with a 24-hour news station.

Optional: Download the PBS story on government video news releases. This can be found at www.pbs.org/newshour/bb/media/jan-june05/vnr_5-13.html#.

Time Frame

This lesson will take two to three standard high school English class periods.

> Day 1: 15 minutes to cue and watch video news releases and 20–30 minutes to discuss them.
>
> Day 2: 20 minutes to watch broadcast news and 15 minutes to discuss
>
> Day 3: 20–30 minutes to draft video news release and allow 30 minutes for an assessment.

Optional class: 10 minutes to watch PBS story and 15 minutes to discuss.

Description of Activity

At the core, this is an ethical discussion that must consider the rights of all parties. Organizations have the right to produce and distribute VNRs;

television stations have the right to air the material they deem appropriate (except for some cases of controversial political issues); and the public has the right to be told the truth through media. Students need to wrestle with the issue of when it is ethical for a news organization to use a video news release. Students should choose a perspective and defend it.

Activity 1

Show students a few examples of VNRs or have them access them through the Internet (as described above). Explain that VNRs are created by organizations and distributed to the media with the intention of informing and persuading the media about an issue. The organization hopes that the media will cover the story in their broadcasts, and even more, hopes that they will cover it from a perspective in line with the organization's view on the issue.

> **Discussion Questions** (formatted as handouts on the companion disc [see Figures 26.1 and 26.2])
>
> ■ Some people believe that organizations are behaving unethically when they create and distribute VNRs. Why do you think that is? What is your opinion?
>
> ■ Some people believe that news organizations are behaving unethically when they run the video news release as a news story in their broadcast. Why do you think that is? What is your opinion?
>
> ■ When might it be proper for a television station or network to use the news release?

Have students complete the worksheet on video news releases. Ask them to share their responses with the class. Encourage critical analysis of the issue as well as position taking and defense.

Activity 2

Show students a prerecorded news program broadcast. How many of the stories could be video news releases? Certainly, any stories about local crimes or the weather are not news releases. Any breaking news would not be a VNR. So what parts might be produced by an organization and presented as news? For any story that might be a VNR, does the story present both sides of an issue fairly? Or does it seem to be trying to persuade the viewer toward one side of the issue? This could indicate whether it was produced by an organization or by a journalist. You might have the students contact the local television station to ask about the source of the story. Even if a local reporter introduces the story, that does not mean he or she wrote it entirely or that the video clips were not taken from VNRs.

Activity 3

This next activity can be done in class or given as a homework assignment. Have students work in groups to draft the text of a video news release. Organizations typically follow a process when producing and distributing a VNR. They choose the topic, thoroughly research it, assess the opinion of significant members of their publics (meaning customers, shareholders, employees, etc.), write the text of the VNR, and finally produce it. Copies of the VNR are distributed to news directors at appropriate news organizations. When news directors receive it, they decide whether to cover the issue in their news broadcast. They also decide whether to use the content of the VNR in part or as a whole in the broadcast.

Ask students to imagine that they work in the communication office for the mayor of the city. Have them choose a current issue to cover in a VNR and then follow the process of producing a VNR through the step of writing the text. Things to consider: How would you present the issue? What information do you think the media would need to know about the issue? Have students discuss how they can ensure that the use of this VNR will be ethical.

This activity could be extended to the creation of the visuals that would be included in the VNR package sent out to news agencies. Laura Brown's lesson on producing PSAs (Chapter 27) provides suggestions for handling video production elements.

Optional activity: Show the students all or part of the PBS story about government use of VNRs. This clip explores the ethical concerns surrounding this issue. During discussion, you might have students express their opinions about the various VNRs that are shown during the clip.

Assessment

Students' understanding and critical analysis of this topic could be assessed through a creative activity and/or a persuasive essay.

Assessment Option 1

A question for students: "If you were preparing a video news release for your school or for a school-related program in which you are currently involved, what material would you include in it?" Have the students sketch out what they believe would be important for the media to know about the program or the school. What process would they follow to produce the VNR? How would they ensure that the use of this video is ethical?

Evaluate students' work primarily on their understanding of ethical concerns about video news releases. Is the content fair and balanced? Does their response reflect knowledge about the responsibility of the organization and the journalist in the production and use of VNRs? Second, consider the creativity and thoroughness of the content of the news release. Has the student considered what the media would need to know to cover the issue? Did the student propose a reasonable process for producing the VNR?

Assessment Option 2

Have students take a position on the ethical use of VNRs and defend it. Is it ethical for organizations to produce them? Is it ethical for news broadcasts to run them? Evaluate students' work by the thoroughness and thoughtfulness of their response. Again, you can use Figure 26.2 on the companion disk as a guide.

Connections and Adaptations

Media literacy education often focuses on the informed consumption of advertising, while students' understanding of news sources is often overlooked. For students to be truly media literate, they need to be critical consumers of news content. One potential source of unfiltered persuasive information is the VNR produced by government, corporate, or nonprofit organizations and run on televisions stations without proper attribution.

Students will develop and practice persuasive writing skills by critically analyzing the use of VNRs and by following the process of producing them.

Work Cited

Center for Media and Democracy. 4 June 2007 <http://www.prwatch.org/>.

Supplemental Reading and Viewing

Barstow, D., and R. Stein. "Under Bush, a New Age of Prepackaged TV News." *New York Times* 13 Mar. 2005.

Media Literacy Clearinghouse (http://www.frankwbaker.com) has an excellent section on video news releases. PBS coverage of the video news release controversy <http://www.pbs.org/newshour/bb/media/jan-june05/vnr_5-13.html> may work well for high school or even college classes.

Ethical guidelines can be found at the Public Relations Society of America site (http://www.prsa.org/aboutus/ethics/preamble_en.html) and at http://www.rtnda.org/ethics/coe.shtml for radio and TV.

27 Creating a Public Service Announcement: Powerful Persuasion in 60 Seconds

Laura L. Brown
Stevenson High School
Lincolnshire, Illinois

Context

Stevenson High School is a school of approximately 4,600 students in the northern suburbs of Chicago. The following lesson is part of my college prep sophomore English course. This project fits in to a comprehensive study of persuasion in many different forms, including public speaking, writing, literature, and media. The course includes a study of persuasive works such as Martin Luther King Jr.'s "Letter from Birmingham Jail" and Henry David Thoreau's "Civil Disobedience." Students also write persuasive essays and write and deliver their own persuasive speechs. After studying persuasion in written and spoken language, we move to examining how persuasion is used in visual media.

Rationale

This unit is an important extension of our study of persuasion into visual media. Students not only need to study and practice elements of persuasion in literature and writing, but they also must recognize and understand how these elements work in the visual media they are bombarded with everyday. By manipulating the media themselves rather than simply studying examples, they become active learners and combine both critical and creative higher-order thinking skills. Technology is the best tool to allow for this transformative learning experience because it provides students with the ability to do things they couldn't do without the technology. Using digital cameras and computer software, they are able to manipulate visual images, sound, and text to create their own unique finished product, and as a result, they gain a more intimate understanding of how persuasion and visual media really work.

Objectives

Students will be able to:

- Create a storyboard that demonstrates outstanding preparation in every detail of a public service announcement (PSA): images, script, text, music, transitions, and effects
- Demonstrate a clear understanding of the building blocks and emotional appeals of persuasion with a PSA that achieves effective application of unit concepts
- Analyze target audience and use appropriate appeals to communicate the message effectively
- Demonstrate good use of visual images to communicate the message effectively
- Use iMovie software to create good continuity within the PSA and demonstrate effort to create a polished, finished product

NCTE/IRA standards addressed: 1, 4, 6, 7, 8, 12

Materials/Preactivity Preparation

Students will use the following materials:

- *Magazine ads and sample PSAs.* These are used as a means to analyze and begin discussion of how images and language combine to create powerful persuasive messages.
- *Topic cards.* Each bears a different message and target audience. I have each group of students draw their topics at random out of a hat.
- *Storyboards.* Students use storyboard frames to plan their PSAs. They must indicate what images they will use by drawing them in the frames and then including additional information about dialogue, text, music, special effects, and/or transitions that are pertinent to each frame. Storyboard forms are available on the companion disk (see Figures 7.1 and 7.2).
- *Computers with iMovie software.* This software makes creating the PSAs possible by allowing students to edit video and add music, voice-over narration, text, special effects, and visual transitions. I used approximately twelve computers with a class of approximately twenty-five students.

- *Digital video camera with FireWire cable.* Students need to do any filming on a digital camera that can transfer video to the computer with the use of a FireWire cable.
- *Other handouts, including rubrics, peer evaluations, and self-evaluations.* These materials are available on the companion disk.

Time Frame

This lesson usually takes ten to twelve 50-minute class periods. I usually spend two classes introducing the project, demonstrating the software, and discussing the samples. Students spend two classes storyboarding and five to seven classes filming and working to create the PSAs on the computer. You need one class period at the end of the project to view the finished products. Very little of this project can be completed as homework, so I generally have my students read a short novel pertinent to our study of persuasion independently as homework during their work on this project.

Description of Activity

Before we begin focusing on the public service announcement, we usually spend a day reviewing emotional appeals and persuasive techniques by examining magazine advertisements. Students work in small groups of three to look at three different advertisements (each student brings in an ad to class). They determine what the message is, who the target audience is, and what emotional appeals and building blocks are used. Figure 27.1 on the companion disk offers a handout that enumerates and defines these appeals and building blocks.

When students have completed their worksheets (see Figure 27.2 on the companion disk), we discuss some of the ads and talk about how the images and text work together to communicate the message effectively to the target audience. Depending on the ads we are using, I might ask, "What do you notice about the colors used in this ad?" or "How does the large text at the top influence the way we see this image?" or "If this ad had a different target audience, what would we have to change?"

When I am satisfied from our discussions that students can apply their knowledge of persuasive techniques to visual media (like the magazine ads), we are ready to begin the PSA. I start by giving students a "real-world" context for their assignment. I tell them that they are now part of the creative team put together to develop a PSA for the Ad Council—an organization responsible for many of the PSAs you see on television every day. Students must use all they know about the art of persuasion to make the most of the 30 to 60 seconds that a commercial spot allows. This time limit is important because it forces students to limit themselves to what is most effective and necessary to convey their message to the target audience. I stress the importance of working together as a team as they use iMovie software to create a 30- to 60-second PSA similar to those they have seen on television. See Figure 27.3 on the companion disk for the assignment handout.

As a class, we view sample PSAs created by other students and those available at the Ad Council website (www.adcouncil.org). This website contains sample PSAs, including many storyboards. These are good models for students.

I also spend some time reviewing information on copyright issues so that students are sure to abide by the law. Our technology trainer, Charlene Chausis, has provided very helpful information regarding these copyright issues on her staff development website (see www6. district125.k12.il.us/staffdev/Copyright.html). I emphasize with my students the "fair use" portion limitations regarding the use of music, photographs, and motion media:

- Motion media (such as movies, commercials, or television programs): 10 percent or 30 seconds
- Text: 10 percent or 1,000 words
- Music, lyrics, music video: 10 percent or 30 seconds
- Numerical data sets: 10 percent or 2.500 fields or cell entries
- Illustrations and photographs: 10 percent or fifteen images in a collection; no more than five by a single artist or photographer

Introducing the software and examining the models takes at least two class periods. Next, students meet with their teams to discuss the assigned message and target audience. Some suggestions for messages and target audiences might be convincing college students to pursue a career in teaching, or convincing teenagers to eat a healthier diet, or convincing parents that they need to be more involved in their teenager's education. The students then determine what persuasive techniques they wish to use and brainstorm ideas. Students then create a storyboard. They plan out what they will film, any still shots, text, effects—everything. The storyboarding usually takes one and a half to two class periods. The storyboard is evaluated with the final product. I insist that students have everything planned before they begin working with the camera or the computer. Then students spend at least three to five days filming shots, collecting images, choosing music, and us-ing iMovie to create a PSA.

During this time, my job is to be a coach of sorts, helping with both the technology and the content of the project. I try to make sure that students follow the appropriate steps (first, planning; second, storyboarding; third, filming and editing). Students sometimes want to jump right into using the software without good preparation and plan-ning. It is also important to build a culture in which students help one another solve problems and encourage one another as they develop and execute their ideas. To ensure that all students are engaged and the burden does not fall on one or two students alone, every so often I ask students to rotate the computer, handing it off to another group mem-ber, so that one student does not dominate the computer work. Another idea to ensure equal participation is to assign specific roles and tasks to each group member.

I always allow my students to teach me new things as we work with the technology. Students often find a better way of doing things or a feature in the software that I am not aware of. I encourage them to show me and to share their discoveries with one another. This allows us to use the tool in the best possible way to explore the boundaries of persuasion as it relates to media. For example, one group of students wanted to include a scene in their PSA that had the camera moving down an empty hospital hallway. Since filming in a hospital would have been very difficult, they had to come up with a different way of achiev-ing the effect. One of the students discovered a feature in iMovie called the "Ken Burns Effect," which pans across or zooms in or out of a still image. He showed me how to use this feature with a still image of a hospital hallway to make it appear as though the camera were moving down the hallway. This was a very effective and creative way to use this feature of the software. He showed it to me, and I in turn encouraged him to share it with the class. That day we all learned something new about how the software works.

Students generally find this project both fun and challenging. The technology often requires flexibility and patience, and I encourage my students to view technical difficulties as opportunities to learn more about the technology and how it works. The amount of flexibility re-quired often depends on the kind of equipment and the technical sup-port available to teachers in the classroom.

To help students feel a celebratory sense of accomplishment at the end of the project, I serve popcorn as we watch the finished products. This viewing is particularly important as a motivating factor for students. Knowing that their peers will see the PSA generally makes students work much harder for a polished finished product. I also encourage students to be critical viewers of one another's work by asking them to complete peer evaluations of the finished PSAs (Figure 27.4 on the companion disk). After viewing all the PSAs, students also complete a detailed self-analysis of their own work. They often rate their own success through comparison to the other finished products; however, even if they are disappointed with elements of the final video, students often demonstrate a thorough understanding of persuasive techniques through this self-analysis. This tells me that all students learn a great deal about persuasion and media even when they experience frustration or limited success with the technology. The process is just as important as the product.

Assessment

I use a rubric to grade the final product. The exemplary project has the following characteristics:

- The storyboard demonstrates outstanding preparation in every detail of the PSA: images, script, text, music, transitions, and effects.
- PSA demonstrates an outstanding understanding of the building blocks and emotional appeals of persuasion. PSA achieves an excellent application of unit concepts.
- PSA shows outstanding audience analysis and uses the best possible appeals to communicate a clear and effective message.
- PSA demonstrates a powerful use of visual images to communicate the message effectively.
- PSA has outstanding continuity. Project is polished and professional looking. Worthy of public viewing!

A complete version of this rubric, which includes characteristics of accomplished, developing, and inadequate projects, is found in Figure 27.5 on the companion disk. For a sample PSA, see Figure 27.6.

The finished product is not the only way to evaluate students' success in reaching the unit objectives. The peer and self-evaluations also reveal much about the extent of student learning. While viewing the ads in class, I ask students to keep notes on each of the PSAs they watch. Then I ask them to name the strongest and weakest PSAs in terms of technical aspects and the strongest and weakest ad in terms of its persuasive techniques. Students must support each decision with specific evidence from their notes. I then ask them to tell me who gets their vote for best overall. I also ask them to compare their work to that of their peers, mark a rubric for their own PSA, and respond to the following questions in writing:

- How well did your group work together?
- Were you satisfied with the final product?
- What would you do differently next time?
- What was your best contribution to the finished product?

This opportunity to reflect on their own work is an important element of the project and provides me with valuable insight to the lessons they've learned from this experience.

Connections and Adaptations

This project fits nicely in any curriculum that includes persuasion and can be easily adapted to suit middle school students. The software is relatively easy to learn, and students have increasingly native abilities with technology that allow them to learn it quickly. Teachers who work in schools with video announcements each morning might arrange for the best PSA to be shown to the whole school. This is an exciting way to give students a very real audience for their work. Teachers with more limited technological resources might consider having students simply create more elaborate storyboards instead of actually filming and editing the PSAs. The storyboards could be drawn, or students could use photographs to illustrate their message.

Many good resources on the Apple website can assist teachers who want to use iMovie in their classrooms. An iMovie tutorial at apple.com/support/imovie contains step-by-step instructions and helpful hints. There is also a how-to guide available for educators using iMovie at education.apple.com/education/ilife/howto.

Index

Editors

Mary T. Christel has been a member of the communication arts department at Adlai E. Stevenson High School in the northwest suburbs of Chicago since 1979, teaching AP literature classes as well as courses in media and film studies. She earned a BSS at Northwestern University in theater and an MA in interdisciplinary arts education at Columbia College. In 2001 she published a book on media literacy with Ellen Krueger, *Seeing and Believing: How to Teach Media Literacy in the English Classroom*, as well as contributing to three books on teaching Shakespeare. Christel has served as director of the Commission on Media and chair of the Assembly on Media Arts for NCTE.

Scott Sullivan is assistant professor of secondary education in the National College of Education at National-Louis University. He taught English and media literacy at the high school level for ten years and has been involved in a variety of media literacy activities and organizations over the last few years. Sullivan lives, works, and teaches in the Chicagoland area.

Contributors

Since 1996, **Karen Ambrosh** has taught video production and media design classes at Audubon Technology and Communication Center, a Milwaukee public middle school. She has a master's degree in journalism and mass communication from UW–Milwaukee and is president of the National Telemedia Council, a nonprofit organization that advocates for a media-wise, literate, global society and produces *Telemedium, The Journal of Media Literacy*.

Frank W. Baker is a media education consultant who conducts workshops with students, parents, and teachers and at local, regional, and national curriculum conferences. A University of Georgia journalism graduate, he worked in television news for nine years. He worked for eleven years as an instructional television/distance education administrator for the Orange County (Florida) public school system, where he conducted workshops for teachers on media literacy. In 1999 his study of state teaching standards, which include media literacy, was published by *Education Week*. As president of the Partnership for Media Education, Baker chaired the National Media Education Conference in St. Paul, Minnesota, in 1999. He currently serves on NCTE's Commission on Media. He maintains the Media Literacy Clearinghouse Web page.

David Bengtson lives in Long Prairie, Minnesota, where he taught English at the high school level for thirty-three and a half years. During this time, he and his students collaborated with media artist Mike Hazard in a series of video poetry residencies, producing ten video poems based on Hazard's writing. These and other video poems by his students have been shown at workshops, festivals, and conferences around the country. He has served on NCTE's Commission on Media. Each summer, Bengtson team-teaches a class titled "Seeing Things with Video" at the Minnesota Institute for Talented Youth.

Jason Block is an English and journalism teacher at Prospect High School in Mount Prospect, Illinois, where he also serves as adviser for the student newspaper, the *Prospector*. During his two years guiding the *Prospector*, the publication has won numerous awards, including the prestigious Pacemaker in 2005, given to twenty-four schools nationwide by the National Scholastic Press Association. Before coming to Prospect, Block taught English and media analysis at Adlai E. Stevenson High School in Lincolnshire, Illinois. His background is in journalism; he spent three years as a professional sportswriter before going into teaching.

Denise Sevick Bortree has a BA in writing and English from Geneva College and an MA in mass communication and an MEd, both from the University of Florida. She is currently a doctoral student in the School of Journalism and Communication at the University of Florida. Her teaching experience includes college-level classes in media literacy and public relations. She researches and writes on the topic of children and media.

Laura L. Brown has been an English teacher at Stevenson High School in Lincolnshire, Illinois, since 1987. She has been a leader in technology integration at Stevenson for the last six years through her work with a staff development program called PowerRangers. This award-winning program provides technology resources, training, and support for teachers so they can make the most effective use of these tools in the classroom. Brown has shared her work at numerous workshops and conferences, and was invited to present her work to the Illinois state legislators in Springfield as one of the Tech 2001 winners.

David L. Bruce is assistant professor at Kent State University in the Department of Teaching, Leadership and Curriculum Studies. Before earning his PhD, Bruce taught high school English and media studies for eleven years. His primary research and teaching interests focus on reading and composing with video, particularly the way in which students and teachers can use print and video to complement each other. He is currently president of the Ohio Council of Teachers of English Language Arts (OCTELA) and director of NCTE's Commission on Media.

Rich Clark teaches creative writing and humanities at Buffalo Grove High School in Buffalo Grove, Illinois. Having received a BA in the teaching of English from the University of Illinois at Urbana–Champaign, he is currently pursuing an MA in interdisciplinary arts from Columbia College in Chicago. Clark has been published in Triton College's *Ariel* magazine and enjoys performing and composing music, writing, and creating installation artwork.

Leda Cooks received a PhD from Ohio University in 1993 and is currently professor of communications at the University of Massachusetts, teaching courses in conflict and mediation, intercultural and interracial communication, gender and communication, the social impact of information technology, and critical pedagogy. Her courses generally include community service learning and community-based research, and she is committed to forging learning, service, and research partnerships between university and community. Cooks's research focuses, among other things, on the role of education in socialization and the mediation of culture. Recent projects include editing a journal as well as coediting and contributing to a book on whiteness, performance, and pedagogy, published in March 2007.

Jacqueline Cullen teaches Freshman Accelerated English and Junior College Prep English at Adlai E. Stevenson High School in Lincolnshire, Illinois. Before her current teaching position, Cullen taught in Woodstock, Illinois, and Waterloo, Iowa. With an undergraduate degree in English and a minor in reading, and a graduate degree in

English education, both from the University of Northern Iowa, her teaching experiences range from working with remedial reading students to AP students. In addition, she has presented at both IATE and NCTE.

Belinha S. De Abreu is auxiliary assistant professor at Drexel University. Previously, as a school library media specialist at the Walsh Intermediate School (5–8) in Branford, Connecticut, she specialized in teaching media literacy. Before her career in education, she enjoyed a fast-paced job in broadcasting, working for NBC in Providence, Rhode Island. De Abreu holds a BA in communications with a concentration in television and public relations, an MLS in library science and instructional technology, and a certificate in media literacy from Appalachian State University, and she is finishing a PhD in curriculum and instruction with a focus in media literacy at the University of Connecticut.

Mark Dolce started and ended his pre-education career as a grant writer for nonprofit legal and social services in Chicago and New York City, respectively. In between grant writing gigs, he worked as a film and video production manager, as a computer network specialist for a large-scale event production company, and as a stay-at-home dad. In 2005 he earned a Master of Arts in Teaching from National-Louis University. He also has a BA in English with honors and an area certification in film studies from Indiana University–Bloomington. Dolce currently teaches English and media at Lake Zurich High School in Illinois.

Stephanie A. Flores-Koulish is assistant professor of curriculum and instruction at Loyola College in Maryland. Her area of expertise and research is critical media literacy education; she also teaches media literacy to other teachers at Loyola College. She previously taught children with special needs and English as a second language in both primary and secondary schools. Flores-Koulish is the author of *Teacher Education for Critical Consumption of Mass Media and Popular Culture* (2004), a study that examines the media worlds of undergraduates studying elementary education and suggests the need for critical media literacy education in teacher education.

Nili Friedman is currently teaching fourth-grade general studies and fifth-grade language arts at the Akiva Jewish Community Day School in Nashville, Tennessee. She earned her undergraduate degree at Brandeis University, where she majored in English and minored in elementary education, Judaic studies, and a humanities interdisciplinary program. She is in the process of completing her MA in elementary education at Vanderbilt University with a concentration in English education. In addition to teaching full time, Friedman works as the family educator at West End Synagogue, where she creates and implements programs for parents and children ranging in age from infancy through high school.

Kate Glass teaches creative writing and humanities/fine arts at Buffalo Grove High School. A graduate of the University of Illinois, Glass has been teaching for sixteen years. She holds an MA in written communications from National-Louis University and is currently working on an MA in fiction writing at Northwestern University. Her poems have been published in *Ariel, Little America*, and other small publications, and she is currently completing work on her third screenplay. Glass lives in Evanston, Illinois.

Kevin Howley received a PhD from Indiana University in 1998 and is currently associate professor of media studies at DePauw University. He is author of *Community Media: People, Places, and Communication Technologies* (2005). Howley's work has appeared in the *Journal of Radio Studies; Journalism: Theory, Practice, and Criticism; Television and New Media*; and *Social Movement Studies*. He also produces documentary videos, including, most recently, *Victory at Sea? Culture Jamming Dubya* (2004).

Elizabeth Kenney is a graduate of the Great Books program at the University of Notre Dame and holds a Master of Arts in Teaching English from the University of Chicago. She has taught at Stevenson High School since 1989, where she has had adventures in teaching American and British literature, world literature, AP English, and, most recently, film and media studies.

William Kist, assistant professor at Kent State University, has been a middle school/high school English teacher, a curriculum coordinator, and a consultant and trainer for school districts nationwide. Author of *New Literacies in Action: Teaching and Learning in Multiple Media* (2005) and over twenty articles and book chapters, Kist has made over thirty national and international conference presentations. In addition to his career in education, Kist has worked in video and film production and as a musician. The recipient of an Ohio Educational Broadcasting Network Commission (OEBIE) Honorable Mention, Kist also received a regional Emmy Award nomination for outstanding achievement in music composition.

Cynthia Lucia is assistant professor of English and cinema studies at Rider University. She has authored *Framing Female Lawyers: Women on Trial in Film* (2005) and has written extensively for *Cineaste*, where she has served on the editorial board for over a decade. Her essays appear in *Feminism, Media, and the Law* (1997), *Film and Sexual Politics: A Critical Reader* (forthcoming), and *The Process of Adaptation* (forthcoming). Lucia taught at Horace Greeley High School and New York University, where she offered "Cinema Studies for the High School Teacher."

Louis Mazza, with a BFA from Minneapolis College of Art and Design and an MAT from the University of the Arts in Philadelphia, is an artist and teacher of media arts, graphic design, and media literacy, based, quite coincidentally, in Media, Pennsylvania. Mazza's work is a hybrid of photography, graphic design, and interactive media that focuses on social connections and collective interactions via the Internet. His teaching philosophy is based on the belief that meaningful learning occurs when students are engaged in personally relevant activities based on social interaction, cultural awareness, creativity, and critical thinking.

Stephen Murphy is chair of the art department at New Trier High School in Winnetka, Illinois, where he teaches video art and photography. Before his career in education, Murphy worked for a decade in television in Boston and New York, primarily at WNET in New York. His credits in film production include work on *Voices and Visions*, the documentary series on American poetry. Murphy has a BFA from Pratt Institute in photography and is all-but-thesis from the Massachusetts Institute of Technology, where he studied film with Ricky Leacock, one of the pioneers of cinema verité. He earned a Master of Liberal Arts from the University of Chicago in 2001. Murphy is currently serving on NCTE's Commission on Media.

Jane Freiburg Nickerson has taught English at Gallaudet University, a liberal arts university for the Deaf and Hard-of-Hearing located in Washington, D.C., for twenty-three years. During the past ten years, she has taught numerous literature and film courses. She received her doctorate in education, curriculum, and instruction, specializing in reading education, from the University of Maryland at College Park.

Thomas O'Donnell has been a reading and English teacher for the last thirty-three years. He developed a love of stories and reading at an early age from his dad, who carried a newspaper with him to read on the bus every day and who read stories aloud to his children at night. O'Donnell's love of movies, as well as books, led to his experimentation with storyboards and his inquiry into how he could use the visual displays of director's craft in moviemaking to help students see the many connections to author's craft in writing. He has had success teaching the storyboarding technique to struggling readers in his strategic reading class and to proficient readers in his ninth-grade English classes at Highland Park High School.

Angela Paradise is a doctoral student in the Department of Communication at the University of Massachusetts in Amherst. Her research interests include the social impact of media, media violence, video games, youth and media, and media literacy. She holds a BA in American studies and communication and media studies from Tufts University and received her MA in communication at the University of Massachusetts. Upon completion of her doctoral degree, Paradise looks forward to pursuing a teaching and research career at a college or university in the Boston area.

Mari Castañeda Paredes received her PhD from UC–San Diego in 2000 and is currently assistant professor in the Department of Communication at the University of Massachusetts in Amherst. Her areas of interest include community action research, political economy of communication, Spanish-language/Latino media, and the property creation of new information and digital technologies. Castañeda Paredes is also interested in media literacy, especially as it relates to communities of color in a transnational context. She is currently working on a research team that examines community–university partnerships in a Puerto Rican neighborhood located in Holyoke, Massachusetts.

Carol Porter-O'Donnell teaches reading and is an assistant principal at Deerfield High School. Her work with storyboarding as a strategy to support struggling readers was the focus of an inquiry that she did with her ninth-grade students as part of her district's professional development program. In addition to finding that storyboarding helps readers to better visualize their reading and understand author's craft, Porter-O'Donnell found that students developed more active reading skills in the work they needed to do to comprehend difficult texts. Her publications include *"What Do I Teach for 90 Minutes?"*, *The Portfolio as A Learning Strategy* (with Janell Cleland), and chapters in *Talking about Books: Creating Literate Communities* and *Delicate Balances: Collaborative Research in Language Education*.

Neil Rigler teaches English and film studies at Deerfield High School in Deerfield, Illinois, where he is also the advisor for both the literary magazine and the improv comedy troupe. He has taught at Deerfield for eight years, after completing MAs in both education and English at Northwestern University in Evanston, Illinois. As a member of the Bard College Institute for Writing and Thinking, Rigler has been teaching in the Lake Forest College Summer Writing Workshop for the past eight summers.

Erica Scharrer received her PhD from Syracuse University in 1998 and is associate professor in the Department of Communication at the University of Massachusetts in Amherst, teaching classes about the media's role in the lives of individuals young and old. Together with her departmental colleagues, she has created partnerships with teachers in local school districts around a yearly media literacy unit on the topic of conflict and violence. Scharrer has coauthored (with George Comstock) the book *Television: What's on, Who's Watching, and What It Means* and is currently working with Comstock on a new book titled *Media and the American Child*.

Charles F. Trafford has BAs in both English literature and journalism and an MA in education. He currently teaches high school English in the Seattle area, where he also teaches college seminars on media literacy. Trafford recently published his first novel, *God's Country*. In addition to teaching, he has worked in television, music, and event promotion. He is currently studying adolescent media habits and their effects on student learning.

Brian Turnbaugh teaches global studies and modern media at Community High School in West Chicago, Illinois. He developed the school's media literacy class with colleague Ross Collin as a summer school class in 2002; the class continues to run as a senior elective. Turnbaugh attended the 2004 Media and Democracy conference at Harvard

University, where he met the editors of this book. He has contributed to *Media and American Democracy*, published by the Bill of Rights Institute.

Kathleen Turner received her BA in English education from Lincoln University in Jefferson City, Missouri. She then taught for a year in the Jefferson City Public School District. She received her MA in English with a specialization in film and literature from Northern Illinois University, where she continues to work on her doctorate. While working on graduate degrees, Turner has been teaching in the First Year Composition program at NIU. She enjoys bringing visual media into the classroom at all levels of education and enjoys finding means of alternative assessment in composition.

Scott Williams received his MEd in education from Loyola University. He developed a six-hour curriculum in alcohol awareness for an independent business he owned and operated. He also owned and operated an independent radio program that aired in the Chicago market. Currently chairman of the board of an Illinois State Senate Scholarship committee, Williams has served in this role for the last eight years. He currently teaches English and is a team leader at Adlai E. Stevenson High School in Lincolnshire, Illinois.

This book was typeset in Palatino and Helvetica by Electronic Imaging.
The typeface used on the cover was Cosmos.
The book was printed on 50-lb. Williamsburg Offset paper by Versa Press, Inc.